THE RADIANT LIFE PROJECT

To the Emmerich Family
So grateful for the years
of friendship and support.
I love you all!

KP.King

The Radiant Life Project

Awaken Your Purpose, Heal Your Past, and Transform Your Future

Kate King, MA, LPC, ATR-BC

ROWMAN & LITTLEFIELD
Lanham • Boulder • New York • London

Published by Rowman & Littlefield
An imprint of The Rowman & Littlefield Publishing Group, Inc.
4501 Forbes Boulevard, Suite 200, Lanham, Maryland 20706
www.rowman.com

86-90 Paul Street, London EC2A 4NE

British Library Cataloguing in Publication Information Available

Library of Congress Cataloging-in-Publication Data
Names: King, Kate (Counselor), author.
  Title: The radiant life project : awaken your purpose, heal your past,
  and transform your future / Kate King, MA, LPC, ATR-BC.
  Description: Lanham : Rowman & Littlefield, [2023] | Includes
  bibliographical references and index.
  Identifiers: LCCN 2023011070 (print) | LCCN 2023011071
  (ebook) | ISBN 9781538181874 (cloth) | ISBN 9781538181881
  (ebook)
  Subjects: LCSH: Self-actualization (Psychology) | Happiness. |
  Psychic trauma.
  Classification: LCC BF637.S4 K548428 2023 (print) | LCC
  BF637.S4 (ebook) | DDC 158.1--dc23/eng/20230323
  LC record available at https://lccn.loc.gov/2023011070
  LC ebook record available at https://lccn.loc.gov/2023011071

♾️™ The paper used in this publication meets the minimum requirements of
American National Standard for Information Sciences—Permanence of Paper
for Printed Library Materials, ANSI/NISO Z39.48-1992.

This one's for all of you brave souls
who are courageous enough to do the inner work
and bring the radiant life that is your birthright
directly toward you.
The world needs you.

And for my Core 4: Danny, Bridger, and Heidi.
None of this is possible without you.

CONTENTS

Author's Note ix

Radiant, the Definitions xi

Foreword xiii

Introduction xvii

CHAPTER 1: The Quest for Authenticity: Seeking a
Fresh Face in the Sea of Masks 1

CHAPTER 2: Culture: What We've Been Spoon-Fed
All Our Lives 19

CHAPTER 3: Nurturance and Deep Rest: The What,
When, and How 39

CHAPTER 4: Healing: A Journey Within 73

CHAPTER 5: Meaningful Growth: Inner Work at
Its Finest 89

CHAPTER 6: Ancestral Trauma, Epigenetics, and
Lineage Patterns 115

CHAPTER 7: The Stories We Tell Ourselves 135

CHAPTER 8: Sharks in the Bathtub: The Tough
Cookies of Your Psyche 155

CONTENTS

CHAPTER 9: Integrity and Alignment: Our
Relationship *with the* Truth 179

CHAPTER 10: Making Stuff: What Creativity's Got
to Do With It 205

CHAPTER 11: Wholeness and Self-Led Living:
Making *the* Shift 229

Epilogue 251

Notes 255

Bibliography 263

Index 269

About Kate King 285

Author's Note

The intention of this book is to provide helpful information on the subjects discussed. It is not intended to be used for the diagnosis or treatment of any specific medical, psychiatric, or mental health issues. Please always consult with your primary healthcare provider if you feel uncertain about decisions that could affect your health. If you feel emotionally unstable and at the risk of harming yourself or someone else, please immediately call 911 or go to your nearest emergency room.

All names and identifying information of the people portrayed throughout this book have been changed to maintain confidentiality.

RADIANT, THE DEFINITIONS

Merriam-Webster Dictionary Definition:

Radiant (adjective) ra·di·ant \ 'rā-dē-ənt

1. a: Radiating rays or reflecting beams of light
   b: Vividly bright and shining: Glowing

2. Marked by or expressive of love, confidence, or happiness

3. Emitting or relating to radiant heat

Synonyms for *radiant*: aglow, beaming, bright, glowing, sunny, brilliant, luminous, lustrous

Cambridge English Dictionary Definition:

Radiant (adjective). US: reɪ.di.ənt UK: 'reɪ.di.ənt

1. Obviously very happy, or very beautiful

2. Producing heat or light

3. Expressing great happiness, hope, or beauty

4. Sending out or possessing heat or light

Kate's Definition:

Radiant ra·di·ant \ 'rā-dē-ənt

1. The experience or existence of being energetically lit from within, glowing and vibrant

2. Possessing and outwardly expressing the qualities inherent in genuine inner beauty

3. Resonating brilliant warmth and light harmoniously within the Self and with others

4. Lustrous vitality and life force energy circulating within oneself and beaming outward

FOREWORD

Having worked with thousands of people, I often hear the question "How . . . ?" How do I live a more fulfilling life? How do I work through my fear? How do I achieve the success I seek? How do I live in alignment with my purpose? How do I know if I am doing it right or wrong? How do I prove myself? How, how, how . . . ?

While there are many tools and resources available to begin the journey of self-awareness and discovery, few exist that really get to the heart of the questions and issues that stand in the way of our clarity. In my deep dive into the principles and practices of spiritual psychology, one idea that has had great impact in my life is that we are consciously awakening into our unconditional loving nature—which is to say that at our most basic level, our very essence, we are *love*.

To live a fulfilling, thriving life, it is essential to heal the wounds and misunderstandings that disturb our peace. To do this, we must understand that healing is the application of loving the parts inside that hurt. We must reflect on moments of our life that have challenged us, and we must practice self-forgiveness so we can come to peace within ourselves. When we achieve such a feat, we can release the bonds that tie us to the misunderstandings that cause pain and suffering. Once we free these misunderstandings (and the typical judgments at the root of our pain and suffering), we can make new choices, love our Self, and free our Self from thoughts and behaviors that limit our expression and experience of love, joy, freedom, and peace.

Many people seek to remove these very experiences of limitation and judgment from their lives and have successfully moved beyond suffering into the expansive awareness of their true essence of *love*. This is an impactful part of what you will learn from *The Radiant Life Project*, among so much more.

Throughout the years I have worked with and known Kate King, I have witnessed her expansive capacity to hold truth, to practice what she teaches in her own life, and to stand within her authentic expression in the service of healing herself as well as the people in her community and across the world. When I dove into the pages of *The Radiant Life Project*, I immediately felt Kate's invitation to reflect deeply on my life and to cultivate clarity in seeing things anew. I experienced a sense of joyful surrender and permission to be me. Kate innately knows how to blend scientific research-based concepts and principles into the practicality and operation of daily life. She sets up the expectation that she will be teaching, and then blends heartfelt stories and science with an invitation to thoughtfully explore your relationship to her concepts and lessons to make your life unimaginably radiant.

The very first chapter begins by sending you on a quest for your own authenticity. Among many unique teachings, Kate shares the powerful reflection of the dance between what she refers to as the shadow and sunny sides of any given topic. This effectively opens an opportunity for you to understand the depth and polarity in your life and asks you to consider that perhaps negativity isn't *bad* but rather a summons for eliciting emotional wisdom, growth, and healing. In concepts like the shadow and sunny side, you will experience the creativity, insight, and humor that make Kate's teachings so accessible. Her words are poetic, painting pictures of concepts she introduces while also cutting straight to the point so that you can immediately understand and apply her lessons.

To live a radiant life is an important and meaningful goal. Kate's work is to help you learn key principles and methods for your utilization as you peel back the layers of your life journey and challenge yourself with thought-provoking questions. This is just one of the surprising gifts (of which there are many) within the pages of this book. In the first few chapters, I felt that Kate was inviting me to be courageous and vulnerable enough with myself to look beneath the surface of my life and really dissect what supports and depletes me. Beyond those first chapters, the book traverses an impactful journey both inward and beyond the concepts of myself and my place in the world that I had previously held. In the final chapters, I felt encouragement and actionable support to truly integrate all I had learned. I enjoyed exploring what inspires me to grow, causes me to shrink, expands my self-perception, and challenges me.

This work spans the depth and complexity of understanding the nuances of integrity and accountability to oneself, as well as how such concepts weave into the fabric of relational connection. In a refined and digestible way, Kate teaches us to use the uniquely curated tools of parts work, ancestral healing, and art therapy for attending to deep trauma and wounding rooted in childhood and beyond. She makes the quest for growth and happiness accessible and applicable with this guiding resource.

Through and through, Kate's work of writing and teaching is a deep and clear template that builds awareness, confidence, and self-acceptance in whomever may read it. It activates revelation, healing, and growth as a rare gem in a sea that is saturated with clinical studies and self-help books. Dive in and illuminate your RADIANT LIFE!

With love and freedom,
Monika Zands, master coach and entrepreneur

Introduction

The boy at the beginning of a story has no way of knowing that the story has begun.
—ERIN MORGENSTERN, "THE STARLESS SEA"

THE ENTIRE WORLD CAME TO A SCREECHING HALT IN WHAT felt like the space of a heartbeat. It was reminiscent of the Hollywood blockbuster vibe of an apocalyptic screenplay. It seemed that, indeed, the world very well may have been ending. As I tend to do in moments of fear, my entire system—mind, heart, and body—went into freeze mode. It wasn't unfamiliar for me to feel immobilized by fear, but it was quite new to be frozen in the company of all of Earth's humanity. It was the onset of the Covid-19 pandemic, and none among us had a sense of the wild ride we were collectively buckling-up for.

This book is not about Covid-19, but the pandemic was an influencing factor that unearthed hidden opportunities for my growth and transformation—as adversity tends to do—and birthed this book as a self-healing toolkit for the masses with just the right balance of challenge and support. This writing aligned with my own exceedingly uncomfortable awakening at the beginning of 2022, which was uncovered by personal and professional burnout unlike anything I had ever before experienced. On the radiance scale, I'd say I was subterranean. I was a lackluster, dulled, and numbed version of myself, and I felt farther apart from my true nature than ever before. It became crystal clear that I needed to take extreme measures to counterbalance my stress and exhaustion. Working tirelessly as a healthcare provider during the pandemic while simultaneously navigating complex sociocultural expectations, an unsustainably expanded social network, my family's well-being, and my own personal fears of the Covid virus nearly drowned me.

To the shock and discomfort of my clients and larger community, I chose to take a four-month sabbatical from my work. You probably have your own associations for what a sacred pause of this kind means, but to me it felt wildly radical, moderately terrifying, and deeply profound. Stepping away from my work was an excruciatingly unfashionable choice to make within an industry best known for helping, healing, and even saving others. *Take care of yourself? I think not. You are a helper, and helpers do not have the convenient luxury of just not helping.* Or do they? Behind curtain number one lies a narrative that could use some tweaking. It reminds me of a quote spoken by my daughter around age three in response to my clumsy attempt to explain my introverted temperament in motherhood. With profound irritation in her voice she said, "But you're a mommy, and mommies don't need space!" When I announced my sabbatical, the response was quite similar, but of course the lingo surrounded *therapist* instead of *mommy*. My choice to step away from the demands of my work was not socially acceptable or normal, and many people judged and criticized me for it. I did not have a reason supported by society to take a break from work, such as maternity leave, death of a loved one, or treatment for a debilitating illness. Still, I took the time. I did so against my own cultural conditioning because I desperately needed rest, repair, and rekindling with my authentic Self. I needed to stoke the inner fire of my soul and life force to bring my radiance back online.

And just like that, *The Radiant Life Project* was born.

By calling *The Radiant Life Project* a *project*, I acknowledge the work-in-progress we all are. I honor the continuous process of growth and discovery in the journey toward the life we are each capable of creating for ourselves. For the sake of living radiantly, hear me when I say this: The single most crucial project any of us will ever experience—the one that has the most profound impact on the whole of your being—is the ongoing project of healing and inner growth. Like climbing an infinite staircase, the project of Self has no particular destination, but with each step it elevates you.

As I made the commitment to climb the staircase toward my radiant life with the initiation of my sabbatical, I noticed an interesting contrast to the wave of judgment that had initially ensued in response to my intentional efforts for rest and repair. An unbelievable number of other therapists, medical providers, caregivers, and community members responded with surprising support and even accolades. I suddenly realized that was I surrounded by many others who had drifted dangerously away from their radiance too. My choice to step out of the madness of our normal societal rhythm had reflected to these people their own imbalances. They had also become so caught up in their many projects that their Self-project had been sadly neglected. These community members responded to my experience of burnout with resonance, but had not yet given themselves permission to extricate their strangled voices from the vice-grip of societal expectations and cry out for help. Somewhere along the way, the authenticity and radiance of these empathic others had clustered together and sunk to the bottom of their ever-growing and demanding priority list.

It was in this moment of realization that I understood the importance of modeling in our relationships with one another. The necessity for such modeling to stem from a deeply honest, human, and humble place suddenly seemed of crucial importance. It was then that I realized this important truth: Only with a stance of undeniable genuineness can we join together to shape the collective expectations surrounding us all. When we link arms and together participate in constructing a platform infused with authenticity, we provide the necessary spaciousness and understanding for ourselves and our communities to not only remain safe, healthy, and sane but also to become radiant.

For me, intentionally stepping away from the shoulds, supposed-to's and you musts of social conditioning was a courageous and necessary movement toward healing. This shift allowed me to support myself while also modeling for my clients and others what the return to Self can look like. I actively marched beyond the trance of society's definition of success, adulting, and professional identity in order to attend inwardly. You may be wondering, *Why would she do such a thing? This sounds like professional suicide! Interpersonal disgrace! A one-way ticket to the sticky swamp of unemployment leading to a lesser lifestyle!* My answer is simple: I stepped outside the box of societal expectations because it did not align with who I actually was in that very moment of time, and what I needed. Simple as that.

The pandemic combined with persistent issues of racism, social injustice for marginalized communities, political unrest, and closed-mindedness toward interpersonal diversity clearly triggered collective hardship. Is it any wonder that the resulting pain and suffering has trickled down to affect each of us in various mental, emotional, physical, spiritual, and energetic ways? Serious problems like these create deeply rooted groupthink patterns that result in large-scale devastation and distress. When such energetics persist, our individual and collective radiance dulls, and we default to cultural numbness and avoidance.

Psychological trauma, mental illness, physical and emotional pain, and disembodied value systems are at an all-time high within our society. Most people are running in an endless rat-race toward—where exactly? Most of us subscribe to insidious beliefs related to money, power, and status that were established long ago as guidelines for existence. We strive toward the endless pursuit of substances, materials, and algorithm-derived popularity with the intention to survive another day in one piece. We have become guided by who we think we are supposed to be rather than who we actually are. When asked this most basic question—*"Who are you?"*—the vast majority of my clients respond with a profound and resounding *"I have no idea."*

With your consent and active participation, you can shift your adherence away from the toxic cultural narratives that hold you back and diminish your inner flame. This book is a groundbreaking guide for deep inner healing and self-growth based on getting clear on who you are as a person—not defined by your online followers, financial net-worth, your parents' hopes and dreams for you, or your position of seniority in your exclusive poker club. It's about discovering your very essence and nurturing the brilliant pilot light that is your lifeforce. This work centers around living in celebration and congruence with your highest and most authentic You.

As you read along, you will encounter invitations called *offerings* throughout the text. Please pause and thoughtfully consider each offering in your mind, heart, journal, and sketchbook while you journey through the chapters. Take advantage of the opportunities to bring this work into your real life by actively exercising the book's teachings in the moment. It's okay to move back and forth from the book to your journal as you sit with new revelations and insights and integrate the information. Though you can return to this text for years of generative growth inspiration, it is not meant to support a future You who lives on a horizon somewhere beyond the present. No, this work is for the You who is here and willing to elevate now. Intentionally invite the deep inner Self forward to explore and experience this meaningful authenticity-based transformative work.

You will notice that I speak about the concept of *authenticity* with reverence and honor. I place it at a rank of priority alongside our human needs for food, sleep, breath, and love. You will soon learn about the profound link between authenticity and radiance. As it turns out, living with both qualities fully intact and on-board is the straightest shot toward a meaningful life. To return home to your truest Self, you must deliberately shed any disingenuous bits you have accumulated from living on autopilot. Such qualities may be based on apathy, victimization, insecurity, unhealed wounds, or other heavy weights upon your precious soul. Without the veil of illusory obscurants, you will find yourself more able to open up and see our world and your Self from a fresh perspective.

Now (maybe more than ever) is a powerful time for each of us to return home to our authentic Selves. When we make contact with the elemental quality of our being, we free ourselves to live with aligned intentionality. From such efforts comes deeper access to the necessary ingredients for building radiance into the next chapter both individually and collectively. Answer me this: If not now, when? One of my favorite Chinese proverbs says, "The best time to plant a tree was twenty years ago. The second-best time is now." The same goes for returning to radiance. If you've been lost for a while, there's no time better than the eternal Now to ignite your soul and return home. You may notice your mind drumming up a laundry list of questions about the how/ why/when/and who, and I've got a one-size-fits-all answer for all of those questions. I call it *the authenticity answer*. I have found that solutions and answers are always available if you willingly dive beneath the fluff and obligations of life to discern what is aligned and real in the moment you are in. Authenticity is always the answer, and it is a direct vein toward a radiant life.

From these pages you will learn to thoughtfully use the authenticity answer in your own life, and you will also learn to become your own mapmaker. You will discover opportunities to integrate the teachings from the following chapters in specificity to your unique needs, perspective, and identity. Together we will investigate cultural messages, scientific teachings, psychological methodologies, creative invitations, and spiritual practices to serve your inner-growth process. We will also take an honest look at the barriers that keep you from accessing the strength and permission you need to live in congruence with your true Self and embody the radiance you so yearn for.

The coming chapters are lovingly packed with tools, practices, teachings, and resources that will bring you into contact with your inner flame. You will traverse a supportive journey that will help you engage layers of healing, release suffering, and return to the radiance that is your birthright. You will learn to remove effortful participation in the endless narratives of who you believe you are supposed to be as an individual, part of a family or system, professional, and member of society. With this empowering self-work, you will not only find encouragement and validation to foster your own growth, inspiration, and movement into brilliant inner alignment but you will also become well-resourced for ongoing systemic well-being.

This book is intended to guide you on a thorough exploration of the life experiences that most challenge you and prevent active participation in your life. You will explore the depths of interpersonal connection and relationships, barriers to authentic engagement with meaningful activities and work, and early wounding that prevents satisfaction and joy. You may even come face to face with factors that influence your very will to live. You will be asked to open your mind and heart to new perspectives and practices and to consider looking at life through different lenses than ever before.

It is my sincere hope that this eclectic blend of gifts and offerings will help you access deep layers within yourself that are primed and ready for healing but may not have been previously recognized as such. The material of these pages may open inner doors you have long forgotten or, possibly, never knew existed at all. You may gain access to memories, possibilities, and experiences yet unimaginable for you. I invite you to act courageously for the purpose of your emotional, psychological, and spiritual freedom. Remain open to integrating new practices and tools that will build upon the wisdom you already possess. By combining new skills with your valuable lived experiences, you can create a sustainable intrinsic foundation from which you can live your radiant life.

I hope that this book will act as a guiding lantern in your discovery of reorienting yourself in relationship to your life. When you forge a new path forward toward meaningful purpose, intentionality, and harmony in the way you live, any limitations you previously perceived become negotiable. I invite you to question belief systems that may be holding you back, overworking you, or perpetuating your pursuit toward the proverbial carrot on a stick that always seems beyond reach. You will be guided to explore and identify patterns you engage with in daily life that no longer serve you. It's time to get curious about your personal flavor of authenticity. You will be summoned to delve into the healthy and unhealthy dynamics of your relationships and inquire about the design and construction of the very thoughts, stories, and values that swim within your psyche.

I invite you to read this book with true openness. Consider that what you have been taught, and all you know about human experience, is not set in stone. Take what resonates with you from these pages and leave what doesn't, but please be willing to consider the possibility that it's time for a radical change. Though the old paradigm of living may have served you well for however long, it's okay if it no longer aligns. If your inner light is not shining with the brilliance of its greatest capacity, I hope you will trust my invitation to welcome a shift.

If you choose to believe in anything, consider this: You were not meant to live a dull, uninspired life on autopilot. I can't tell you why we're here in existence, but I would bet my piggy bank its not to live half asleep and dreary. Becoming honest about the misalignment within your Self (and working toward changing it) is a rewarding and healthy pursuit. Contemplate the prospect that the entirety of your life, everything you believe and value, can be reworked. With such an expansive mindset, you can allow space for your wounds to truly heal and your magnificent desires to bloom freely. Nothing is off-limits for this powerful work, no matter how deeply engrained or socially entangled it may be. Become courageous enough to invite gentleness in. Hear the whispers of your soul and body. When you listen to your Self as the source of wisdom, you will learn to honor your true nature and attend to the needs and desires within. From an empowered perspective, you can bravely step off the rollercoaster of life, set down the expectations and obligations society has heaped upon your shoulders, and stop living a life you did not actively choose in exchange for one that truly fills and nourishes you from the inside out.

Let's dive in, shall we?

The Quest for Authenticity

Seeking a Fresh Face in the Sea of Masks

Who we are is far more meaningful than anything we will ever do.
                    —Robert Schwartz, *"Your Soul's Plan"*

The orchid hypothesis, discussed in David Dobbs' 2009 article "The Science of Success" in the *Atlantic*[1] talks about two very different types of children: *orchid children,* who present as deeply sensitive, potentially fragile, and in need of more delicate care, and *dandelion children,* identified by their seemingly resilient, hearty personas that bounce back quickly from the world's challenges and do not need careful tending. The delineation of these two types originated from a scientific study by Marian Bakermans-Kranenburg in 2004 that considered the ways genes shape behavior—specifically in children.[2] Several key behavioral genes were discovered in the study's children that seemed to increase their vulnerability to specific mental health conditions and imbalances or mood sensitivities. Children with the key genes would later be identified by psychologist Bruce Ellis and pediatrician W. Thomas Boyce as *orchid children*.[3] As research progressed beyond the initial 2004 findings, various studies narrowed in on the topic. A great deal of learning about what is often called the *genetic vulnerability model* followed, surrounding the discovery of specific genes that predispose children to mental health conditions. Although such research may seem dooming, scientists began to notice an incredible upside when they implemented a slight reframe: The genes previously considered problematic in orchid children also tend to increase the children's potential for incredibly high propensity toward creativity, empathic attunement, and other magnificent gifts that come with heightened sensitivity.

In my therapy practice, I often ask my clients to consider both the *shadow side* and the *sunny side* of a topic. This process invites a person to notice where the seemingly undesirable or negative qualities of a situation are counterbalanced by a positive, beneficial perspective if only they remember to expand their minds beyond their initial perception. Thinking like this is necessary for noticing how a devastating breakup, for example, provides freedom from an unhealthy relational dynamic. The shadow side is the pain of heartbreak, while the sunny side is the healthy release from an injurious tether. This is not shallow optimism; it requires a pivot of attention in the service of reading between the lines of a situation to notice the blessings buried in the rubble that you may not have seen before. Nothing in life, especially emotional or psychological qualities of human behavior, is one-dimensional. Like the shadow side/sunny side approach, the orchid hypothesis invites us into a new perspective of sensitivity that allows for expansion beyond an initial negative judgment. A mindset shift such as this opens us up to notice the wildly imaginative and spectacular facets of human experience that we may have missed by looking through too narrow of a lens.

Akin to most talents and gifts that exist within each remarkable human being, the nurturance and gentleness with which the orchid aptitude is handled makes an immense difference in how it manifests. If their sensitivities are not appreciated and nourished, orchid children are more likely than their counterparts to shut down, slide into mental illness, inflict harm upon themselves, and even become a danger to others. On the flip side, when people with this more tender temperament feel safe and supported in attuned environments with gentle caregivers, sensitive children tend to develop into undeniably brilliant, abundantly creative people with a plethora of admirable gifts to share with the world.

As with all humans, dandelion children also benefit from wholehearted environments, however their well-being does not depend on it nearly as much as that of orchid children. The resilient and steady temperament of dandelion children enables them to share their unique gifts with the world while remaining more durable when it comes to the bumpy potholes of life. In nature, a dandelion seedling will grow wherever it has been planted—even if it must grow through the unfriendly cracks of a city sidewalk. Like their namesake, dandelion children do not need optimal conditions in order to thrive. They possess the genetic predisposition to successfully grow into robust, healthy adults even if they are not provided an ideal starting place. But we can't all be tough dandelion children. All of nature holds the crucial balance of soft/hard, large/small, sweet/bitter. The world needs variety, and it would be a much darker, more heartless place without the gift of orchid children to balance the scales of humankind.

Offering: Muse for a moment on whether you identify most as an orchid or dandelion. Explore the gifts and challenges you have experienced in relationship to your temperament in your journal.

I share this powerful scientific work with you to highlight the importance of the individual differences among and between us. Although human beings have much in common with one another, we are not all built and wired the same. Depending on your genes, the amount of nurturance you received in your childhood and young adult environment, and whether you lean more toward the *orchid* or *dandelion* ends of the temperament spectrum, your authentic Self will need unique sustenance, stimuli, care, and support in order to radiate its brilliance into the world. Honoring differences such as these without shame or value judgments about which is better or worse allows for each person's essential Self to exist as whole and valuable in its natural form. The point is not to force an orchid child into a dandelion temperament or vice versa. This will fail every time, and it will damage that precious Self. If you happen to identify with the orchid temperament, I invite you to lean in and fully embrace that valuable facet of who you are. Lovingly place your hand over your heart and tell yourself that you are exactly who you were meant to be—your tenderness is one of your gifts.

THE LAYERS OF US
Oftentimes when practicing authenticity work, a person may discover that they have buried the more delicate, vulnerable

qualities of who they are for protection. An art therapy exercise I enjoy exploring with clients involves investigating the layers of masks and psychological armor they wear (mostly unconsciously) to protect such aspects of their innermost Self from visibility, exposure, and risk. In this particular directive, I like to use blank wooden matryoshka dolls, commonly known as Russian nesting dolls—you know, the ones where you can pop open the doll to find a smaller doll inside of it, and a smaller one within that one, and smaller and smaller until you discover the final tiny doll that no longer breaks open.

In this creative metaphor, we are each flesh matryoshka dolls with elaborately constructed layers that act as convincing masks to protect us from the world. For this directive, I ask clients to paint and decorate each doll to represent their most commonly used masks in order of their dominance.

One client of mine, whom I'll call Miriam, was seeing me for relationship dissatisfaction in her marriage. Miriam painted her outermost doll with flowers and warm colors, representing her surface-level presentation of herself to the world as a pleasing, compliant, likable person. She called this her *Lovely Lady* persona. Just beneath the flowery layer rested a different Self she revealed exclusively to her spouse, close friends, and family members. This second layer was her self-proclaimed *Weepy Girl*, who carried deep unhappiness and sadness. Miriam depicted *Weepy Girl* with long dripping lines of blue and gray rain. On the next layer in, she used red and black hatch marks to represent the pain and agony of her *Pissy Rebel* identity, witnessed only in the dark moments of contention in her marriage. Miriam addressed this layer hesitantly and described it as the raging and resentful part of her. Miriam brought two more layers to life beneath the

Pissy Rebel before finally encountering what she simply called *Me*. She painted this innermost doll with brilliant rainbow colors. Miriam spoke about her internal *me* with reverence and love, explaining its representation of her most basic essence. Through her creative process, Miriam had found her authentic Self.

I like to use art when exploring layers. As Miriam's story exemplifies, therapeutic art making is incredibly insightful and expressive. Writing often results in a similar effect. Regardless of the method you choose to use in this type of exploration, it is important to understand that we all have layers. It is normal and healthy—and a natural response to being a person in this wild jungle called Life.

In addition to understanding the many layers within, it is also important to acknowledge that the path toward a radiant life is a complex and meandering one. I do not believe it is possible for any of us to live in total alignment 100 percent of the time. It's just not realistic to expect this of ourselves, no matter how authentically we live. The outer layers of our psychological nesting dolls exist for a reason, and it makes sense that they come forward from time to time to mask us however they believe they need to. The point is not to rid ourselves of our matryoshka layers. Instead, this work is meant to acknowledge that various layers exist within each of us. We must learn to appreciate our shields for the adaptive functions they serve, and then intentionally return to our authentic Selves.

Meditation is similar in that the goal is not to remove all thoughts from our human monkey minds. The intention of meditation is to be present with the thoughts that arise, notice and observe them, and then return to the breath and centered practice. In meditation it is thoughts that derail us, and on the journey toward a radiant life it is matryoshka masks. In both scenarios, it is essential to practice grace and self-forgiveness when we notice that we have strayed from our true Selves, and then lovingly bring ourselves back to the task at hand—in this case, the congruent experience of inner authenticity.

Anchoring is a helpful practice that aides in accessing Self. When you feel caught in a whirlwind that feels perceptibly not You, anchoring helps to clear the storm. Just like a ship uses its anchor to lock into solid ground, there are qualities within you that serve the same function. These are the elements of your essential Self that you are already aware of; the parts of you that you know well and feel sure of. When you rest your focus on the aspects of your Self that you inherently trust as true, there's a natural separation—like oil from water—that illuminates who you know yourself to be. These are your anchors, and they lock directly into your core value system, which is a dominant ingredient in your recipe for authenticity. An example of an anchor from my life is nature. I know without a doubt that being in nature, especially on a long walking trail surrounded by trees and colorful flora, is integral to my essential Self. I am healthiest, happiest, and most whole when I make daily contact with nature. If I find I have strayed apart from my authentic Self, or need realignment, I can discern whether my nature anchor is intact. Like good medicine, intentionally returning to nature will heal and refresh me every time. A friend of mine anchors in bodies of water because the buoyancy of floating brings her back to her Self. Maybe your anchor is related to animals, family, yogic stretching, or photography. Anchors can also be internal qualities like your sense of humor or creative drive.

Offering: Take a moment to write about three of your anchors in your journal.

Now that you have discovered some of your anchors, consider journaling about their function in your life so that you can gain clarity about how to access them.

FINDING TRUE NORTH

Now let's shift from anchors to compasses. Far above us, the North Star, or Stella Polaris, perches high in the velvety heavens. Talk about radiant! Because of its location in the sky, this guiding star doesn't appear to move around as other stars do. Polaris is a fixed point that has been used as a compass by sailors, explorers, and hunters throughout history when no other landmarks were in sight. Martha Beck beautifully juxtaposes the North Star with our human potential for high-integrity authentic living in her book *Finding Your Own North Star: Claiming the Life You Were Meant to Live.* Humans, as well as perhaps all other animals, possess an inner True North, just like our reliable North Star in the heavens, that continuously steers us toward our essential Selves. It is from that interior home within our Selves that the radiance within each one of us can emanate. In some ways, our True North points us toward survival, as wired by Mother Nature for the continuation of our species. Other aspects of True North, for humans at least, are more subtle. These relate to our drive to pursue alignment with our value system, core beliefs, and high spiritual purpose. The pull toward these deeper and more profound inner priorities is a powerful attractive force toward our radiant potential. When we're authentically aligned, we can feel the resonance of being in congruity with who we truly are at our purest level, and we shine brightly into all areas of our lives.

But what if we get lost? As happens in the night sky under thick cloud cover or weather patterns, the shimmer of our North Star can become obscured behind the distractions of our busy minds and emotional hurricanes. When we can no longer see or feel the pull of our North Star, we can use an internal compass system to help us find our way back to it. Tools like intuition, instinct, truthful mirroring from trusted sources, and honest cognitive and emotional processing are all helpful built-in mechanisms that can return us to True North. When using a trusty compass, you can bet that whichever direction you turn, its needle will always point at Polaris. Similarly, your dependable internal tool kit will bring you safely back into congruity with your authentic Self when you float astray.

During a time in my life when I was deeply investigating my inner compass and ensuring my alignment with my own True North, I purchased a necklace for myself as a totem, or tangible reminder. I was specific in choosing a necklace that embodied my personal concept of the energetic quality of True North in its color, shape, and feel. I wear this necklace to this day, even as I type these words, as a reminder that I have a guiding North Star within me that I can always access. I trust implicitly that my authentic Self will always guide me through life with connection to who I truly am, and it will remind me to make choices that are congruent with my purpose and live radiantly. When I lose sight, experience ungroundedness, or feel my self-trust wavering, I place my hand upon my North Star necklace and return to the home base of my authentic Self. A physical item like my necklace can be a helpful touchstone to remind you of what matters and who you are. I recommend that you consider what carries meaning of this kind for you and try to keep your totem nearby for moments when you need it. A friend of mine keeps heart-shaped rocks she finds in nature at her front door as a totem. I know someone else who infused this type of meaning into a hand-written statement she carries in her wallet. Your personal totem can take any shape or form you'd like; what is important is that it carries the sacred reminder of your innermost truth.

Offering: What might be a meaningful totem for you? Jot down or sketch your ideas in your journal or sketchbook.

You may notice as you tap into the magnetism of your True North that certain grievances may arise in your dynamics with other people, as well as insecurities within your Self related to how you are being perceived in your newly aligned state. These are natural speed bumps along the road to authenticity. The key is to remain as true to your alignment as possible regardless of the judgments, criticisms, or doubts of everyone surrounding you. In Western culture, we are not taught to follow the beat of our own drum; we are taught to fit in. Capturing the radiance of your authentic Self may cause you to stand out—if not obviously, at least in subtle ways that will undoubtedly be perceptible to those who have grown comfortable with you in your misaligned state. Although they may have the best of intentions, if these people resist your growth and alignment, it means they have benefitted from your self-abandonment and are committed to your adherence to the outdated Self you once were but no longer are.

Brene Brown calls people like this *flame blower-outers.* They do not protect and nurture the flame that is your true Self but rather hold investment in either blowing out your light or keeping it small. Although you can offer a conversation to help such people in your life better understand the changes you are undergoing as you venture toward your True North, their participation, agreement, approval, and permission are not necessary for your growth process. You have the spiritual freedom to grow, change, heal, and reorient yourself in your life whenever you choose, in any fashion that you see fit. You do not need anyone's permission or blessing to capture your radiant life, nor is it anyone else's right to dictate who you are.

Now, let's dive into a few powerful practices to use in regaining alignment with True North when you find yourself astray:

Values: The values at the core of your authentic Self are the qualities of your life that matter most to you and anchor and ground you. These are the essential beliefs you hold about yourself, the things, people, or experiences you most passionately believe in and will fight for, and the pieces of your world that you hold most sacred. Given the potency of values, it is alarming how easily many people stray from honoring theirs. The good news is that once you become aware that you have either floated apart from or betrayed your values, it is easy to regain alignment with them because they are so essential to your being. Values fit into a person's energetic frequency the way a key fits into its lock. Once a person regains contact with their values, the resonance feels so right that it's easy to reintegrate the value and live more fully from its influence.

Offering: A simple exercise to help you identify your values and discern whether you are living from them is to write a list of what you care a lot about. You may write words like family, fitness, physical appearance, the safety of animals in the rainforest, etc. Write until you have thirty items on your list (I know, it's a lot. Dig deep).

These are what I call your *library of personal values*, and they highlight the bundle of the bits of life that matter most to you. It can be hard to consistently live in total congruity with so many values, so let's whittle it down further. Comb through your list and circle your ten highest-priority values. Finally, select three values from your circled ten that are of ultimate importance beyond all else in your life. These are your *core values*. They are the things/people/experiences that are most sacred to you. If they zapped out of existence, these would be the parts of your life you would desperately miss, and their absence would leave behind a painful void. Next, get radically honest with yourself and discern how closely you are living in coherence with these core values. If family is at the top of your priority list, but you rarely spend time with your loved ones because of your hectic work schedule, you're not living in alignment with that value and something needs to change for you to live more authentically. If you value your mental health above all else but you frequently place yourself in situations where you feel anxious, depressed, or depleted, you've got an inconsistency. The first step toward returning to your values is noticing where you have strayed, so for your own sake just be honest about how you have self-betrayed in this way, and from that vantage point you can make positive change.

Intentionality: The degree to which you are intentional with your behaviors, relationships, actions, and words has an enormous effect upon your adherence to your True North. If you are coasting along on comfortably numb autopilot, not actively making thoughtful decisions and being passive or avoidant, you're definitely astray. Buying into mass belief systems or participating in groupthink at the deficit of thinking for yourself makes you a bit like a drone plugged into the matrix. With an unconscious mindset, you will not have the capacity to tailor-make your life to the unique and special flavor that is authentically yours and yours alone. This is not to say that you shouldn't participate in groups or communities—you definitely should, because all humans need connection. Just don't believe everything you hear or allow yourself to be guided by anyone but yourself. Never disregard your own brilliant intelligence and intuition for anyone or anything. In short: WAKE UP and think for yourself. Then make thoughtful, considerate, clear choices in your life that align with who you truly are and follow the path that leads to your unique radiant life.

Offering: In your journal, list three places in your life where you often slip into cruise control. Then, through introspective writing, investigate how you can reclaim your power.

Your "Sweet Spot": We all lie somewhere on the introvert/extrovert spectrum, and honoring the way you fill up your energetic tank is essential for authentic living. An introvert cannot be made into an extrovert by mass exposure to people, events, and busy parties, and an extrovert will not enjoy forced solitude. These qualities within us are not something to change but to embrace. When you lean in to your true nature and follow the threads toward what lights you up and leaves you feeling satisfied, peaceful, and full-hearted, you are in alignment with True North. Because introversion and extroversion are nuanced, not binary, you get to find your sweet spot where you engage, retreat, participate, and observe in the special blend that is your particular comfort level. When you release pressure or obligation and simply honor your internal compass, you will say yes to the forms of connection and activity that align for you and no to the ones that don't.

Offering: On a scale from one to ten (one being extremely introverted, ten being extremely extroverted, and five being neutral), write in your journal about your place on the introvert/extrovert spectrum. Consider how well you honor your temperament and if there are circumstances in your life for which you push yourself out of your true nature.

BE REAL, BUT STAY KIND

To close this chapter on authenticity, I want to speak to something that often trips people up as they start navigating toward True North. Living in congruity with your essential Self and moving away from the people, things, experiences, and behaviors that do not align with who you truly are is a major ingredient in the recipe that cooks up a radiant life. With that being said, it can sometimes be tricky to remain kind and respectful in your authenticity territory. Being cruel or unkind in the name of realness is not the name of the game. Telling someone a harsh truth is still harsh, even if it is true. There are many possible ways to be true and real without being hurtful.

I speak from experience with this, because it was a huge learning curve for me to understand how to balance the honest truth as I saw it with the fiery righteousness within me that was ego-based and hurtful. This was especially challenging when I tried to have conversations about experiences where I felt hurt or mistreated, and I had a particular agenda about wanting to rectify a painful experience by making someone feel badly about what they had done to me.

One such experience rolled out in a series of three conversations I had with my mother where I gave voice to the hurt and woundedness I had experienced in our relationship. Where I went wrong was not my intention to communicate my pain but my delivery—it was far less than kind. I have a strong Aries spirit and, admittedly, I have the capacity to singe. At that point in my life, I had to learn that it was not my job to punish someone who I had felt hurt by, but to communicate my experience and offer genuine effort toward repair. What I needed to express to my mother was real. It was important and valid and true. However, the way I conveyed my pain was laced with so much venom that she was unable to hear the broken-heartedness of the hurt person sitting in front of her. She was so blinded by my fiery emotional darts that our conversations had no chance of providing healing for either of us.

I didn't understand this at first. During our conversations, I thought I was being strong, assertive, and effectively using my voice to express my truth. Later when I recounted my experience with my therapist, she did not respond with the pride or accolades I expected for being brave, strong, and real. Instead, she answered with difficult feedback that I will always remember. She said to me, "No, Kate. What you did was burn your mother's house down. That is not the work we are doing here. It is not kind to burn anyone's house down, no matter what they have done to you." And she was right. I had slammed my mother with such violent blame, accusation, and anger that in those conversations I had harmed her too. Two wounded people is not better than one. It is not fair to hurt the person who hurt you, nor is it reparative in any way. Sure, it may feel cathartic, but healing, no.

Offering: In your journal, write about a time when you figuratively "burned someone's house down" with words, actions, or emotions that you later realized were cruel or counterproductive (even if you're just realizing it in this very moment).

I learned from those conversations with my mother that high-integrity communication is thoughtful, considerate, respectful, and kind. It's not always easy to express difficult and painful truths with such qualities intact, but it is well worth the extra effort to figure out how to do so whenever a situation of this kind arises. Here are a few helpful tools for this kind of authentic expression and communication:

- **Use "I-statements."** When I expressed my feelings toward my mother, I could have said *I felt hurt when you did that* instead of saying *you hurt me when you did that.* Approaching my mother with constructive conversation rather than aggressiveness and blame would have quelled her defensiveness and made a heartfelt conversation more possible.

- **Practice accountability.** Take responsibility for your part in the dynamic, and own your missteps and errors. Rather than saying *You never want to help me, and you are so critical of my choices* I could have said *I* *should have more clearly expressed my needs and my desire for you to support me.*

- **Give the other person the benefit of the doubt** that they did the best they could and they're imperfect just like you. Instead of saying *You don't care about me or my feelings* try something like *I believe you care about me, but maybe you didn't know that I was sensitive to this particular issue.*

With love, respect, and thoughtfulness, it is entirely possible to behave in ways that are both authentic and kind. Take it easy on yourself when you practice this, because it is something that takes care and intentionality. If you mistakenly (or intentionally) burn someone's house down like I did, a sincere apology is in order. A good apology does not include excuses, defensiveness, explanation, or blame, and it does not guarantee that you will be forgiven immediately or ever. If you burn someone's house down or cause harm or damage, please understand that your apology must come without expectations but with the sole intention of making amends. It can be really challenging to humble yourself and admit that you were actually the dragon in the room when you had been adamantly focused on the other person playing that role, but this is a crucial aspect of authenticity.

Not every brick on the road to a radiant life is comfortable, happy, or easy. That's alright—it's not supposed to be. Authentic living can be really hard sometimes. Keep going anyway; I promise it is worth it. Remember: Hardship often brings hidden gifts to conscious awareness. With intentional work, such realizations later develop into unimaginably meaningful ripples that can affect the lives of yourself and others.

Culture

What We've Been Spoon-Fed All Our Lives

Keep some room in your heart for the unimaginable.
—*MARY OLIVER*

WESTERN CULTURE TEACHES THAT A PINCH OF JOY, A DASH of ease, and a heaping spoonful of happiness boil together into an ideal life. I've personally never met a person who has perfected this recipe, and I doubt I ever will. In my experience, each human life is composed of a much more complex set of ingredients—yes, happiness and joy, but so much more. Fear, wonder, stress, hardship, exuberance, anxiety, and many more ingredients also exist in the dynamic and multifaceted life of a human being. There seems no way around the inevitability of hardship, and yet a meaningful life is well within reach. How? Let me tell you.

A meaningful life is not the same as a perfect, stress-free, easy life (per our culture's definition). The truth is much more dynamic and nonlinear. Humans are meaning-makers, and adversity tends to strengthen the meaning we make about our experiences. The radiance that is always available to you is mutually exclusive from your hardship and suffering. Both exist simultaneously, and it is important to understand that each endures to enhance the other. Contrast is necessary because it allows us to notice the edge between darkness and light—and appreciate the differences. Without the cold ocean depths, we wouldn't appreciate the warmth of coral reefs—and so it goes with experience. Radiant embodiment of joy, happiness, and love lose their depth if we haven't also experienced grief, pain, and struggle. We need contrast like we need air.

Anyone who has experienced difficult times, even brief moments of real challenge, can likely attest to the reality that we learn when we struggle. The entire globe experienced this reality during the Covid-19 pandemic, which inadvertently unearthed gifts (albeit shrouded in trauma and stress) in the form of awakening our souls to the brokenness and misalignment of our collective way of life. Our most difficult life lessons and experiences are immensely valuable aspects of our growth journey, and the same is true relationally. The most challenging people in each of our lives are our greatest teachers if we can only see them as such. Experiences of relational discord, misalignment, and human cruelty, uncomfortable as they may be, provide the necessary material for us to do the work that leads to our growth and evolution.

Offering: Which challenging relationships have been important teachers in your life? And how? Explore this in your journal or talk to a loved one about the lessons your relationships have taught you.

Another powerful way we learn through struggle is evidenced by our brains' integration of a new skill or hobby. Nobody is born a master chess player, but I'm sure we can all conjure up a mental image of the talented people who learn to strategize and maneuver those black and white pieces with incredible mastery (*Queen's Gambit,* anyone?). You can bet that the learning process for a master chess player wasn't automatic or easy, but it certainly built their brain to operate on a magnificently high level for their matches through care, effort, and plenty of time spent wrestling with challenge.

Not a chess master and can't relate? Here are a few other real-life examples for the modern human:

- A medical patient's valiant pursuit of vitality while navigating a chronic illness.

- The herculean effort of a mental health warrior pulling himself out of bed in the morning when caught under the weight of depression.

- A terrified person inundated with fear of failure and criticism who musters the courage to stand at a podium for public speaking.

- Parents everywhere bringing newborns home from hospitals without even the slightest clue how to swaddle.

Challenging experiences of all shapes and sizes hold the potential for us to access intellectual, emotional, spiritual, and psychological improvements. It is good medicine to do things that feel hard. Growth doesn't happen nearly as often when we are feeling comfy-cozy easy-breezy, and with growth comes an ever-increasing capacity for radiance.

This is not to say that ease is insignificant—quite the opposite. We all need breathers to gear up for the inevitable challenges of the future. As Bethany Webster wisely states in her book *Discovering the Inner Mother*,[1] "Act only when inspired. Otherwise rest."

The sweet, precious reprieve of rest is an important aspect of the cycles that persist in life. We must inhale/exhale. We must give/receive. We must exert/rest. Human beings are built with resilience in our blood, hope in our bones, and the capacity for inspiration in our very tissue. Rest is the magical ingredient that brings power to our infinite potential.

Operating from a resourced system supercharges the limitless depth and wonder of each and every soul on this planet. It's easy to remain within the single-dimension of the known when we are stuck in the throes of stress, exhaustion, or the perilous climb up one social/political/professional ladder or another. Just remember, there is still much we can sense but cannot prove about the miraculous human experience; similarly, the full enchantment of our astonishing oceans and outer space galaxy remain mysterious to even the very brightest of scientists. Think how far we have come as a species, all we've learned, and all we know. Then consider all we have yet to learn. The possibilities are infinite, but what we know for sure is that we are not robotic creatures who can eternally exert and produce. To reap the greatest benefit of our labor, we must build the relief of cessation into our everyday proceedings. We will more thoroughly discuss rest in Chapter 3, but for now just know it's an important piece of the puzzle.

The vibrant triad of rest, authenticity, and meaningful purpose intertwine in a reciprocal dance to support our human souls. Though profound, such notions can easily slip into lofty nebulous territory when applied to the day-to-day meandering of people on planet Earth. The irony of these seemingly innocuous concepts is that despite their existential depth, they have become cliché because everyone's sick and tired of trying to manifest them in a culture that doesn't know how to unplug.

On a whim, I asked my mailman what he thinks gives life meaning and purpose. He broke out into nervous laughter and simply replied, "Beats me. Let me know when you find out." See? Cliché, and laughable. But maybe there's more. If you are willing to move beneath the linguistics that have become socially overused and superficially tossed around, I think we each know in our guts that there's something here worth exploring, if only we had the spare energy reserves and glowing arrow pointing our way.

Every friend, family member, and client I have polled on the topic of meaning and purpose admit that they have wrestled with questions surrounding the tricky, almost indefinable concepts as they consider why they're alive and what to do with the ever-perplexing nature of their being.

Offering: Journal about the following questions to gain deeper insight:

> *What do you think the meaning of life is?*
> *What do you think your purpose is?*
> *How do you feel about these questions?*

A shockingly small number of people take their "meaning and purpose" thought process a level deeper into authenticity territory to consider their genuine gifts and interests rather than simply assuming the cultural landslide of *should* and *supposed to's*. Every person I polled explained their reality of feeling suffocated under life's responsibilities. After a long day of chores, work, and obligations, they reported feeling too depleted to even consider such an existential topic. *Yeah, regaining alignment with my soul's purpose sounds fun. Let me get back to you when I finally win this rat-race and shoot a superhuman dose of motivation and inspiration through my system.*

We have become so busy running around in the modern game of Life that considering the very reason for living has grown to feel like a luxury we cannot afford. If this is true, then what's the point of being here at all if we are simply spinning like hamsters on an endless wheel? Something that seems abundantly clear to me is that we all want our lives to be meaningful. We do not want to waste away in a bone-draining existence without living the illusive experiences of contribution, peace, joy, and love that make it all worthwhile. Despite our constantly depleting energy reserves, most people spend years journeying toward achieving such an end, as if it is an actual end to achieve. But what if it's not? Maybe we have it backwards.

I wonder if the trick to unlocking the type of meaning we yearn for is to think about our experiences in a new paradigm-shifting way: Life does not have meaning *despite* its difficulties (like some kind of enormous workaround process avoiding discomfort and suffering). Meaning comes on-board when we *include* our challenges and ambitions by braiding them into the cacophony of our messy, brilliant, humbling human experiences. This is how we access radiance: by delicately blending all of life's shades and colors and integrating the subsequent ripples they create. This is what makes life worth living—but only if we remember the secret ingredient, which (every single time) is authenticity.

It is my firm belief that authenticity is the answer to any and all of your questions. It may not be the answer you want to hear, the easy or fast one, but it's the true answer. If you want to know who you are, what you care about, and who's hat to hang yours next to at the end of the day, tap into your inner compass to ascertain your answer. Anything else is artificial sweetener or straight-up poison.

HUMAN CONNECTION—WE'RE IN THIS TOGETHER

Speaking of meaning and purpose, I think most of us agree that our connections to one another greatly enhance this thing called Life. I came across a phenomenal study on the topic of human connection[2] that I would like to share with you. Researchers hooked up a sample of people's brains and bodies to sensors, and measured their neurological and physiological activity while they all listened to the same story about human kindness amid the unspeakable hardship of genocide. The study discovered undeniable consistency between participants in their heart rate variance (in this case, their heart beats slowed in similar ways), as well as consistent breathing changes among participants (in the form of slower breathing) while they experienced the story. Excitingly, the results display evidence of a powerful mind/body connection in regard to how our brains' exposure to meaningful stories can affect consistent healthy change between different people.

As it turns out, we tend to react in similar ways to similar experiences. At our very core, regardless of our individual, cultural, or even personality differences, we share a common baseline. The big takeaway for me was this: People have more in common than we could ever imagine. In this particular study, stories ignited a sense of connection within the participants that allowed them to relate to the narrative characters and resonate with their experiences in real time. Just as the study participants' heart rates and breathing patterns changed in predictable ways when they were exposed to particular stimuli, our psyches react consistently when we are exposed to life challenges like aging, relational discord, exhaustion, or a global pandemic, to name a few. Although we are all unique and different, many qualities bind us together as a species. Our response to human kindness being one of them, and the drive toward a meaningful, radiant life is another.

HUSTLE AND BURNOUT

I have seen evidence of many consistencies between clients in my psychotherapy work. One example is the large number of people who land on my therapy couch self-identifying as a *perfectionist*. The frequency of people for whom perfectionism is an issue absolutely astounds me, but it shouldn't. With the societal messages surrounding standards of beauty, success, belonging, and lovability in our culture, it's a miracle that anyone exists without perfectionist tendencies. Creating and sustaining a facade of perfection majorly contributes to the hustle and burnout culture in the West. I define *perfectionism* as a facet of social anxiety based on a perceived need for approval and belonging. Perfectionists tend to believe that they must be judged as flawless by themselves and others in order to earn safety, love, and status. A cousin to perfectionism in the relay of socialization is *comparison*, through which many of our dreams and ideals for self-worth and value become smashed to smithereens against the impossible measuring stick of never-enoughness.

No amount of expensive clothing, perfect make-up, inflated bank accounts, or popularity will result in a challenge-free life. Despite our best efforts to fit the mold of flawlessness, we tend to feel confused by its unattainability. One reason for this is that we have been culturally conditioned to pour constant energy into obscuring the deep fatigue within ourselves from hustling so hard for so long. We are taught to move faster, chase more, and never feel satisfied. We prize productivity, and measure success by how busy we are, how much is in our bank account, and how desirable our résumé is. All of this comes at the high cost of our relationships, inner peace, and life satisfaction. As the character Nigel so aptly states in the movie *The Devil Wears Prada*,[3] "Let me know when your whole life goes up in smoke. That means you're up for a promotion." We share collective beliefs that a larger salary, whiter teeth, or a younger romantic partner will bring greater ease and happiness into our lives, while on some deep level we know we are being tricked—not to mention drained of every energetic resource within us. At the end of the day, true radiance—the kind that emanates from within, not the artificial sparkles on the cheeks of airbrushed models—is not born from perfection. Instead, it is derived from the wholehearted embracing and embodiment of the complex totality of who we truly are—cracks and flaws included.

Offering: Wouldn't it be wonderful to sidestep the spiderweb of endless grasping and striving? Imagine feeling the sensation inside yourself of enoughness. Satisfaction. The light and warmth of genuine radiance. Envision feeling full enough from within to truly and actively appreciate, enjoy, and participate in your life rather than being constantly drained by it.

Now write about it in your journal.

Constant comparison and competition have led many of us to feel isolated in our suffering, while believing that everyone else experiences lives filled with perfect emotional balance, issue-free relationships, and infinite joyful ease. Such thinking builds inner beliefs that you are doing things wrong/bad (dull), and everyone else is right/good (radiant). This type of polarized thinking leaves you holding the short end of the stick in your own life and is a fruitless drain of precious energy.

I invite you to try something new: Look around yourself. Perceive more deeply than usual beneath the surface of casual observation. Notice the mother pushing her wiggly baby in a stroller, the businessman power-walking into his office, the exhausted parking lot attendant coming off his night shift. Look and really see the humanity in each of these people. Remind yourself that everyone you see has blood pulsing through their veins, breath moving through their lungs, and adaptive strategies for managing their core issues. Every single one of these people is built like you are: human and full of flaws, likely in need of deep rest, and yearning for a strong magnetic pull toward a radiant life that fulfills and nourishes them from the inside-out.

Pema Chodron teaches the affirmation "just like me"[4] to help her students remember that we are all more alike than we sometimes want to admit. Chodron's practice helps us train our brains and minds to cease judgment and, instead, adopt a perspective of compassion. When you witness pain in another person, remember that you also know what hurt feels like. *Just like me.* If you see someone raging in rush hour traffic, think, *Just like me.*

Everyone does their best to effectively manage the ever-terrifying demands, stressors, and responsibilities of their existence. It's much less isolating when you realize you are not separate because of the wounds and experiences you carry but rather an integral part of humanity's wholeness. Zoom out your perception and witness the world as more than just a competitive jungle where you have to fight for survival and delay nourishment until the weekend, your next vacation, retirement, or precisely never. Instead, see if you can make it happen in this very moment.

Offering: Stop reading for a hot second and close your eyes. Greet yourself lovingly. "Hello, you dashing sunflower of a human! I just realized that I have the capacity to pause life and check in whenever I want. How's it going in here? Anything to report?" Then take a listen. Ride the breath for a few cycles, and simply notice how you're doing—really doing. Notice the slight headache or tension. The rumblings of hunger now that you realize you've missed lunch (again). Your longing for fresh air. Whatever you sense in your body, just be with it. It's OK to feel discomfort. See what happens if you greet your experience kindly rather than resisting it. Then write about it.

Allow yourself to marvel at the truth that we all exist together in a gravity-fueled container that holds constant space for our souls to move through the same uncertain experience of life toward the ultimate goal of consciousness, growth, and radiance. Soften your perception and accept the limitations of being human. Acknowledge the necessity to counterbalance your powerful forward momentum with beats of peaceful reprieve and introspection.

When you actively slow down and bring balance into the larger picture of your life, you will likely notice that your system naturally seeks a particular rhythm. If you allow space for this tempo to sync up, your sleep schedule will regulate, your mental energy will equalize, and your stomach will signal hunger at similar times each day. Naturally, our bodies enjoy balance and predictability. By gifting yourself this basic pleasure, the regularity of homeostasis will become noticeable in many areas of your life.

When you become familiar with your natural cadence, you will notice the spectacular inclusion of ebb and flow in your experience. Ebb and Flow are the two sisters of Mother Nature's great plan, it seems. Consider the movement of inhalation and exhalation, and there they are. They exist in the ocean tides, and with the waxing and waning moon. Seasons also follow the sisters' familiar and distinct rhythm. When all of nature so brilliantly reflects the graceful hand-off between ebb and flow, why do we burn ourselves out by resisting this natural cycle?

Burnout is what happens when anything (natural or material) neglects the rhythm of ebb and flow. This can happen to a vehicle when it has been run too hard and fast without time to cool its engine, and it can happen to people in much the same way. Hustle culture tells us that we are meant to run like machines, but it forgets two important factors:

1. Even machines burn out at some point.

2. We are flesh and blood and bone, and we have mortal limitations embedded in our DNA.

Collectively, we are taught in the West to like the idea of *hustling*. Our culture attaches a certain aura to hustling that generates mass-societal approval of lifestyles that include high productivity, wealth, status, and materialism. This links with the simple yet fallible equation: hustle + more hustle = more of everything you have been conditioned to want (money, success, happiness, love, the works). Nowhere in this line of thinking is there space to cool our engines, reflect introspectively, or check in with our values. The messages in hustle culture teach that more is better, faster is necessary, bigger always wins, and the striving must persist until a person earns the ultimate fantasy reward of vacation or retirement. Cue the cameras toward a seasoned yet ageless You reclined on a luxury beach with a martini in hand and a smile on your face. Remember the brochures for ideal retirement that have been embossed into our brains if only we promise to subscribe to hustle culture? I do. And I consciously choose to unsubscribe because it's a load of lies and artificial sweetener.

The real equation looks more like this: hustle + more hustle = deep burnout, exhaustion, and a vague sense of purposelessness toward living. We tend to neglect the sticky underbelly of our numbing behaviors until we have safely separated ourselves from our pain. We don't seem to notice that when we numb our pain, we numb our joy too. The emotional system of a human being cannot selectively choose only certain areas for apathy, so numbness becomes a blanket that covers the entirety of our emotional experiences. This blanketing unintentionally dulls the most beautiful aspects of human existence, and though void of pain, we tend to feel hollow and empty. Whatever the opposite of radiance is, this pretty well captures it.

As for a more realistic picture of retirement after a life of worker-bee hustle? It looks a whole lot more depressing, painful, and resentful than the idyllic picture on the fraud brochure. If (and I do mean *if*) a person makes it in one piece to retirement, the stress and drama from decades of marination in toxic hustle culture most often cranks out seniors with jacked-up nervous systems, fragmented relationships, and the necessity for a team of people to take care of their failing minds and bodies. Aha! The Wizard has been exposed as the quirky fraud he's always been behind the curtain. Hustle culture is as much a myth as the magical wizard of Oz, yet so many of us fall into its seductive trap anyway. Why? Because we all have the best intentions to pursue a radiant life. We've just meandered down the wrong yellow brick road to find it.

Offering: In your journal, list three ways you participate in hustle culture, and how you can shift the dynamic for each item in your list.

The Wizard of Oz isn't the only children's movie that teaches important adult lessons. As a mom of two little ones, I often find myself entranced by an animated story while tightly sandwiched by cozy bodies on the couch. I occasionally find myself moved to either tears or awe by the creative imaginings of companies like Disney/Pixar during family movie nights. Somehow the writers and producers of these animated films have discovered how to join together entertaining storylines, engaging characters, profound emotional depth, and bite-sized culturally resonant lessons for the subliminal absorption of our young ones. One such movie that prompted me to pause, rewind, and replay was

Encanto.[5] Most specifically, my heart resonated with a song called *Surface Pressure.* This powerful song was sung by a character named Luisa who had been cast by her family and community into the role of *the strong one.* Luisa sang about the intense internal pressure she felt in response to the load of external pressures heaped upon her shoulders to the extent where they became internally reinforced by her own expectations of how she asked herself to exist in her world.

Pretty insightful for a children's movie, yes? Maybe you self-identify with Luisa, or perhaps you know someone else who lives like her. Regardless, I imagine we can all agree that although strength and durability are common cultural expectations, they are an unsustainable way of life. Carrying the burdens of the world on your shoulders is too much for any person—no matter how strong they seem to be. So why do we continue to maintain, project, and propagate unhealthy habits and behaviors upon the conscience of ourselves and others?

Offering: Why do you think we continue to maintain, project, and propagate the unhealthy habits of hustle culture? Thoughtfully consider this question, and bring it to your journal for processing.

CULTURAL MESSAGES

One culprit that propels us grievously apart from the balance of a mind/body/soul system that knows authenticity and balance is the cultural conditioning we have been spoon-fed since before we could utter our first baby babble. Little ones witness the bigger ones in their lives (caregivers and other influential adults), unsteadily carrying the heavy burden of adult responsibilities with massive stress and strain that manifests in oh-so-many unhealthy ways (addiction, reckless impulsivity, chronic numbness, and emotional dysregulation, to name a few).

Then, in a repetitive dance of duplication, the little ones habitually grow into their own version of the same thing. With my clients I often share the phrase, *hurt people hurt people,* to exemplify this phenomenon. I firmly believe that people don't mean to hurt one another nearly as often as they do, but they do nonetheless; generation after well-meaning generation. Monkey-see-monkey-do, which results in the infamous passive-aggressive statement lashed-out during many a strained argument, *You're just like your mother!* And perhaps you are. The good news is you don't have to be, if you don't want to be. In Chapter 6 you will learn how to become a pattern-breaker, how to step into the uncharted territory of living differently than your ancestors and actively deviating from society's insatiable standards.

Thanks to evolution, the creatures of Earth were wired to study previous generations to learn how to fit in and survive in our world. We absorb messages from voices we hear around us, faces we see on television and in airbrushed ads, and characters we encounter through books and media sources. Human beings are constantly drinking in messages about how and who we are supposed to be in order to meet the mark as a successful person of worth. Groups and generations of people operating under similar value systems ultimately create culture, and much of this is beneficial. Not everything you learned from your parents is complete idiocy, and I know you know this. The trick is to consciously pick and choose what to integrate from the bucket of cultural teachings to which you have been exposed. You must thoughtfully discern which resonant bits to keep, and throw the rest back into the void.

For example, in the culture of the West, we are not taught to rest. When I took my sabbatical in 2022, I chose to throw this arbitrary standard away like the box of week-old sushi it is, and I invite you to do the same. We are taught that rest is lazy and weak. We learn from an early age that in order to achieve what we're supposed to in life, we need to fiercely and adamantly pursue illusory measures such as wealth, status, possessions, and popularity at any cost. *More, more, more. Nothing is ever enough, and self-nurturance is for losers and quitters.*

I am utterly baffled that our society judges tenderness to be mutually exclusive from strength, when in reality it is an essential ingredient that promotes vitality and potency from the inside out. How incredibly shortsighted we have become when the more delicate, loving aspects of life are not only viewed as weak and pathetic, but also somehow threatening to our pursuit and expectation for a well-lived life.

In our traditional patriarchal culture, polarization has become a streamlined way of thinking about most everything. We have learned to think about ourselves, our relationships, our lifestyles, and our work through the filter of good/bad, right/wrong, strong/weak. The mentality surrounding such binary thinking does not allow space for balance. It is an all-or-nothing zero-sum perspective of living that objectifies warm tenderness as the villain that threatens success and achievement. Thinking along these lines has wrongly taught successive generations of people to abandon the feminine aspects of their psyches in favor of the dominant masculine.

I want to be very clear that I am not speaking of *feminine* and *masculine* in a way that delineates sex and gender.

All human beings—male, female, non-binary, gender-fluid, and trans—possess masculine and feminine qualities within themselves, like the iconic yin and yang from Chinese philosophy. We all need quiet to balance loudness, softness to balance fierceness, and water to balance fire. The combination of masculine and feminine energies within each person is as natural as the shades of darkness and daylight are to our planet. Masculinity is not reserved only for the men among us, nor femininity for the women. These are fluid and dynamic energetic elements. The fact that young children are not commonly taught to allow and embrace both the masculine and feminine qualities within themselves is one insidious root of our cultural toxicity.

When we are saturated by masculine-dominated polarized thinking, more always seems to be better than less, which fuels an insatiable hunger for power and greed. Faster speed and productivity take precedence over pacing. Qualities such as largeness, loudness, and strength seem preferable to their opposites. Masculine culture tends to reduce the continuum of shades into stark black and white to tidily stuff life into limited boxes based on a narrow spectrum. Tell me, where is there space for the possibility of radiance with black and white as our only options?

Many incredible books have been written about *The Patriarchy* and its outdated, detrimental effects upon our society, so I won't delve deeper into that topic. One great resource is the book *Burnout: The Secret to Unlocking the Stress Cycle* by sisters Emily and Amelia Nagoski. For the purpose of this book, it is enough to simply acknowledge that the controlled perspective we have been taught to accept as *normal* fits like Cinderella's delicate glass slipper on her cruel stepsister's massive foot: restricting, achy, and flat out wrong.

RESILIENCY AND GRIT

Resiliency and grit are two concepts that are embedded in societal messages that preach who and how we are supposed to be to achieve a meaningful life. These qualities, like all others, exist on a continuum and are not binary. I like to apply my shadow side/sunny side approach when talking about resiliency and grit because of their dynamism and complexity. On the sunny side, resiliency and grit keep us going when the going gets tough. They propel us through adversity and hardship, and they help us prove to ourselves (and others) that we are capable of unimaginably more than we ever previously thought. Sounds positive, right? In Western culture, the sunny side is the only side we are ever exposed to on this topic until we find ourselves undeniably equipped with a fried nervous system. You see, the belief that we must continuously endure discomfort when life seems to be endlessly laced with hardship only serves to obscure our human limitations.

The overarching message that *life is supposed to be hard and there's no way around it, so buckle down and deal with it* perpetuates a dangerous pattern in our collective mindset. Buying in to the self-fulfilling prophecies that life is always hard, we must always be tough, and there is no option but to continue in the grind feels a lot like Sisyphus'[6] doomed eternity of pushing a boulder up a mountain only to have it roll back down each time. The shadow side is that when resiliency and grit reign supreme, you're on the express train to resentment and burnout. When we praise resiliency and grit within ourselves and one another, we spread the message that ease and freedom are inaccessible, impossible luxuries we cannot afford. We perpetuate the belief that tenderness and rest are bad or wrong. This only continues the relentlessness of our striving, sprinting, and autopilot numbing, which effectively keeps us apart from our authentic Selves and the radiant life we deeply yearn for. We also rack up physiological challenges when our nervous systems are constantly on guard and grinding, which we will discuss in Chapter 4.

Though resiliency and grit are valuable tools to access for short periods of time, it is important to deactivate them as well. When we successfully unplug from the message that *life is always hard and we've got no choice but to tolerate it,* we prevent ourselves from becoming caged within a rigid world of survival and torment. As with most everything in life, these qualities must balance not only within our Selves but in our outer societal and cultural systems as well.

Offering: Write about your relationship to resiliency and grit.

CHAPTER 3

Nurturance and Deep Rest

The What, When, and How

*The most important thing is remembering the most
important thing.*

—*SUZUKI ROSHI*

THE HUMAN BODY WAS DESIGNED WITH REST IN MIND, AS
part of our basic wiring, whether we respect this fact or not.
Much of the time, the power and strength of our mental
processes drive us continually forward toward being productive and remaining busy. This chapter will discuss the
many emotional, psychological, and energetic reasons for
integrating rest into our days and how doing so helps us
access the juicy radiance we all deeply yearn for. In addition
to the needs of our minds, souls, and hearts, our physical
requirement for rest is also essential. In fact, the human nervous system contains an entire branch assigned to that very
function. The *autonomic nervous system* (ANS) is the branch
of our nervous system that controls the automatic manage-
ment of our body's functioning, such as our breathing, heart

rate, and digestion. This vigilant part of our anatomy scans our bodies four times per second to discern if we are safe.[1] Furthermore, the ANS is divided into two branches: the *sympathetic nervous system* (SNS) and *parasympathetic nervous system* (PNS).

Dr. Stephen Porges' Polyvagal theory teaches that the parasympathetic branch of our nervous system has two component parts that join together with the sympathetic to round out our ANS. All of this happens without our conscious awareness. The building blocks of our ANS developed as an autonomic hierarchy[2] composed of the dorsal vagal building block that developed first (about 500 million years ago), followed by the sympathetic branch about 400 million years ago, and finally the ventral vagal around 200 million years ago.[3] The *ventral vagal system* (when we are calm and regulated) and *dorsal vagal system* (when we are shut-down and numb) both exist in the parasympathetic and relate to the down-regulating of our nervous system.

When our bodies feel safe and sound, we effectively access a ventral state where we can focus inwardly, cool our engines, and relax the hormones and neuromodulators that are responsible for activation and stress responses. Our bodies can take stock of our internal needs to keep our systems in good running order. Nutrients from the foods washing through our digestive tract are most effectively extracted and put to use when we are in Ventral, and our bodies attend to detoxification and internal system repair.

When our internal state is primed for protection against danger, however, ventral vagal first gives way to the sympathetic for an active response to the presenting threat (fight/flight). If our systems ascertain that we cannot fight or flee from the presenting danger, and our lives feel imminently threatened, our dorsal vagal response activates to shut us down and allow us to collapse into numbness. Such a response is our bodies' best effort to make us comfortable while enduring an unsafe situation that we cannot escape.

It is no accident that the parasympathetic has been aptly named the *rest and digest* portion of the human nervous system. When the ventral vagal system of the PNS is active, many crucial internal functions freely operate. It is important to understand that we have the capacity to experience ventral, sympathetic, and dorsal nervous system states because they all serve important functions. It is normal to flux through all three states throughout any given day, but it is important to return to the home-base of ventral to reap the benefits of a regulated nervous system. Problems arise in our physiological, emotional, and mental spheres when we get stuck in either sympathetic (anxious/agitated) or dorsal (hopeless/numb) for too long.

Here's an example for how a person can move through all three branches in response to one experience: Franco began his morning feeling steady and calm (ventral). He was ready for a productive day at work where he would execute the tasks required of him, and he felt prepared (even optimistic) about how his day would unfold. Upon Franco's arrival at his office, he opened his email and noticed an atypical influx of emails with headlines expressing urgency and emergency related to a major client. In the beat of a second, Franco's heart began to race, his pupils dilated, and his mind zeroed in on the content of the emails (sympathetic). He became flooded by the urge to *do something* to decrease the anxiety and fear flowing through his system in response to the unexpected problem. Franco spent hours managing his employees and speaking with his client in an effort to mitigate the issue, but by 9 p.m. he had not found the answer he needed to decrease the alarm. His energy was depleted, his mind was weary, and he felt a discernable *who cares* response to the presenting issue (dorsal). With no more tricks up his sleeve, and a continually angry client, Franco felt hopelessness wash through him. He could do nothing but retreat home and fall into the comforting embrace of Netflix and chocolate ice cream until a fitful sleep finally cocooned him.

Notice how each autonomic state Franco moved through had a particular function for getting him through his day, and each state responded differently to what he experienced. Because the building blocks of the ANS are hierarchical (meaning that they must be moved through in a predetermined, predictable fashion), Franco accordingly moved from a regulated state (ventral) to an actively dysregulated state (sympathetic), and finally to a collapsed dysregulated state (dorsal). For Franco to reregulate his system, he would need to move backward through the hierarchy to regain balance in his system by starting in dorsal, passing through sympathetic, and finally arriving in ventral. When Franco woke up the next morning, he moved toward regulation by first experiencing the *ugh* sensation of dorsal but motivating himself with the anxious/ambitious energy to *do something to fix this problem* with sympathetic. Hours later, Franco discovered the key to solve his client's dilemma, and was thus returned to the calm regulated state of ventral.

NURTURE

Now that you have a foundation for understanding the autonomic nervous system (we'll build on this in Chapter 4), let's talk about less scientific methods for rest and self-nurturance. Even with the best of intentions, real self-care can sometimes be a tall order to tackle. This is especially true for a busy-bee modern person for whom multitasking and productivity have become as much a way of life as eating and breathing. Self-care (and I mean deep self-care—not just a quick mani/pedi between meetings) is a culturally conditioned no-no. Sadly, cutting ourselves off from the vital repose we require diminishes our life's radiance because we become trapped in a dull autopilot existence of striving and surviving. This locks us into the activation of our SNS, where we lose contact with the nurturing PNS for the purpose of prioritizing survival. In such a state, our bodies believe we are perpetually unsafe. To counterbalance the innate survival response within all of us, we need regular inclusion of soothing, calm, restful experiences that ultimately signal safety to our bodies.

To maintain a healthy rhythm and balance the dense energy of stress and pressure, we desperately need nurturance—and a lot of it. In fact, we need bushels and barrels more than any of us ever think we need. Within the psyches of most people, there seems to be a deep-seated fear of softening toward ourselves and accessing the kinds of deep rest that will truly revitalize us from the inside out. People tend to get so caught up in fearing rest as a means to avoid facing the stillness of their own soul that they consequently throw their mind/body/spirit equilibrium dangerously off-balance.

The mysterious and ethereal concept of *balance* is something many people reportedly seek, and it has grown to be a hot topic throughout many branches of holistic healthcare and wellness circles. Listen closely to coffee shop or dinner table chit chat and you will undoubtedly hear the murmurings about a *balanced diet* or *work/life balance,* among many other common phrases about the imbalanced scales of our lives. Even with increasing awareness about the rewards that come with finding the sweet spot of a balanced lifestyle, it always seems to remain slightly out of reach. A big reason for this is the pace of modern living, which leaves very little room for a deep inhale/exhale. But there are also two other important culprits: procrastination and affirmation.

The continual avoidance of looking our stressors in the face and actually managing them from their root origin results in a certain type of procrastination that is alarmingly seductive. This happens when a person knows there's a problem but keeps shuffling it under the rug to handle another time. The inconvenience of facing the issue develops over time into a flat-out avoidance similar to the notorious dieter's promise that they will stop binging on Twinkies on Monday. When a person is nestled in this pattern, it's easy to look around and notice how many others are also distracted by the speedy pace of life. This acts as an insidious affirmation that if we're all stuck together in the rapidly churning whirlwind of modern-day living, it must be okay. *It's not ideal, and it feels wrong, but we're all in it together—so hey! Let's just keep it going.*

It is common to think that as long as our experience is within the realm of *normal*, there's no need to change it. This is problematic in the case of self-care, deep rest, and true nourishment because *normal* does not necessarily equate to *healthy*. When we avoid doing the work it takes to integrate true sustainable balance in our lives by telling ourselves it is normal to live sizzled to a crisp with burnout, we become part of the problem—not just for ourselves, but for our families, societies, and cultures, too. When we fall in line with the cultural norms that work against building a radiant life filled with meaning and wholeheartedness, we actively sell out to the hustle. We render ourselves as yet another drone in the maddening matrix of unconscious living, and we do not evolve.

Deep within our souls, I believe that many people understand that our subscription to these societal norms perpetuates the hollow dullness we feel as an undercurrent to our lives. We exist in a maddening relay of work, families, social events, extracurriculars, materialism, obligatory participation, and doing what we feel we have to do in order to fit in—then rinse and repeat. So many of us crave calibration in our psyches and nervous systems while simultaneously remaining multiple arms' lengths (at least) away from the real rest and soul nourishment we deeply yearn for. Softness and gentleness have become ruthlessly edged to the outer banks of our collective experience, seemingly reserved only for the times in life when someone is so undeniably not okay that they have landed in a sick bed, hospital, or psychiatric ward. Do we really want to wait until it gets that far?

Today, right now, this actual moment is the perfect time to redesign our relationship with rest and nurturance. It is certainly a patience practice to get more comfortable with inviting and allowing deep self-care into our lives. When we do achieve such a feat, even in small amounts, we support our inner compass and more effectively navigate the tides of our ever-demanding modern experiences.

THE GIVER TRAP

Interestingly for many, a gaping chasm exists between giving nurturance and receiving it. I have found that many of the most tender, loving, generous people among us tend not to shine their warmth inwardly toward themselves. These individuals may use their caregiving behaviors as part of a sophisticated inner mechanism based on projecting their own needs onto others. This pattern only builds dynamics that unintentionally perpetuate the fearful energy of codependency and insecurity. Regardless of the specific psychological purpose of such a role, people who embody the *superstar caregiver* persona often get set on cruise-control in relational dynamics where they take impeccable care of everyone else, and ultimately experience severe burnout and illness due to imbalance.

If you are a *giver*, you might identify as being a caretaker, parent, teacher, supportive aid, empath, listener, good neighbor, nurse, or an *oh, bless her soul* kind of person. There is so much to appreciate about those who emanate such giving energy, but there is a shadow side as well that is worth investigating for the sake of cultivating a radiant life. In Jungian psychology, the *shadow* is not something to be feared but simply an internal quality or pattern that we keep hidden away for fear of it being uncomfortable, unacceptable, inappropriate, or threatening. Every single person has shadow elements of their psyche, just as each individual has light aspects. By honestly opening ourselves to lovingly investigate our shadow elements, we make space for unconditional love surrounding the complex nature of our Selves. When we embrace the natural dualities that are common among all people, we contribute to large-scale healing for our communities and our world.

In the West, women have historically fallen into the role of the limitless caregiver in their families, social networks, and even workplaces. Counter to women, men have often fulfilled dynamics of imbalanced ambition and emotional constriction. These are dominant stereotypical patterns in Western culture (and other cultures), and they are directly related to our patriarchal conditioning. Importantly, these cultural undertones seem to be slowly but surely shifting as we collectively shine light into these shadow elements of our society. Together we must release ourselves from the stifling boxes of such stereotyping in order to access true freedom and authenticity. The work of awakening consciousness and living radiantly includes counterbalancing the palpable energy of the wounded feminine and masculine archetypes with the power of deep self-nourishment. Let's find a way to maintain the healthy qualities of the above-mentioned dynamics while also developing a sense of equilibrium, shall we? Yes, it's possible.

Now, when I talk about nurturance, self-care, and rest, I am not talking about sleeping in on a Saturday twice per year when the kids are at Grandma's house. I'm not talking about pausing once every few months for a 50-minute massage before throwing yourself back into the grind. Little glimmers of self-care can certainly help, but they don't pack enough punch to deliver the deep nurturance a modern stressed-to-the-max person needs to truly recalibrate—let alone thrive. A nourishing life is one where rest, reprieve, introspection, and gentleness toward the Self are an integral aspect of the daily rhythm. A person whose lifestyle incorporates deep nourishment will successfully fill their emotional, physical, energetic, and psychological tanks in regular doses of tender care and attunement.

THIS THING CALLED SELF-LOVE

Since most of us haven't been effectively taught about deep nourishment, this concept may require some patient brainstorming as you discover which methods of self-care resonate most in your system. Don't default to the cliche glass of wine in a bubble bath before you learn whether this actually fills your soul or not. I, for one, can't stand bubble baths. Some people like bodywork, others gravitate toward writing, doodling, playing tennis, gardening, grooming puppies, or sharing intimate conversations with trusted friends.

Think about what fills you up, and what depletes you. Notice when you have walked away from an experience thinking, *Wow, that was wonderful! I should do that more often.* That's resonance.

Offering: Thoughtfully consider the things, people, and experience that fill you up and deplete you. Next, list and explore them in your journal.

When considering the social and active elements of self-care, it is important to mindfully attune to your place on the introvert/extrovert spectrum. The impact of experiences such as socialization, caregiving, intellectual stimulation, or alone time can vary greatly depending on whether you recharge successfully while in the company of others, or if you would rather snuggle into a book nook for a dose of blissful solitude.

If you think of self-care as selfish or indulgent, I invite you to change your perspective. Keeping gentleness as an off-limits indulgence only fosters a toxic adherence to cultural judgment, which effectively restrains your access to true Self. Such rigid thinking is consistent with the masculine-dominant perspective that tenderness is weak. Coping and avoidance strategies of all shapes and sizes have been built around this mentality throughout our societal container to repress the powerful energetics of oppression, inequality, shame, and resentment that live inside our collective unconscious.

Consider this chapter an invitation to rebalance your yin/yang energy and invite more feminine attributes into your system. After all, if you don't care for yourself in a deep nourishing way, I think we both know it won't happen. Most people are intimately familiar with the slippery slope that follows when too much time has been spent without self-care. It starts with irritability and burnout, and leads toward an avalanche of depletion, resentment, instability, and even illness. Remember the infamous flight attendants' directive: *Put your own oxygen mask on before helping someone else.* It is not possible to be all the things for all the people if you don't first nourish yourself. After all, you can't pour tea from an empty pot.

Self-love is not a frivolity; it is as essential as air. The part of you that believes taking care of yourself is an extravagant indulgence is misguided and potentially linked to trauma. Such distorted thinking is based on old narratives that may have granted you limited success in the past, but potentially no longer align. With this in mind, I encourage you to gently address your triggered response to rest.

Offering: Write about any triggers, resistance, or responses that arise within when you consider the topic of rest. Notice if you have certain rules, limitations, or justifications surrounding this topic, and consider where you learned to relate to rest in such a way.

Help your system learn something new that will provide multilevel benefits of healing. Simply notice your resistance toward tenderness and ask yourself what it's really about. You may discover that a scared younger version of yourself is trying its best to survive in a dog-eat-dog world. Perhaps you can recall the memory of a harsh caregiver's voice punishing you for exposing emotional vulnerability. Resistance and avoidance do not eradicate your deep need for gentleness; they only perpetuate the energetic equivalent of repeatedly filling a bucket with water only to notice that the bucket has holes and it will never remain full for long. It is not enough to occasionally squeeze in time for the things that nourish you. You need to make them a priority and grant yourself these necessary pleasures on the daily.

NOURISHMENT IN RELATIONSHIPS

Two important elements of deep nourishment are the integration and maintenance of aligned relationships with healthy people. If you find yourself guilted or shamed for saying no to social gatherings, or you notice the people in your life taking more from you than they give, you can bet you are out of alignment in those relationships. In some cases, an honest conversation that leads to shifting the give/take ratio does the trick. For other dynamics, the only healthy action is to cut ties and move along. Though it may seem painful and awkward to end relationships that do not honor your authentic Self, trust me when I say it's worth it tenfold in the long run as you cultivate a radiant life. If you find yourself bending over backwards to meet the contact and connection needs of another person at the expense of your own, you have strayed into self-abandonment territory. In this situation, you allow their needs to supersede your own, and effectively teach your system that you are less important than the others in your life.

The differing degrees of separate individuals' needs is not an automatic recipe for friendship doom, but it is an important factor to identify and navigate early on in the relationship. Differing opinions about gossip and privacy, vehement political opinions that lead to arguments, mis-aligned value systems, and contrasting desires for frequency of contact all land in this territory. In situations where members of a friendship have unique and dissimilar needs, both parties must respect and honor the contrast without demands or pressure if the friendship is to thrive.

I once had a friendship where my need for connection was far less than my friend's, and it ultimately broke us up. The tough reality of our incompatibility became starkly apparent when after many years of meeting the frequency and intimacy of my friend's social needs at the expense of my own, I refused to abandon myself in that fashion anymore. During our relationship's downfall, we had a conversation where I equated our incongruous needs to house plants in my effort to explain the imbalance between us. I said:

If your social needs are like a house plant, I cannot water it as often as you want/need me to. I can water it sometimes, and if it can be like a cactus or succulent and not require or expect weekly watering, I will joyfully do so when I am able. If the plant needs weekly watering, however, please understand that I cannot and will not do that. Feel free to get more watering from other people and sources, but I cannot provide that frequency for you.

To summarize a long story, my friend responded with annoyance and resistance. She demanded that her plant be watered at the frequency she needed, and expressed her opinion that it was our responsibility as friends to water each other's proverbial house plants as often as necessary, even if one plant consistently needed more watering than the other person was willing to give. Needless to say, at the end of it all, the relationship didn't survive. The win for me was that I walked away feeling aligned with my integrity from being honest about my limits and needs.

In the realm of boundary work, I recommend thinking about setting healthy boundaries as a journey through three necessary gates: honesty, respect, and kindness. Rolling out your boundary with the inclusion of these three facets does not guarantee an ideal response of understanding and appreciation from the other person (let's face it, people don't like boundaries), but it does provide you with the knowledge that you did what you needed to do in the service of your highest good with strong integrity. It's worth stating that this work is simpler and more effective if you set your boundary at (or near) the moment when the transgression occurred—not weeks, months, or years later. Moving through the three gates of boundary setting is easier if you have not tolerated resentment toward the other person for so long that you have no patience left. Once you reach such a level of frustration with a relationship, it's difficult to keep yourself from explosive boundary setting. This is when you say what needs to be said, but it comes out laced with venom, aggression, and victimization. An outburst demanding a boundary can be effective, but it doesn't feel nearly as satisfying as one set with honesty, respect, and kindness.

If the person you are in contact with does not honor your boundary, that's on them. Please avoid the sticky trap of thinking that they must agree with or appreciate your boundary in order for it to be valid. In the most emotionally intelligent relationships, members can maturely respect and honor one another's boundaries (even celebrate them!), but let's face it, maturity isn't always the defining quality in a person. So protect and honor your Self and your authentic needs, and then release your attachment to how the other person responds. You are only accountable for the way you delivered your boundary, not for how it was received.

Regardless of whether misalignment exists within a friendship, romantic partnership, casual acquaintanceship, or family relationship, if you tolerate interpersonal incongruity for too long, you can bet you'll feel strained on a soul level. No matter how much you want a relationship to work out and last for the long haul, soul strain does not result in a life of nourishment—nor does it pave the way to a radiant life. Ending a connection with someone or moving them to a lower priority in your life does not mean they are bad or wrong, and it does not mean you are bad or wrong for shifting the dynamic. It simply indicates that the two of you are incongruous when it comes to each of your authentic needs for connection, contact, and intimacy. The good news is that when you free another person from a misaligned relationship with you, the result is mutually beneficial; even if at first it seems hurtful or riddled with grief. Letting go of one another allows for precious space to open for both parties to seek authentic connection elsewhere. Somewhere out there are people who need the same flavor of connection you need, and they're looking for you too, but you will not have space for aligned relationships if your life is densely filled with mediocre connections.

At a pivotal time in my life, I found myself driving down the street when I noticed writing on a local church sign that said, *What you want wants you.* I am not a religious person, but nonetheless the message comforted me. Even to this day it continues to serve as a reminder for me to allow space for truly aligned people and experiences. I no longer spend an ounce of my time twisting myself into a pretzel in placeholder friendships or obligatory experiences that keep me from my radiant life.

Somewhere along the meandering path of my journey, I made a commitment to myself that I will only have people in my life who can tolerate and respect my *no*. This is crucial for me. As a deeply introverted and sensitive person, I need to say *no* a lot more than is socially acceptable, and it is important to me that my loved ones don't take it personally, feel rejected, or get upset when I behave in coherence with my integrity. If your friend resists when you decline their invitation to happy hour in order to soak in a warm bath, you're in a misaligned relationship. If your social group gets sour when you back out of brunch because you're tapped out from an exhausting week, they're not your people. Let them go, and make space for others who will celebrate your adherence to self-care and the integrity of your *no*. This goes for professional relationships as well. It might surprise your boss when you request a weekly hour off to speak with your therapist, but a good manager will prize your mental health and understand its link with your productivity at work.

Find new friends, coworkers, and companies that prioritize and appreciate self-care, and reciprocate support within these relationships. Attunement and respect build interpersonal experiences that foster deep nourishment on a regular basis, which profoundly benefits all involved. The embodiment of high-integrity nourishment also provides healing for wounded parts of yourself and others that have been precariously held together with chewing gum and duct tape after sprinting for far too long. Integrating aligned relationships into your life is a deep act of self-love, and it greatly contributes to the construction of a radiant life.

Just as relationships play an important part in the nourishment of a human experience, there are many other crucial facets of self-support that contribute too. Glennon Doyle, in her book *Untamed*, writes about true self-care as building a life you don't have to escape from on an emergency basis. I can relate to how easy it is to get carried away by the over-scheduled, success-driven, drama-fueled aspects of life. This seemingly endless cycle drains our living energy while simultaneously demanding more in a relentless marathon that never seems to end. In my own participation with this cultural dynamic, I can remember having once felt like a living engine for far too long. I was a hyper-efficient multitasking worker bee, and I didn't know how to cut the ignition and cool down. I got a lot done, but there was a price to pay.

Years ago, I came face to face with my limit. I finally got married to the love of my life after together standing against unbelievable cruelty and violence toward our relationship by close family members for almost a decade. As if the stress of weathering such an emotional storm wasn't enough, we scheduled our wedding for the weekend after I completed graduate school, worked a full-time job, wrapped up a clinical internship, and dealt with complex social demands. Eventually, I landed haphazardly on a sunny beachside chaise lounge with heart palpitations and hives. My system had endured enough, and it wanted me to listen. This was the beginning of my long journey toward integrating reliable nurturance (the real kind) into my life, and it has remained an ongoing practice ever since.

GRATITUDE

One of my favorite nurturing tools to support a depleted and weary system is the cultivation of gratitude. There's something about the energetic resonance of gratitude that provides a sense of buoyant resiliency to all experiences, and neuroscience confirms its benefits as well. *Neuromodulators* are chemicals released in the brain and body that make certain brain areas more or less active and create a trickle-down effect in the body. The main neuromodulator associated with gratitude is *serotonin*,[4] and it resonates through the body like the combination of warmth and levity. When serotonin starts flowing through a person's brain, a physical process activates making them more likely to lean in and seek continued exposure to the someone or something that ignited the feelings. Since gratitude is a full-body experience, it's not enough to simply think grateful thoughts. To pack the largest impact, it is important to invite the sensory experience of gratitude into the body to feel its uplifting resonance.

Offering: Consider qualities of your life you feel grateful for, and notice how your body responds. Do you feel the neural activation described above inclining you to lean toward the feel-good sensation? Is there a warmth inside, or a sense of color, tingling, or lightness? To gain more depth into your sensory experience ask yourself how you know when you are feeling gratitude. In your journal, write about the sensations you experience, and how they let you know that your inner system is experiencing gratitude.

When you create a bridge between your mind and body by allowing thoughts to expand into somatic sensations, gratitude evolves into a deeper experience.

Stanford University professor, neuroscientist, and ophthalmologist Andrew Huberman teaches the importance of intention and genuineness in the experience of gratitude. Huberman explains that we can't lie to ourselves by saying we are grateful when we're not, because our brains know the difference. Real gratitude can only be felt when the experience has been wholehearted and genuine. We actually have specific brain circuits that look for authenticity,[5] so if we don't give toward ourselves and others with true sincerity, we undermine the potency with which our gratitude will be experienced from the receiving end. A takeaway here: Don't bother writing those thank-you letters or text messages unless you truly feel sincere gratitude. The brain of your intended recipient will filter your gratitude out as inauthentic and it won't accomplish what you had in mind. It's like what Jennifer Aniston's character said to Vince Vaughn's character in the 2006 romantic comedy, *The Break-Up*: "I don't want you to do the dishes. I want you to want to do the dishes." No matter how you spin it, efforts to love, help, and appreciate ourselves and one another just feel different when they are sincere. Thanks to neuroscience, we now know that our brains have a wired-in B.S. detector.

Another enlightening discovery highlighted by Huberman is that expressing gratitude does not result in the most fulfilling and long-lasting experience in a person's system— receiving gratitude does. Simply thinking of what you are grateful for and verbalizing or writing it down, though it can feel positively warming, does not affect the parts of your brain that are most impacted by the neurochemistry of gratitude. Huberman defines our *pro-social neural network* as a dominant brain system associated with how we process gratitude. This neural network is directly related to our *middle prefrontal cortex*, which impacts how we perceive the experiences of our lives. Remember, in order to feel gratitude, our brains must first perceive that something lovely is happening, we're glad it's happening, and gratitude is in fact flowing through our system. This results in the following cascade of pleasurable chemical responses in the brain and body.

Unless you happen to be the recipient of a vibrant fan-mail following, not a lot of us happen to regularly receive exuberant expressions of gratitude for our easy absorption every day. This begs the question of how we can find ways to receive more gratitude in order to make this practice consistent enough to create positive changes in our lives. Neuroscientist Antonio Demasio and his colleagues delved into this very question in one of their studies.[6]

Research subjects watched stories about other people's gratitude experiences while their brains and bodies were observed. Participants witnessed story characters who had lived through the unspeakable hardship of the Holocaust. In the story, the characters experienced gratitude as a result of the kindness and warmth offered by others. By simply observing the characters' feelings of gratitude toward those who offered them kindness, the study participants experienced feelings of gratitude within themselves. Participants' brain imaging also showed neurological activity in the gratitude circuitry of the brain as though gratitude had been received by the test subjects firsthand.

This study highlights the power of narrative story upon the human psyche. If stories themselves can shift the physiology of those observing them, deeply nourishing experiences that lead to feelings of gratitude and other healthy psycho-emotional experiences are well within reach for all of us. Simply kick back, grab some popcorn, and enjoy a favorite movie, show, book, or memory where loving deeds are completed and appreciated between the narrative characters. Then soak in the glow of gratitude. It's something we can all relate to and deeply need.

For a better long-lasting gratitude experience, emphasize the *practice* in gratitude practice. What we know about the brain is that neurons that fire together wire together, so the more we practice feeling gratitude, the easier it will be to access it in the future. Consistent repetition improves the strength of our brains' wiring and integrates the many benefits of a regular gratitude practice. These benefits include decreased inflammation, increased serotonin, improved mental health, improved feelings of nurturance, and many more. Bottom line: practice, practice, practice. Then enjoy the fruits of your labor by reveling in the biophysiological rewards for your mental and physical health.

FINDING PEACE WITH TARA BRACH'S RAIN

Along with gratitude, another beautiful practice for self-nurturance is Tara Brach's RAIN.[7] This technique is a game changer for improving insight into the multitudes of stress daily life can trigger. Additionally, RAIN can help create an internal space from which you can source a sense of peace amid the mysterious variety pack of everyday experiences. Brach has a background as a psychologist and Buddhist teacher and practitioner, and she melds these gifts together helpfully in RAIN. Her simple process directs you to intentionally move through the following steps regarding a difficult experience or emotion you may be confronted with in any given moment:

> R: *Recognize.* Cultivate your inner observer. Bring your awareness away from the external hustle-bustle and toward your inner experience to notice what you feel in the moment. Then name your experience.

A bicycle just zoomed by within an inch of my body, and I am feeling afraid and ruffled.

A: *Allow.* Just let the experience be there. Don't move to change it or make it go away. Brach uses a phrase in her teachings to demonstrate this by saying "this belongs."

It's ok that I am flooded by fear and bewilderment in this moment. These emotions belong. I don't need to make them go away.

I: *Investigate.* Get curious and notice how your present feelings, thoughts, and sensations exist in your body.

I notice a tightness in my chest and nausea in my stomach.

N: *Nurture.* Ask yourself what you need to support yourself in the experience you are presently having. Please note, this is not a question that asks how to make your uncomfortable feeling go away. It is more about how to show up for yourself and meet any needs you may have in order to support and care for yourself in the present moment.

I need to sit down for a moment. I see a bench where I can rest, practice some deep breathing, and calm my fear response before I continue on my way.

After the Rain: Just like after a physical rainstorm, a palpable sense of quiet presence and peacefulness can be experienced after moving through RAIN. Simply notice yourself in the embodied state you have cultivated and be present with the centered feeling of expansive awareness.

Offering: Now you try. In your journal, move through Tara Brach's RAIN to process a current experience in your life. If nothing particular feels present, think back to a recent time when you felt emotionally charged, and with that experience in mind, move through the steps.

Brach's RAIN process helps with the cultivation of unconditional self-love and attunement to your inner experience. It teaches your system that you can trust yourself to show up in a helpful way when difficulty and intensity arise. As neuroscience teaches, the repeated practice of a skill creates well-worn pathways in the brain for automatic firing. The more you notice, align with, and support your inner experience and needs, the brighter and bolder your familiarity with unconditional self-love will be.

If radiating the warmth of loving presence has not been your past default setting, practice attending to yourself in a sensitive manner to facilitate acquaintance with inward-facing love. The more you attune to yourself in challenging moments, the more automatic self-love will be. Soon it will become as instinctive as putting on your socks or bringing a cereal spoon to your mouth.

TRUST AND G FOR GENEROSITY

In many ways, self-love and inner trust go hand in hand. Trust can feel extremely delicate for those among us who know the pain of heartbreak, betrayal, and disappointment. I like to remind my clients (and myself) that the heart is a resilient organ. When given the chance, it has an almost otherworldly capacity to heal. Though the devastation of broken trust in a relationship can create deep wounding, it is our ruptured trust within ourselves that causes the most damage. A profound act of nurturing self-care available to us all is the intentional mending of trust within ourselves.

When I was a competitive freestyle skier back in the '90s, I blew out my knee. After intricate surgery to restore the many bits and pieces of my knee that had been injured, my doctor told me something I will always remember. He said, *Your injured knee will now be much stronger than your other knee because the repair made it sturdier than it was before. Now you'll have to take special care not to injure your good knee because of how durable the injured one has become.* This example paints a good picture of what therapists often refer to as *rupture and repair.* Just like with the physical body, if we attend to an emotional break or strain with patient awareness and healing intention, the repair will make it stronger than ever before.

Brene Brown's work has identified what she refers to as the *anatomy of trust*[8] with seven components in her BRAVING acronym (boundaries, reliability, accountability, vault, integrity, nonjudgement, and generosity). BRAVING applies to both self-trust and interpersonal trust. Dr. Brown's work related to trust is full to the brim of gems we could spend many pages discussing, however the one I most want to highlight is "G" for *Generosity.* I have come to call this type of generosity *emotional generosity.* To avoid confusion, I want to make a distinction between the psycho-emotional practice of generosity I'm about to discuss and the more commonly known generosity that pays for another person's sandwich or comes wrapped in a sparkly bow.

Emotional generosity, when turned inward toward the Self or expressed outwardly toward another, offers an invaluable gift. Softening your filter enough to change your perspective creates room for the pleasant surprises that often come after you learn you were wrong about someone or something. In the court of law, a person is innocent until proven guilty. With emotional generosity, we extend the same method of thinking. Here is an example to help bring more vibrancy to the concept:

Susan had a rough few days wrangling her rejection and abandonment triggers. She had made some mistakes at work, which led to her boss delivering a stern lecture and revoking her level of responsibility. Adding to her stress, Susan and her husband James had adamantly avoided speaking to each other in person, and instead had been arguing via text message for two days. Their marital rift was triggered by an insensitive comment that was spoken at dinner in a moment of anger. It was easy for Susan to start thinking thoughts like, *I'm a disaster and everyone knows it. I'm going to get fired, and my husband is going to leave me for our brilliant adventurous friend, Nicole, whom I'm pretty sure he secretly adores. I'm going to be unemployed and divorced by the end of the week because I am such a pathetic failure.*

Ouch, right? Can you relate to this type of cruel self-admonishment and catastrophic thinking? Though thinking like this may be a default setting built from years of self-punishment and criticism, it's not the only way to move through a presenting challenge. If Susan were to take an emotionally generous perspective of her situation, it could sound like: *It's been a tough few days. I feel broken down and afraid, but this does not make me a failure. Instead of fearing the worst, I am going to try for repair with James and express my hurt feelings. My marriage may have some challenges, but there are many other beautiful qualities I have neglected to notice because I have been flooded by fear. At work, I will continue to do my best to correct my mistakes and try hard to regain my boss' trust. In the meantime, I will remember that I am highly qual-ified for this job, and I will engage my passion for my work to help motivate me.*

And just like that, self-criticism can transform into hopeful motivation. Folks, this is the beauty of emotional generosity, and it is a powerful tool for self-nourishment.

Offering: If you find yourself seeking deep nourishment while feeling lost in a challenging moment but you're not sure where to begin, simply ask yourself, "What kinder perspective of this situation might I be missing right now?"

Another helpful prompt to aid in accessing emotional generosity is to inwardly ask if you are treating yourself and everyone else in your present situation the way you would treat your dearest love. We tend to offer the softest, most open-hearted perspective toward those we most cherish. Frequently, the way we relate to ourselves and those closest to us is nowhere near as gentle. While holding a challenging experience in your mind, envision how you might approach the situation if a treasured person or adoring pet were tangled within it instead of yourself. If you don't have anyone you consider so dear, simply visualize an innocent child or baby animal (that usually does the trick for anyone with a pulse). Challenge yourself to soften into an emotionally generous perspective where you can access the most gracious, open-hearted assumption and perspective about all you already know in the present situation, and all you may not be aware of.

Implementing emotional generosity as an integrated lens through which you see the world takes practice, but it also gifts many rewards. When you start to see all people as basically meandering around the planet doing the best they can with what they've got, giving as much as they are able, and aware of only what they are aware of, the impulsive charge toward judgment and criticism releases. The openness that becomes apparent when harshness transforms into generosity allows for the opportunity to learn something entirely unexpected and new, and also offers the chance for a nourishing experience of compassion. When we remember the common humanity[9] in life's sampler platter of experiences, compassion becomes a binding ingredient for fostering wholeness in our relationships with one another and within ourselves.

In addition to compassion, expression is another key player to help funnel the experiences you have lived during your time on Earth into meaningful manifestation. *Expression* is the opposite counterpoint to *repression* on the behavioral teeter-totter of life. Repression holds energies within. This builds pressure and can feel akin to containing a vast ocean of menacing waves inside. Expression is the act of moving energy through and beyond a person's system. This loosens tension and allows for release and relief. We will delve into creative expression in Chapter 10, but for now, allow yourself to think of expression as anything that moves energy through and beyond yourself.

One of my favorite terms from graduate school is *sublimation*, which is a process of expression where the energies moving through a person become transformed into something new. This can occur when a person effectively channels their emotions into an expressive painting, when they dance out their feelings, or when a build-up of pressure transforms into a shower-sung concert. When Dr. Galit Atlas described the writing process of one of her books about mourning shortly after the death of her beloved life partner, she said that the pages of her book were made from her tears.[10] That's about as good an example of sublimation as I've ever heard.

Offering: Consider how you most effectively sublimate. Allow yourself to explore this topic in thought, through generative conversation with loved ones, or in your journal. If you sublimate through art (or another tactile task) engage your creative or tactile process with sublimation in mind and notice how it feels.

A client of mine, whom I'll call John, experienced this phenomenon when he began an intense workout fueled by immense anger from an argument with his partner. Through physical movement with heavy pressure, deep breathing, and focused cathartic energy release, John felt less anger and an increased capability to have a calm, coherent conversation for repair. His initially painful emotional experience was replaced by a calmer, more focused presence that helped him channel various emotional layers into attuned discussion with his partner, including the grief and pain embedded in his anger. After the sublimation completed, John not only experienced a sense of relief, he also felt introspective and curious rather than consumed by anger. John moved through the surface-level presentation of anger to more thoroughly explore the gifts buried within his rage like the pearl of an oyster. John discovered that his anger masked a deep sense of hurt and rejection his partner had unintentionally triggered by making a flippant comment about his appearance. From this new emotional space, John was able to make meaning of both his triggering experience and the repair that ensued with his partner. His sublimation allowed John to more deeply understand the functionality of his emotional waves that were in search of catharsis and transformation.

In this way, expression can be deeply nourishing and healing. Moving energy through our bodies ultimately opens interior gateways to deep rest by purging the negativity and stress that hold us hostage within a fired-up sympathetic nervous system. Once we are able to down-regulate into a calmer parasympathetic state, we can experience free-flowing access to the kind of deep rest and nourishment our systems require.

Methods for expression are as wide and varied as people are. Anything that helps you move energy through your mind, heart, and body will feel expressive. Perhaps you like to go for a long run or walk when immersed in heavy internal feelings. Maybe journaling feels more accessible, or art making. Many people enjoy the catharsis that comes from external processing with a trusted friend or loved one. For you it might be deep breathing, playing or listening to meaningful music, stretching your body, dancing, or shooting a few games of pool with your buddies. Whatever helps you move energy out rather than keeping it in is expression. This results in widespread health and balance across many physical, mental, emotional, psychological, and energetic systems, and it contributes immensely to our ability to unplug and access the healing benefits of rest.

It is important to note that not all forms of expression are healthy and nourishing, and it's crucial that you know the difference. Screaming at the top of your lungs at your child or community bus driver in the name of self-expression can feel like release, but it hurts rather than heals. Anyone who has done something like this (and I think we can all relate to some degree) knows the feeling of remorse and guilt that follows such an expressive episode. True nourishing expression is not followed by a hangover of regret and shame.

Similarly, violence against humans, animals, or property may feel cathartic, but it ultimately does not result in the benefits of healthy release. Anyone who has spent weeks or months nursing the broken bones shattered by angrily punching a wall or another person can attest to this. Blowing off steam with a few drinks before driving recklessly down the freeway may feel burden-free and host an impulsive *screw it* mentality, but this is not healthy expression. Healthy expression allows for release without harming, belittling, endangering, or unleashing poisonous emotional darts upon anyone or anything.

THE HEALING POWER OF FORGIVENESS

Is generosity doable? Sure. Compassion? Why not. But forgiveness? That's where I lose many people in the layers of deep healing work necessary to build a radiant life. Forgiveness seems to be one of the most bitter pills a person can swallow, and it is all based on a massive misunderstanding. People tend to think that forgiveness offered to someone who hurt them condones the person's wrongdoing and makes it okay. No. The power of forgiveness does not lie by excusing abuse, harm, thoughtlessness, or cruelty. The true potency of forgiveness comes when a person finds relief by no longer carrying the painful grudge they have been harboring in response to being hurt. Though it's nice if you can get to a place where your forgiveness repairs strain or betrayal in a relationship, forgiveness is not about freeing the other person from the wrongdoing of their transgression—it's about freeing yourself from carrying the toxic energy you assumed with your hurt.

Offering: Is there a hurt you've been carrying? Write about it in your journal or create artistic imagery that explores your experience in a visual context.

A certain Jewish Hasidic parable tells the story of a quarrel between a king and his son. It goes like this: Something (I'm not sure what exactly) went awry in the relationship between a king and his son, leading to a horrible argument with much bitterness and hurt. In a fit of rage, the king exiled the prince from his kingdom. Years passed, and over time the king's heart softened. Seeking repair, the king sent his ministers to seek out the prince and ask him to return home to the kingdom. When the ministers found the prince, he was still deeply wounded from his tumult with his father and declined the king's invitation. The ministers returned to the kingdom to tell the king of his son's refusal to return, and the king sent them back to the prince with a new message: *Return as far as you are able, and I will come the rest of the way to meet you.*[11]

Yowza. Now that's what forgiveness in the service of repair truly looks like. Not only did the king invite his son home in an effort to make amends, but he expressed his commitment to the relationship by demonstrating his willingness to humble himself to any degree necessary to make things right. I often remind my clients that a good apology contains three essential parts:

1. Take accountability for the hurtful act you executed.
I did that. I raged at you, and I know it was immensely hurtful.

2. Express a sincere apology (you have to truly mean it).
I am truly sorry for what I did, and for the pain it caused you.

3. Ask what you can do to make it right, and then follow through.
What can I do to make this right?
Or, as the king said, *"I will come the rest of the way to meet you."*

Although forgiveness can be a difficult practice because of the special blend of humility, accountability, and remorse that contributes to its stickiness, practice it anyway. It will free you from the poison of burdensome grudges, and it may even heal and elevate your relationships.

As you practice forgiveness, healthy expression, emotional generosity, and other nurturing lessons from this chapter, you are building an effective toolbox that will replenish your soul and lead you toward a radiant life. Please source from these practices when you feel weary, and when your containment strategies feel thin and unsteady. Continue opening your mind and heart to new experiences, behaviors, and people who leave you feeling filled up.

Life is a shape-shifting concoction of messiness, beauty, and confusion much of the time. I trust that with these tools and others you have yet to discover, you will learn to peacefully coexist with the more volatile and sensitive parts of yourself. Begin by displaying intentional engagement in your life while truthfully acknowledging your need for rest and repair. This is a courageous act of self-love. Allow yourself to feel proud of the lengths you have traveled, and take a breather. There's plenty of time to bravely move toward all that still lies undiscovered within you and ahead on your path.

CHAPTER 4

Healing

A Journey Within

Be patient toward all that is unsolved in your heart
and try to love the questions themselves.
                                          —*RAINER MARIA RILKE*

IMAGINE A YELLOW SCHOOL BUS WITH EVERY SEAT FILLED
with children of varying ages, dispositions, and temperaments. Then imagine that the driver of the bus is a child too.
You know there must be an adult somewhere, but where?
This is the premise of the therapeutic modality of Internal
Family Systems (IFS), which was developed by Richard
Schwartz.[1] IFS teaches that each person possesses a true
Self within; who we are at our most basic essence. When
we operate from Self, we are clear, compassionate, creative,
and filled with peaceful, insightful qualities. Also within
every person are what IFS defines as *parts,* or aspects of
ourselves that have fractured away from true Self when we
faced hardship, trauma, and pain in life. Parts believe it is
their purpose to drive the bus to safety. Most parts were

created in childhood in response to difficult life situations, but we can also develop parts later in life. The two kinds of parts that exist within our internal systems are *exile parts* and *protector parts*. Exile parts hold the wounded, fragile energy of our inner children's pain, and they are held beneath our awareness by protector parts who do their best to keep exile energy hidden away. The two kinds of protector parts are *managers* and *firefighters*. Manager protector parts hold our lives together with high-functioning skills and behaviors such as perfectionism, hyper-organization, intellect, and other such methods. Firefighter protector parts are the emergency service squad who come running to our defense with extreme measures like addiction, impulsivity, and other behaviors that help dull our pain momentarily, but these parts have no regard for the collateral damage they leave in their wake.

The main intentions in IFS are to learn how to return to Self, recognize the function protector parts play, and shine loving awareness upon exile parts to help them reintegrate in our system. When this is achieved, protector parts become free to assume new healthier roles within us. The goal in IFS is not to get rid of any parts or to think of certain parts as good or bad. A basic assumption in this therapeutic method is that all parts are important and valuable. They do their very best, with whatever they know, in any way they are capable, to safely make it through life in one piece. Due to the fragmented nature of parts, they are often stunted in age, knowledge, and maturity at the point where they came into being. If an exile part developed when a person was attacked by a dog at age four, a protector part that evolved to protect that exile from feeling such danger again would defend it by embodying the energy of fearful aggression toward anything that feels threatening—dog or not. As a result of this survival strategy, whenever the person feels unsafe and unconsciously activates this protective mechanism, they essentially operate from the perspective of a four-year-old. If you have ever found yourself in an argument with a loved one and thought to yourself, *This person is throwing a fit and behaving like a toddler!* It's likely that you are in direct contact with a triggered toddler-aged protector part, and it is doing whatever it knows how to do to defend itself.

The healthiest thing we can do when engaging what Richard Schwartz calls *parts work* is to become unblended with our parts and return to Self. This is easier said than done. It involves becoming aware that you are flooded by the energy of a part, then consciously working to see that particular part from the curiosity and compassion of true Self. If you can see the part as something other than Self, and even visualize it as a projective image of a creature or animal, you will have created enough space to disidentify from the part. The You who can witness the part cannot be the part. When you are able to see the part as an aspect of your system, but not the totality of your being, you can un-blend from its energy and see clearly once again.

Here's an example of this process: James was enraged. He was running late for a meeting to pitch a multi-million-dollar advertising campaign to a big client. As the head of his managerial team, James had worked tirelessly to design and develop a campaign he felt incredibly proud of. But then James got stuck in bumper-to-bumper traffic that seriously delayed his arrival. He screamed at the traffic, cycled thoughts of disbelief and failure through his mind, and sweat through his newly pressed dress shirt. James was flooded by the energy of a protector part. His fear of failure (exile) had been managed by maintaining a high-achieving lucrative career, always being on time, and keeping a strong reputation for being reliable and responsible. When James practiced IFS in that triggered moment, he began by noticing that his system was being flooded by the angry aggressive energy of a part. He said to himself, *I am really activated right now. I notice my increased body temperature, pressure in my forehead, and tension throughout my entire upper body.* These observations allowed James to sense more deeply into his body, and he recognized the familiar protective part that often showed up when the possibility of failure was present. With this information, James observed the intense, anxious, and fearful qualities of his protector part and related to the part with compassion. He inwardly verbalized, *I know it is frustrating to be stuck in this traffic jam. You really care about making it to the meeting on time, and you value your work.* Then, with continued compassion, creativity, and clarity, James worked with his protector part from the perspective of Self to bring his system into a less activated state where he felt calmer and more capable of handling his situation. *I cannot control the traffic. I have strong faith in the quality of my campaign, and I trust that the client will understand the situation and be willing to reschedule. I will make phone calls to the client and to my office explaining the traffic, and we will make a plan. That is all I can do in this moment, and I must remain aware and safe while I drive.*

Whether you decide to take a deep-dive into the complex inter-workings of IFS theory and practice—which I will not do in this book—or just hold it gently in your mind as a casual tool, please remember to always be respectful of the exquisite intelligence of your adaptive inner child.[2] These young parts within us do the very best they can, with what they know from their limited perspective, to keep us healthy, stable, and sane. Appreciate and honor them, but don't let them drive the bus. If you need help returning your parts to the passenger seats where they belong, please find a qualified IFS practitioner and allow them to help you navigate.

Offering: In your journal, write about an experience when one of your parts was driving the bus. If you're feeling artsy, create an image of a school bus being driven by one of your parts. The part need not look like you, or even be highly specific. If you can find congruence with the energetics of the part through line, color, and shape, that's enough. Perhaps your school bus is being driven by a wild minion, or a red triangle with steam emanating from it, or a sketch-like stick figure of yourself at age four.

Scattered throughout the following chapters, you will read references to IFS and parts work, as I find this methodology to be an incredible resource for inner healing work. Truly, in both my professional clinical work with clients and my personal work, IFS has by far been the most beneficial modality I have discovered. I can honestly say that it has changed my life, and I think you will feel similarly once you begin looking at the many facets of yourself through the lens of Self and parts.

TRAUMA

Back in Chapter 3, we touched on the sympathetic nervous system (SNS) branch of the autonomic nervous system. Let's dig a little deeper for a more comprehensive understanding: The sympathetic[3] is the part of the automatic nervous system (ANS) that is responsible for keeping you safe, alive, and whole (mostly in a physical way) by activating you to *do something* to achieve safety. This is the part of your system that reacts to potential threats with, *Oh! I can do something to keep you from harm. Run away! Battle this out!* If for whatever reason the fight/flight response of the SNS doesn't work, the system defaults back to the dorsal vagal function[4] of the parasympathetic as a last resort which says, *Maybe they'll leave you alone if you play dead. And if you become a victim, at least it won't hurt so badly because you'll be numb.* In addition to the fight and flight responses of the SNS, sometimes a person can get caught in *freeze*, which is when the body gets caught between the sympathetic and dorsal systems in an immobilized state that is filled with massive tension and internal energy. My husband can attest that this is my default reaction to surprising or shocking experiences. I have been rendered frozen in an unexpected sprinkler downpour (more than once) during family picnics, and I also tend to freeze up when I am unexpectedly confronted interpersonally with anger or accusation. Inconveniently for me, it is typically not until long after another person would have fled the sprinklers or engaged relational discord that I find myself able to do so.

The *fawn* behavior is a lesser-known mechanism that can initiate in any nervous system state to keep us safe in the face of danger by collapsing emotionally and psychology into compliance, people pleasing, and smallness. Most often when people habituate to the fawn response, they have been conditioned to do so through traumatic relationships. *I feel publicly humiliated when Mom tells other people about my learning disability, but I'll just deal with my shame internally because if I confront Mom it will make her mad and I'll never hear the end of it.* Such dangerous relational dynamics teach that a person will be safe if they remain helpless and compliant. Messages like this can be taught in the face of overt danger, and they can also be taught subtly through a lifetime of microaggressions.

The term *microaggressions* speaks to the type of trauma that happens over time when a person is exposed to small, seemingly trivial or insignificant attacks that slowly chip away at their self-worth, perceived value, or experience of safety. Though one microaggression hurts, it is most likely survivable—like getting a bee sting. Multiple bee stings, however, can greatly harm or even kill a person. Microaggressions in large quantities over years (or even decades) can bring a person into deep emotional trauma and inhibit their functioning. Often when people are victims of microaggressions, they believe their experience of trauma to be oversensitive or crazy because that's the message their abusers send them. *Gaslighting* is a behavior used in dynamics such as these when an abuser manipulates their victim's perception of reality and makes them feel unsure if their experience is true. Though gaslighting can also be an intrinsic part of the types of trauma that result in fight, flight, and freeze, it is the fawn response that most often initiates to cope with traumas related to manipulative behaviors and ongoing microaggressions that persist long-term.

Whether the SNS reacts to the insidious trauma of microaggressions and gaslighting, a singular event like a catastrophic accident, or anything in between, its priority is to keep us alive by focusing all of our energy toward safety. In response to a threat, the SNS initiates many protective functions that include (but are not limited to) increasing our metabolism and blood pressure, releasing adrenaline and other neurotransmitters and hormones into our bloodstream, increasing oxygenation, dilating our pupils, and many other changes in our organs and inner-systems to prime us for defense and survival. The sympathetic rollout spectacularly readies our bodies to react and remain vigilant until the perceived threat has passed before notching down into the parasympathetic for rest and processing.

Though the SNS displays an impressive response to danger, it can be detrimental if we get trapped in a sympathetic state long-term. This is what happens in posttraumatic stress disorder (PTSD) and other chronic trauma responses. When our brains and bodies believe that we are in danger, they remain in a warrior stance to protect us, but there is no built-in timer that ceases this protection. In the case of ongoing exposure to threat (like a person in an abusive home or a soldier on a battlefield), the SNS fires its protective power in such a prolonged way that a person can find themselves utterly depleted and hardly functioning.

Our bodies were designed to regain balance and move in and out of the different nervous system states with ease, but trauma drastically alters our ability to do so. Oftentimes, trauma doesn't end when the traumatic experience stops. It continues to live within a person as a persistent state of unease based on a core belief that the world is unsafe and they are unsafe in it. Prolonged hypervigilance keeps systems like these ready at all times to fight and protect. Traumatic memories, flashbacks, and narratives about danger all compile to trigger unconscious biological mechanisms connected to a person's SNS that prevent them from down-regulating into the PNS.

It is important to understand that trauma comes in all shapes and sizes, and no one type of trauma is more valid than another. The Substance Abuse and Mental Health Services Administration (SAMHSA) has developed a definition of trauma[5] based on the combination of a given experience that they call the *three E's.*

1. The event: What happened—without emotional attachment or charge.

    Jamie's car was hit by a drunk driver while waiting at a stop light. She was flung through the windshield, knocked unconscious, and obtained multiple injuries. An ambulance drove Jamie to the hospital for medical treatment.

2. The experience: How the person experienced the event emotionally and psychologically.

    Immediately upon awakening at the hospital, Jamie reported feeling helpless, terrified, and bewildered that a person would drive drunk and put her in danger when she had done nothing to deserve the damage and injuries she acquired as a result of their actions.

3. The effects: The lasting effects from the experience in a person's mind and body.

    Jamie developed PTSD and anxiety as a result of her experience. After her recovery, she reported feeling intense fear while driving and being a passenger in a car. Jamie began working with a trauma therapist to heal the psychological wounding that occurred from her car accident.

The complexities that arise in response to trauma can derail a person's ability to feel safe in infinite ways. Sometimes trauma is the result of a singular event, like Jamie's car accident, while other traumatic experiences happen repeatedly such as that of a child in an abusive home. Trauma can happen any time a person becomes physically, emotionally, or psychologically affected by an experience from which they cannot return to baseline regulation and normal functioning. The continuum of traumatic experiences different people encounter is vast. A person's ability to rebound after challenging experiences depends greatly upon the internal safety narratives that are based on their early relationships and life experiences. If a child was raised by cold, disinterested parents who neglected their emotional needs and inadvertently (or directly) taught them that they were on their own, that child would be more likely to grow up thinking, *The world is a cold and uncaring place. I need to make my own way and cover my own back to stay safe and get my needs met.*

THIS IS YOUR BRAIN ON TRAUMA

Neuroscientist and child psychiatrist Dr. Bruce Perry has developed a wealth of resources in his work about the effects of trauma on the human brain. Dr. Perry eloquently teaches[6] that all experience moves through the brain from the bottom up. The innermost core of the human brain, sometimes called the *brainstem and diencephalon* or *reptilian brain,* is where our most primitive, survival-based, reactive brain mechanisms live. This part of the brain exists not only in humans, but in all living creatures. Its job is essentially to keep living beings alive. This innermost part of the brain is responsible for physical safety, reproduction, breathing, basic motor functioning, sleep, and waste excretion. Experience starts here, and if something flags this part of the brain as unsafe, involuntary measures such as running away, physical aggression, or curling into a ball can ensue before the person has time to fully process the experience. After the initial information passes through the lower structure's filters, it moves up.

The second level of the brain, sometimes referred to as the *limbic* or *mammalian brain* (because it can be found in all mammals) is where most of our behavioral responses and emotional processes happen. If an experience picked up red flags when it passed through the lower structures of the brain, the limbic system will then attach emotional reactions to those red flags before passing the information upward again.

The topmost level of the human brain, the *cortex* or *neo-cortex,* houses a capacity for sophistication that is only found in humans. It is because of our cortex that we can build bridges, explore outer space, and solve crossword puzzles. The topmost part of our brains is where we access higher-level thinking, planning, strategy, and analysis, and it's the last stop on the train of experiential processing. By the time trauma makes its way to the cortex for cognitive processing and analysis, a person may have picked up so much physical and emotional distress from the lower levels of the brain that they either cannot process their experience (overwhelm) or feel entirely disconnected from it (dissociation).

I have treated many trauma survivors who rationally know they are safe and sound, yet their bodies remain hyper-vigilant and primed for protection. This is because some-where in the communication between the brainstem and the cortex, neural connections developed in support of the belief that the world is unsafe. Many people in these situations develop coping mechanisms to contain the fear and reac-tivity of their trauma such as dissociation, numbing, impul-sivity, and other behaviors. Therapy, properly prescribed and utilized medication, and intentional practice all become important pieces of the puzzle to treat such displacements of psycho-emotional experience. Teaching a fired-up nervous system to rebalance itself can often take time and patience, but with skillful support it is possible, helpful, and necessary.

SELF-COMPASSION AND SURRENDER

If I know one thing about trauma healing (really all healing—not just from trauma), it is that compassion is the piece of the puzzle that tips the experiential scales from arduous to meaningful. Without an open-hearted warmth toward oneself while excavating and navigating inner work, recovery tends to feel flat and unsustainable. The single most important person who needs to be on board with your healing and growth process toward a radiant life is Y.O.U.—and I don't mean only the part of you that wants healing so you can check the box and move on with life—I mean all of you. Self-compassion is akin to a lifeboat that saves you from endless darkness and offers a blanket and bowl of soup to soothe your weary soul. Without the generosity and love of self-compassion, life (not to mention healing) feels a whole lot harder.

The big kahuna of self-compassion research and practice is Dr. Kristin Neff.[7] Dr. Neff has an entire body of resources on the topic, and I highly recommend that you delve into it head-first as though you were blissfully soaring toward a swimming pool filled with mint-chocolate-chip ice cream. Yes, it's really that good. Neff's definition of self-compassion[8] involves noticing your suffering, attending to yourself with care and support, and honoring that hardship and imperfection are part of the shared human experience (she calls this *common humanity*). Dr. Neff also differentiates self-compassion from self-pity, which carries the energetics of distain, disgust, and feeling sorry for oneself.

Once you've got your own back in a way that feels both strong and tender, there are no feats you cannot face. Like a loving caregiver, when you attend to yourself with unconditional love, support, and understanding, your tank feels fuller and you can more easily navigate challenges. One further way to support yourself is to take a dimmer-switch perspective rather than an on/off stance toward your healing work. When you set an expectation for your process to unfold in layers, you effectively allow yourself to grow incrementally and with healthy titration. Growth of this kind is more stable and sustainable because it unfolds slowly and does not overwhelm your system with massive change all at once. In healing of all kinds, maintaining stability within your system is essential, and this is absolutely true with trauma work.

Offering: This is an Art Therapy Exercise: You will need to whip out some colored pencils, a graphite pencil, or a piece of charcoal, and grab your sketchbook. From left to right, create a continuum of gradation starting with the lightest possible hue of your color and building to the darkest. If you are working with a gray pencil, for example, when you are finished you will have a hue spectrum from white to black with many shades of gray between. This art therapy exercise offers you a visual representation of the spectrum of healing I reference above, and it allows your brain to grasp the process of gradual change rather than binary contrast.

For the most part in my clinical practice, it seems that people have a pretty good grasp on self-compassion and how it can benefit them. On the flip side, the concept of *surrender* tends to be a bit more complex. Many people misunderstand surrender to be an experience of apathy or not caring (which it is not). As it turns out, it's actually pretty difficult for a person to genuinely not care about their life—no matter how unhappy they may be. The parts of the brain that keep us physically safe and protected also contain an intrinsic motivation to protect us psycho-emotionally—even from ourselves. This is why so many suicide attempts result in failure (a good kind of failure). Even in the darkest dark when we feel trapped and hopeless, somewhere deep within our Selves there is a little voice that encourages us to keep living. Keep trying. Keep caring. No, surrender is not giving up and giving in. Surrender is allowing ourselves to release agenda and attachment, to drop resistance, to become present in the truth of the moment, and to trust. Release, presence, and trust.

My absolute most favorite story of surrender comes from the Tibetan saint Milarepa.[9] It goes like this: One day after collecting firewood, Milarepa returned to his cave to discover that demons had taken residency within it. Milarepa's first thought was that he had to get rid of the snarling monsters, so he chased them around and tried to forcefully remove them from his home. This did not work, and in fact it even enhanced the demons' ferocity. When he realized that his aggression was fruitless, Milarepa tried to teach the demons about his spiritual practices, which also failed to motivate their departure. Finally, Milarepa looked into the demons' eyes and proclaimed that it appeared they would be sharing the space together. He told the demons that he was open to whatever they had to teach him. In response, all of the demons except for one particularly nasty one disappeared. Then finally, in an act of ultimate surrender, Milarepa placed his head inside of the large demon's mouth. "Eat me if you wish," he said. At that moment, in response to the pure surrender Milarepa displayed, the terrifying demon bowed to Milarepa and disappeared.

Milarepa's story beautifully demonstrates how aggression, attachment, and striving can often work against us. Sometimes the only thing to do is to surrender, and it can bring unexpected results. I often think of Milarepa when I am facing a particularly difficult challenge, or when I notice rigidity and attachment within myself. Truly, the most painful experiences, relationships, fears, and circumstances most of us face in life do feel like psychological monsters. What would happen if we just looked them in the eye, expressed our willingness to learn, and placed our heads in their big scary mouths?

Offering: In your journal, make a list of three to five of your monsters. For each monster, write about what makes them feel so scary.

Healing is most certainly a process, and it's true that it can take a long time to move through the layers. I encourage you to be compassionate, loving, and patient as you meet each part of your Self. Notice the gifts that lie embedded within the hardship, and greet them with curiosity and openness. True healing cannot be rushed, and you must listen to your inner system to ascertain appropriate pacing for your inner work. Trauma specialist Peter Levine[10] wrote about the importance of *titration* in his work, which encourages thoughtful pacing when engaging healing work. Think of titration like dipping your toe into your inner layers as you would with a cold mountain lake. If you jump in too fast, your system could become overwhelmed and destabilized by the immersion. But if you ease yourself in slowly, while allowing breaks to recover and retreat before easing in again, the experience will feel more controlled and accessible. You will still reach full immersion, but you will have maintained a supported system throughout your experience.

Most often when navigating my own inner work, I have been surprised that when I meet my psychological demons head on, they are rarely as ferocious as I originally thought. Instead, the parts of myself I have feared most ended up being valuable messengers and guides that introduced me to new levels of depth within my Self that I have enormously benefitted from exploring. As long as you commit to the long haul with yourself and you offer internal compassion and support along the way, the journey can feel immensely gratifying and purposeful.

Meaningful Growth

Inner Work at Its Finest

For a seed to achieve its greatest expression, it must come completely undone. The shell cracks, its insides come out, and everything changes. To someone who doesn't understand growth, it would look like complete destruction.
—CYNTHIA OCCELLI

WHEN WORKING TOWARD AUTHENTICALLY LIVING A RADIant life, it is important to make the distinction between *who you are* and *where you're at*. This also applies to how you see and know others. If you judge who you know yourself and others to be based on where you/they currently are in your/ their growth process, you will not accurately locate the truth of who you/they are beneath all of the trauma, conditioning, stress, and masks most (if not all) people have acquired throughout their years on Earth. How you present yourself both inwardly and outwardly is not necessarily *who you are*. It might just be a reflection of *where you're at*.

Let me iron this out more clearly with an example: Samuel was known by most everyone as a shy, introverted, quiet person. His voice was soft and easily drowned out when speaking in a group of more than two people. When Samuel needed to print a document at work, he would walk quickly and stiffly down his company hallway toward the printer and avert his gaze from people to avoid conversation. When a cluster of colleagues would gather in the office kitchen, he remained at his desk, and if he could not help but be present when the gathering began, Samuel wordlessly disappeared without anyone noticing. He politely declined so many social invitations that he stopped receiving invitations. Samuel could often be seen engaging in solitary acts such as walking his dog alone in nature, going to the movies stag, and staying home under the light of dim reading lamps on most Saturday nights. Based on these observations and perceptions of Samuel, the people in his life thought they knew him—that this behavior indicated who Samuel was. But they were wrong.

What the passerby could not observe about Samuel was the crippling social anxiety lying upon his chest like a sleeping bear. This weight was with Samuel wherever he went, and he had not been able to free himself from it despite his multiple stints in therapy, internet dating efforts, and awkward attempts toward casual conversation with the butcher in his neighborhood market. None of Samuel's coworkers knew that he had a trauma history beyond the imaginings of their wildest nightmares or that he awakened multiple nights per week in a cold sweat of profound fear and confusion. Thinking that Samuel's apparent introversion, or even his anxiety, defined who he was did a massive disservice to the mind-blowingly magnificent essence of Samuel at his core. Samuel's brilliance was obscured by his mental health struggles and trauma. The few lucky folks who did truly know Samuel could attest to his brilliant mind and kind heart. They could boast about his thoughtfulness and witty sense of humor. They knew about his fondness of furry creatures, and his weekly volunteer work at the local animal shelter. The people who truly knew Samuel had gently pushed beyond his surface-level shyness and social avoidance. They patiently waited for genuine trust to build while getting to know Samuel. Over time, these friends were able to see not just *where Samuel was at* in his healing journey, but also *his most basic authentic Self.* And fortunately for these individuals, they found an incredible, loyal, generous friend in Samuel.

Here's the bottom line: You cannot know yourself or another person if you do not allow yourself the patience, attunement, and curiosity to dip beneath everyday personas and surface-level reactions we all have to life in order to witness the authentic Self within. You are not what has happened to you. You are not the projections of who others want you to be. You're just not. There is so much more to you than the emotional, behavioral, and psychological lint you've picked up throughout your life. Consciously or unconsciously, everyone is walking along their own yellow brick road of healing and growth, pacing ever closer to their radiant life. To take a snapshot of a person midway along the path, weary and covered in dust, and say *This is who you are!* is just too one-dimensional, wouldn't you agree?

Offering: Let's practice. In your journal, write a sentence or two about "who you are." Then write a sentence or two about "where you're at." Finally, explore any similarities, differences, or overlap between the two in another few sentences of writing.

Think of the authentic Self as a faithful inner propeller mechanism like the North Star from Chapter 1. This driving force is an energy that will never quit its steady hum, and it serves as a patient guide as you negotiate whatever life throws in your direction. Regardless of the hand you were dealt, your authentic Self will help you discover and optimize the ultimate freedom and purpose that come with living from your truest essence. This true You anticipates the twists, turns, and mountains of learning that lie ahead, and it acknowledges the lived-history behind you. No matter what you encounter along the road, whom you become influenced or wounded by, and what magnitudes of success or hardship rain upon you, the core essence of who you are is never lost. Heaps and piles of filmy confusion might superimpose themselves upon your true Self, like trauma and social anxiety did for Samuel, but nothing can blot out the pilot light that is your most essential Self.

ENTRY TO THE LAND OF EMOTIONS

Emotions are a good place to start when considering the variables that influence our journey along the yellow brick road of life. Jill Bolte Taylor, a scientist and the author of *My Stroke of Insight*,[1] provided a powerful insight with her *90-second rule*. This is a neurological process from Bolte Taylor's work related to the power of choice we hold related to our emotional experiences. As it turns out, there is a specific chemical process that can be observed and tracked in the human brain when a person has an emotional reaction. This specific neurological process persists for approximately

90 seconds before it dissipates. The beauty of this illuminating information is this: Your emotions flow through your brain and body for a remarkably short amount of time. Anything you feel beyond the 90 seconds of your physical system's neurochemistry is your own attachment to the emotion. Basically, if you still feel snagged or triggered after 90 seconds, you have chosen (on some level) to remain in the muddied waters of your emotional experience rather than simply letting it end.

A symbolic image I like to use with clients is a layered bean dip. Just like the delicious party appetizer, our inner landscape in any given moment exists in layers. When we assume that the topmost layer of our emotional experience is the extent of our feelings about whatever we are facing in the moment, we do ourselves an immense disservice by neglecting the deeper strata beneath it. Can you imagine if you only ate the topmost layer of a multilayer dip? You would really miss out on the good stuff.

In this kind of emotional work, we begin by noticing the layer that presents first, followed by the question, *If this were true, then what?* By questioning the topmost layer, you affectively orchestrate a tunnel of curiosity that can take you into the next layer down for investigation. By observing each layer and questioning what it would mean if it were true, you can follow the thread of your emotional experience until you reach the base-level core emotion that resonates as the end of the thread. Once you reach such a landing place, you can attend to the origin of your emotional experience and more clearly understand yourself and your triggers. Most often, the core emotional experience is an unhealed wound from childhood, an outdated core belief, or an attachment to a significant life experience from your past. Here's an example:

Layer one is usually the initial emotional trigger:
My partner made an insensitive comment about my weight and it really pissed me off!
This is the first layer ◊ Anger.

If your partner harshly judges your weight, then what?
I fear that he doesn't find me attractive.
This is the second layer ◊ Insecurity.

If he doesn't find you attractive, then what?
He might lose interest in me and have an affair with someone else.
This is the third layer ◊ Fear of rejection.

If he loses interest in you and has an affair with someone else, then what?
He might leave me and then I would be alone.
This is the fourth layer ◊ Fear of abandonment.

If he leaves you and you find yourself alone, then what?
No one would ever love me again.
This is the fifth layer ◊ Dependency.

If no one ever loves you again, then what?
It would prove that I am truly unlovable and unworthy of love.
This is the core emotional experience ◊ Fear of being unlovable and unworthy.

Notice how far we traveled from the initial presentation of anger to the more difficult, yet more deeply truthful core emotional experiences. Once the topmost layers have been cleared, we can more easily access and attend to the core wound (or wounds) with direct focus and attention. This process can go on and on for many layers, often arriving at a core emotional experience related to unworthiness, lack of lovability, lack of belonging, or worthlessness. Sadly but truly, these are the most common childhood wounds I have found in my clinical experience, and I believe they are common throughout our culture due to the early messaging children receive as they learn how to survive in the world. In response to their core wounds, people learn to behave in ways that they believe will ensure that they will be loved, accepted, appreciated, and valued, even if the feats they perform directly oppose their authentic Selves. Perfectionism is a good example because it is a psychological survival mechanism that operates under the assumption that *If I behave perfectly and do everything right, I will be loved and valued.*

The purpose of engaging the bean dip exercise is to take you deeper than the initial presenting emotion in order to find the core emotional experience that has snagged your trigger. Typically, a person will traverse monumental emotional territory between the top layer of the bean dip, so to speak, and the bottom layer as they investigate deep unhealed inner terrain. Just as anger often masks the experience of hurt because it feels safer and more guarded to feel the flames of anger than the stab of hurt, many other emotions tend to eclipse one another as mechanisms of self-protection. Through the Internal Family Systems (IFS) lens, this is how protector parts work to keep us from feeling the fragile discomfort of exiled parts that carry deep wounding energy we would rather avoid than face.

Offering: For the sake of practice, take a moment to explore your bean dip in your journal. Consider which emotions you default to most often. You may choose to explore anger, anxiety, shame, or any other. Ask yourself how these experiential qualities serve to shield you or keep you at arm's length from deeper pain. Next, consider what you might find if you dipped beneath the surface presentation of one of these familiar emotions. Gently consider who the exiled part may be, and how that part is being guarded by a protector part.

Perhaps you already know the next layer beneath the mask, or maybe clarity still remains ambiguous. If you do encounter awareness of an exile part, first and foremost offer thanks to the protector for allowing you to witness the fragile exile it had been defending. It is crucial when engaging parts work to never force entry past a protector part; this only shuts down the system and creates mistrust between Self and parts. Instead, if you come into contact with a protector part, acknowledge and appreciate it for the job it does to keep your system safe. If, and only *if*, you are able to develop trust with that part through the process of IFS, it may grant you access to meet and attend to the exile behind its shield. This can be a delicate and complex process best handled with the skillful support of a trained IFS practitioner. For now, simply observe the parts you do have awareness of, and see if you can access compassion toward those wounded and defending parts of yourself. It's okay if the experience feels vulnerable, sad, or even relieving. Making contact with the deeper parts of yourself that have been protectively hidden away from your awareness can feel quite complex.

The value in peeking beneath the mask of your automatic default emotions to see those lying beneath is knowing yourself more deeply, healing past wounding, and becoming less fearful and more accepting of your many layers. The experience is akin to a child's fear of the dark lumpy monster squatting in their bedroom corner, only to discover in the light of day that it was only ever a harmless pile of clothes. Mark Nepo says in *The Book of Awakening*, "fear gets its power from our not looking."[2] The bean dip exercise allows you to courageously look at that which feels scary and deepen into the fear to allow yourself to be led toward another breadcrumb along your journey toward a radiant life.

Something interesting about emotions is that they are vastly multidimensional. Not only do emotions present differently between different people, they also show up in unique ways within the same person from one experience to the next. Even when you are flooded by an emotion and engaging in unhealthy or reckless behaviors from its influence, there are no bad or wrong emotions. Can they get out of hand? Absolutely. Returning to the concept of IFS parts work for a moment, certain dysregulated parts within us can become triggered when they feel unsafe, thus igniting protective mechanisms in a cascade of emotional responses and reactions that, despite the best intentions of the protector part, sometimes work against us. The emotions that fuel our protective parts are tools our inner systems use to alert and communicate with us, but our parts can unintentionally distort messages by applying them to outdated narratives. When this happens, the communication about the trigger becomes completely misguided. Have you ever had a strong emotional reaction about something only to later discover that you were completely off-base? *He's definitely cheating on me. He's not answering his phone and running three hours late. I am enraged!* Then twenty minutes later, he walks into the house weary from a stressful workday. In this example, a protector part that had been hurt before and vowed to never allow betrayal again applied a narrative from an old relationship to a current situation that turned out to be completely different. In this way, our emotions can veer into the realm of catastrophic thinking before we have a full-picture understanding of what is truly happening in the moment. When this occurs, we essentially apply outdated information to a present situation and react as we wish we would have in the past—except the current situation may be wildly different than the past situation we are unconsciously referencing. You can see how this rarely delivers a desirable result.

When we are able to remove the flooding from our emotions, we can see how they are an important part of our interior toolbox. Emotions serve as sophisticated bridges between our minds and bodies, and they act as messengers while we interact with the people and experiences in our world. There are destructive and productive versions of all emotions, and an entire spectrum between. If we are willing to see our emotions as the emissaries they truly are, we can source wisdom from their flare-ups. It is important to remember that the pulsing energy of an emotion doesn't make the narrative we're telling ourselves about is true, and it certainly doesn't mean we need to urgently act from that vigilant place.

Consider relating to your emotions as though they were colorful bubbles arising from your interior core. If you can name and visualize the qualities of your emotions and remove the charge from them, you will simply see them for what they are. Without the tether you would normally attach to the emotion, you can notice subtleties and nuances about it that can be hugely informative. *I notice bubbles of anxiety arising from my lower stomach area in response to the presentation I am about to give. They are green and blob-shaped and bouncing all around. I feel nauseous.* Noticing the visual and energetic elements of an emotion allows you to ask the emotion what it is trying to say and source self-support in the moment. *If I take a gentle walk down the hallway, the bubbles seem to bounce around less. Fewer bubbles emanate when I breathe deeply and remind myself that I am an expert on this presentation topic.* Working with an emotion like this may or may not eradicate the discomfort of its presence, but it will amplify your understanding of its message and grant you access to support yourself.

A tool I like to use when I feel intense emotions arising is Tara Brach's distinction between *reaction* and *response*.[3] By simply noticing and observing the wave of feeling rolling through me and relating to it as though it is a messenger, I can much more easily consider what within myself is being triggered and *respond* with kindness and care to that sensitivity. This practice involves accessing an internal experience of *equanimity*, which is balanced mindful presence. As Brach so eloquently states,[4] equanimity involves having "a heart that is ready for anything." It is important to understand when practicing balanced mindful presence that equanimity is not the same as detachment, indifference, or passivity. Those qualities are sometimes made synonymous to equanimity, but they are not the same. True equanimity does not serve as an excuse to avoid the sticky bits of life. Instead, it leads a person toward responsiveness rather than reactivity. When a person responds, they intentionally pause during a triggered moment and create space to thoughtfully attune to both their arising internal experience and the external situation. As Brach says, "You become the ocean that has room for the waves."

When I practice equanimity, I first notice and attend to my inner needs *(take a deep breath, remove myself from the situation, drink water)*. I then execute any external actions necessary in order to move through the experience *(set a boundary with someone, ask for help, cancel plans)*. Gently responding to a trigger or emotion in this way helps me attend to myself with compassion, and thoughtfully consider important next steps. If I simply *react* from a charged emotional space without slowing down and holding space for the emotion to share its wisdom through equanimity, I will most likely breathe fire toward someone in an outburst that is likely exaggerated and unnecessary, and nine times out of ten I'll regret it.

Offering: Write about your response and reaction tendencies in your journal. If you have a loved one you enjoy sharing deep conversations with, explore this topic together. Notice how different people often experience response and reaction in highly unique ways.

Offering: A quick internet search will turn up the timeless poem The Guest House *by the one and only Mewlana Jalaluddin Rumi, who was a Sufi poet born in 1207. Rumi captures the energy of equanimity quite unlike anything I have ever read. If you know* The Guest House, *I invite you to read it again in this context. If you haven't yet discovered this magical poem, look it up. I'm sure you won't regret it.*

STACKED BRICKS AND SPIRALS

I would like to share my *stacked bricks* analogy to explain how inner work must happen in layers. Healing is like a tower of stacked bricks; if you want to disassemble the wall, you have to grab the topmost brick first. If you destabilize the stack by snagging a brick from the middle or bottom, the entire system can come crashing down. This happens with inner work, too. We have to work with the layers that are on top and ready first. Though we may want to work on a layer far below the surface, it does not serve the highest good of our system to set it up for collapse. With this in mind, it's best to wait to heal deeper layers until we arrive there naturally.

Another important piece of this teaching is that the same topic will often have many layers at differing depths within the stack. Clearing a brick from the top doesn't mean you won't someday find another brick lower down with a deeper perspective on the same issue. Entrenched triggers, issues, and growth edges tend to need more than one iteration of focus. In Chapter 7, I teach my *Sharks in the Bathtub* theory for this particular experience, so hold onto your hat. It is normal to return to the same topic repeatedly, each time accessing deeper layers of healing within your system.

My stacked bricks analogy is similar to the spiral perspective of healing, which is a popular concept that floats around various spiritual and psychological communities. In the *spiral theory*, healing is akin to a spiral where a person keeps returning to the same topics, but from different perspectives where they can engage the issue from new vantage points and work with it differently. This is one reason why we see elements of our lives through different lenses as we move through time—because we are moving up the spiral. Up, up, up we go. There is no moving backward in life.

Recall the cliché *Life is about the journey, not the destination*. It's a silver-lining billboard we've seen to the point of becoming collectively desensitized to its truth, but that doesn't make it any less true. Tara Brach shared a cartoon she discovered where a dog sat upon the proverbial mountaintop next to a wise guru. The guru said to the dog, "The bone is not the reward. Digging for the bone is the reward." Maybe it's less cliché if the subject of conversation is canine.

I have seen a theme in many of my clients (and I know it well within myself, too), that we believe if we can just check all the right boxes for *healing* and *growth* we will arrive *there*, in a nirvana place, where everything is silky-smooth and easy. I think we all know in a deep intuitive place that there's no *there* to get to, and yet the striving continues.

I remember hearing from a client of mine about the seemingly endless mountain she felt she was climbing in her self-exploration process. She explained how she kept feeling like she was getting close, thinking she could sense the summit to end her arduous climb, only to recognize that she had reached (yet another) false summit. If you are not familiar with mountain climber lingo, a *false summit* is one of the great tricks of God, The Universe, or whomever you believe to be in charge of this virtual reality called life. When a climber sees what they hope is the summit ahead, a stream of relief and excitement begins pulsing through their veins. *I'm almost there! I have come so far, and I have finally made it. It is so close I can almost taste it.* Then, the climber approaches the summit and suddenly realizes it was a hoax. What looked like the summit from a lower vantage point actually turns out to be a mound of dirt and rock that simply obscured the miles and mountains still left to climb. The happy psycho-emotional cocktail of neuromodulators like dopamine and serotonin, as well as a down-shifting parasympathetic nervous system (to calm you) jolts to a stop. You then become deeply exhausted and frustrated when you realize that so much work still lies ahead. This is akin to the moment when you realize the issue you thought you healed has popped up again in an entirely new dreadful form, and it's time to double check that your web of inner-support is strong enough to hold it.

This has happened with many of my clients, it's happened in me, and I bet it has happened with you, too. How do I know this? Because every one of us ebbs and flows in relationship to the qualities of our lives that challenge us, cause us pain, and stubbornly refuse to go away. The next time you find yourself at the grocery store, in line at the bank, or browsing the stacks of your local bookstore, consider that everyone surrounding you is dealing with their own emotional trigger points and narratives, no matter how polished and put together they may appear. On a bulletin board in my office, I have this quote from Plato pinned front and center for all to read: "Be kind, for everyone you meet is fighting a hard battle."

Plato's words act as a valuable reminder to me when I get so caught up in my own lived experience that I forget I'm not the only person on the planet. Just as I am the main character in my own narrative, so is every other person in theirs. If I leave space in my heart for the possibility that others surrounding me deal with their life pain and struggle differently, I also allow for the distinct probability that whomever I feel reactive toward likely needs more of my compassion than my contempt. Through the lens of common humanity, I believe that every one of us is doing the best we can to navigate this wild, unpredictable, unfair, and sometimes agonizing human experience. In truth, we could all use a lot more kindness.

THE SEASONS OF LIFE

Just as we are all fighting our own battles, it is important to remember that you and everyone around you is in a specific and important season of existence. One of the reasons I appreciate Plato's quote is because it invites us to live life from a trajectory that we cannot possibly possess enough information to fully understand. Have you ever had the experience of being introduced to a concept or idea at a certain point in life and feeling an immediate, *Nah, that's not for me* response, and then a decade later coming across the same concept or idea and thinking, *Wow, I totally need and relate to this?* That's an example of the way we move through seasons in our lives where we express and perceive in different ways than we previously had.

Occasionally it's easy to notice when you are in passage toward another season of life, like a college graduate leaving behind their formal education and leaping head-first into the workforce. Other times we may leave one season of life and slide into another without much awareness until the transformation has been achieved—bada-bing, complete! Whether you find yourself moving through the seasons of life with grace or chaos, it is crucial to catch up to yourself in your new chapter and ask, *Where is life leading me next?* Remember, life expresses itself through us in both individual and collective ways, and it is important to realign with your authentic Self when you notice you've landed in a new season.

Sometimes new seasons in life come about with aging, progressing through healing barriers, igniting life transitions, or difficult experiences like the death of a loved one or onset of a health condition. No matter when or how you find yourself in a new season, take a breath, look around, and notice the subtleties of the season you are in. Perhaps this new chapter requires a slower pace than the last. Maybe imminent challenges exist that demand immediate mitigation. Or perhaps there's a new relationship dynamic to get curious about.

Offering: What season are you in right now? Explore your experience of your present season in writing, shared conversation, thoughtful introspection, or artistic expression.

Katherine May illustrates this interior changing of seasons quite beautifully and humorously in her book *Wintering: The Power of Rest and Retreat in Difficult Times*. May takes her readers through the winter soul-season, explaining how certain times in life exist for dormancy, hibernation, and a slower cadence of inward focus. She is clear in her writing that winter does not last forever, yet it is a meaningful holding space for inquiry and healing to incubate and integrate. May writes, "When I feel the drag of winter, I treat myself like a favored child. I ask myself what is this winter all about. What change is coming?"[5]

In the introspective season of wintering, we are presented with the opportunity to slow down our roller-coaster lives and ask ourselves some difficult and important questions. Over-giving is among the many snares a person can wrestle with as they spend time in the quiet space between seasons. I will speak about what I call *caregiver distortion* to display one possible area for inquiry during the courageous navel-gazing time of wintering. In *The Book of Awakening*, Mark Nepo wrote a statement that many caregivers among us may relate to—I admit, a layer within myself winced when I first read it. Nepo spoke of the tipping point between giving to others from authenticity vs. giving with an agenda. He wrote, "Accept this gift, so I can see myself as giving."[6] Ouch, right? And also so honest, so common. It is absolutely crucial to sit in the sticky mud of this potent statement if you identify as a giving person. As Nepo's writing continues, he elaborates on the possibility that life as a caretaker can be as addictive as the life of an alcoholic when the giver becomes hooked by the particular high that comes with feeling important and needed. Just like with a substance, our bodies can learn to release a cascade of feel-good hormones and neuromodulators to make outward giving feel like an internal reward (*I give you my time/energy not only so that you can feel supported and nourished by receiving it, but also so that I can feel good about myself being needed by you*). Although mostly unconscious, this dynamic is akin to an elaborate labyrinth that only leads back to the Self.

When an inner-dynamic like caregiver distortion occurs repeatedly over time, it becomes a pattern intrinsically linked with a core belief that the only way to receive love is by giving your time/energy/cookies/whatever to others. Thus, being loved by others is conditional upon your endless giving to them. Like all core beliefs, this isn't necessarily true, but the brain and body come to believe it is, so they automatically repeat the behavior in different relationships and experiences to achieve the grand prize of feeling loved and valued. This reinforces that the belief is true by evidencing it in action in a tiresome loop that seems okay on the surface but easily collapses when nudged more deeply.

Not until months, years, or even decades into the dynamic of caregiver distortion does a giver come to realize how transient the satisfaction of caring for others in this way truly is. Those with caregiver distortion must come to accept, sooner or later, that lasting satisfaction cannot come from external sources. Looking outside oneself for affirmation and gratification is reminiscent of *hungry ghosts* from Buddhist mythology. These are beings who exist in a limbo state between realms and are doomed to endless hunger and yearning despite great effort to ingest all they can to satiate themselves.

In a moment of caregiver distortion, a giver doesn't consciously feel like a hungry ghost (that's layers deeper than conscious awareness wants to notice, thank you very much). They are most likely striving to meet a most basic human need—to love and be loved. Most commonly the intention with agenda-laced giving stems from a well-meaning person unaware of the toxicity of their motivation—and please remember that not all giving stems from a toxic place.

Love is necessary for all humans, but it becomes distorted when a person attempts to mask their feelings of unworthiness and unlovability by glossing them over with the thin varnish of approval, appreciation, or validation from others. Caregiving of this kind may seem like a convenient workaround for a while, but those in this dynamic eventually realize that such a flavor of giving renders them unable to feel true compassion of any real depth because their care is sourced from an emotionally needy place loaded with agenda. The giving is not freely given, and that is what makes it toxic. To unwind the dysfunction of caregiver distortion, those who unconsciously engage this dynamic must build a consistent practice of self-love into their lives. They must learn to integrate the truth within themselves that they are inherently whole, lovable, and worthy exactly as they are—without having to do anything to earn, prove, or achieve it. Yikes, bikes! I know.

Offering: Jot a few notes on caregiver distortion in your journal. Is this an experience you yourself have had, or one you may have witnessed in another? Notice how caregiver distortion may present different barriers and serve unique functions for different people depending on their personal story, temperament, or trauma history.

I speak of caregiver distortion because I know it first-hand, and I've wrestled with this particular dragon to the extent that I can now tenderly engage it without getting burned to smithereens—though, admittedly, a stray spark here or there will still occasionally sting. *Dang, I'm still human after all.* Rest assured, it is well within your capacity to heal this layer of wounding with intentional focus and inner work, and it's an important piece of the radiant life puzzle. If you notice a pattern within yourself like caregiver distortion, or any other repetitive behavior or thinking structure that seems so deeply entrenched that you cannot quite stretch your mind around it, please bring a skillful and qualified therapist on board to help you navigate. Sometimes these deep layers benefit immensely from the trained support of a proficient guide. We all have dark layers and blind spots, and it can be helpful to explore yours with an objective, compassionate professional wielding a strong flashlight. When you look more honestly and more closely, you may discover that your wound is wrapped in the shadow of a deeper wound, a limiting belief, or a powerful emotion like fear.

FEAR AND TRIGGERS

Feeling afraid is completely okay. What's not okay is to live an afraid life. Fear is inherent not only in every human being, but every living creature. It is part of our hard-wired protective system with the important job of alerting us when our safety seems in question. Thanks to the sophistication of our minds and the higher-thinking capabilities that come with having a cortex in our brains, the fear response within humans has adapted to be quite highly sensitized—and sometimes distorted. When a small animal hears rustling in the bushes, it makes sense that they prepare to protect themselves in the event that a predator should leap toward them. We have this instinct as well (as discussed in the sympathetic nervous system section in Chapter 3). Unlike other species on Earth, however, we have adapted to experience fear in response to our social metrics, bank account status, degree of perfection in all things we do, and other human-only concerns that so often land a person either in therapy and/or on anti-anxiety meds.

Fear can sometimes act as a cage that results in our feeling cornered or trapped in either ongoing suffering or the perceived prevention of that very thing. It is important to understand that when investigating your cage of fear, you must take accountability for the role you play in perpetuating your stuckness. This does not mean you must adopt a false stance of fearlessness or numb yourself to the point of dissociation in order to bust out of your cage. It simply means that once you understand the role you play in keeping your fears alive and looming, you can find spaciousness within that suffering like pauses between breaths. Calm yourself enough to look around within the cage of fear you have constructed, and get curious about its function and necessity. If you are able to settle more calmly into your fear by investigating it through a new lens, you can expand the moments where your cage feels less stifling, even find gaps between the bars where you can breathe freely and see beyond the fear. Ultimately, the goal of this work is to respect and honor fear without allowing it to distort and reduce your participation in your own life.

Offering: What types of fear cages have you found yourself locked within? Write about your fear cages in your journal. If you wish to explore this topic artistically, create an image that represents the different qualities of your fear cage. Consider how certain materials might best capture the metaphor of your experience. If your cage feels flimsy and pliable, perhaps use yarn or watercolor lines. For a more rigid cage, consider metal wire or thick ink lines. If you choose to represent yourself inside your fear cage, consider how you might accurately represent the felt experience of being trapped within the cage.

The fear response in all of us is related to our lower brain regions, as discussed in Chapter 4, but that's not all. Our protector parts also defend valuable aspects of our lives and identities such as belonging, culturally defined success, relational safety, and emotional stability. Remember, protector parts believe it is their sole responsibility to keep us from ever feeling the way we felt when we were wounded. Regardless of whether a protector part is a manager or a firefighter, they will do everything in their power to keep the fragile exile energy from bubbling to the surface and wreaking the havoc they most fear.

For example, Frances grew up in a chaotic and disorganized household. Her family ran perpetually 20 minutes late, and she often felt embarrassed by her parents' lack of planning and timeliness. Often when caught up in the chaos of their household, Frances' mother would be so frazzled that her daughter's needs for love and attention got overlooked.

Unintentionally and unknowingly, this dynamic created an exile part within Frances that believed she was unimportant and easily disregarded. To defend the wounded energy of her exile part, Frances unconsciously developed a protector part that was highly organized, responsible, and timely. This part took it upon itself to set an alarm on Frances' watch with ample time to corral and filter the chaos of her family. Frances inadvertently took on an over-parentified role in her household to manage the schedules of her entire family, but the protector part didn't mind; in fact, she felt proud of herself for finding a way to overcome the chronic chaos of her family system. Little did Frances know, when her protector part was herding her family, the exile part within only received continued affirmation that certain conditions must be in place for her to be loved and lovable. Both the protector and exile parts took on the belief that Frances could only get her emotional needs met when everything operated smoothly and according to schedule. For the most part, when Frances achieved the herculean task of organizing her family system, the conditions were met. But when she was unable to achieve such a feat every single time, the pain of her exile wounding floated to the surface and triggered an absolute meltdown of Frances' self-worth.

So you see, the protector parts we put in place to manage and mitigate our fear can only be effective until they can't. By design, we humans are imperfect and unable to exercise super-control over all things in our lives, so it is inevitable that exile energy will occasionally leak through the cracks. The key to working with fear is to first become aware of your parts that have been working overtime to either avoid or manage the scary thing. Once you notice the dynamics at play between your parts, you can attend to your default patterns and bring further awareness and compassion to challenge them from the loving perspective of Self. A skillful IFS therapist can help you delve into this work, but you can expand your awareness of these parts today.

Offering: In your journal, list three to five of your protector parts. Next, write about the different ways each protector part serves you, and what its positive intentions are for your system. Then, list three to five of your exile parts, and explore the beliefs of these exile parts.

JOY, SCARY JOY

Dr. Brené Brown's research[7] shows that the most vulnerable emotion human beings can experience is joy. Due to the immense risk inherent in allowing ourselves to feel the resonance of joy and potentially lose it once we manage to somehow grasp it, fear comes into play in many ways, two of which Dr. Brown calls *foreboding joy* and *dress rehearsing tragedy:*

Foreboding joy sounds like: *uh-oh. This feels too good to be true. I better brace myself to lose this because there's no way I'm going to be able to keep it.* It is a natural protective mechanism to prepare oneself for the loss of something valuable in order to soften the inevitable crash-landing when we lose something we truly want and care about. What happens with foreboding joy, however, is a complex and sometimes confusing mash-up of joyful open-heartedness and cold prickly fear. Ironically, the self-protection that comes with foreboding joy is so vulnerable and fear-fueled, it can greatly diminish the very joy we are dead set on hanging onto. Parents are one group of people who understand foreboding joy in the moment they hand their newly minted 16-year-old a set of keys to drive their own car. The mixture of pride, joy, tender-heartedness, and terrifying fear that comes along with such autonomy is no doubt a complexity that includes a healthy dose of foreboding joy.

Dr. Brown's second concept, *dress rehearsing tragedy*, is one I have grown quite skillful at in the years of my life. Illogical as it may be, some part of me believes that if I run the worst-case-scenario of a given situation through my mind (ad nauseum), I will somehow be more prepared to handle it if it manifests. This is absolute hogwash, as any worry-prone person will likely agree. The truth is this: No matter how much we dress rehearse tragedy, hardship still holds the power to take our breath away and bring us to our knees despite our supposed mental preparedness. The illusion of protection we spin through our minds when we dress rehearse tragedy only serves to diminish our joy by removing us from the present moment where we can actually experience it.

No matter how much we face and explore our fears, the truth is that sometimes the vulnerability and fragility of joy is just too scary. Dress rehearsing tragedy and foreboding joy serve as shields to protect us from our fear of the implications of such powerful and complex life experiences. Although fear is part of the psyche that will not go away, luckily for us, it is something that can be tamed and attended to with conscious awareness. Fear is like a Tootsie Pop: You have to break through the hard outer layers of narrative, socialization, and conditioning to get to the inner core, which is the crux of your fear. Moving through the layers of what you're scared of in the service of entering the core of your fear is profound and meaningful work. There are many mechanisms to guide you along your journey, such as IFS parts work, exposure therapy, intentional goal setting, and accountability practices, and many more. As a starting place, notice when you tend to diminish powerful emotions like joy and engage in self-sabotage. Simple awareness can help immensely as you build a radiant life that is not fueled by fear.

Offering: Do you forebode joy or dress rehearse tragedy? In your journal, explore how Dr. Brown's concepts show up in your life.

CHAPTER 6

Ancestral Trauma, Epigenetics, and Lineage Patterns

The credit belongs to the man who is actually in the arena.

—*THEODORE ROOSEVELT*

WHEN YOU VISIT A MEDICAL PROVIDER OR HEALER FOR THE first time, be they a primary care physician, psychiatrist, or energy worker, you will likely be asked to complete intake forms that include your family history. It is pertinent for your provider to understand if your mother or grandfather had high cholesterol or severe depression for preventative care, and also to understand the workings of the system from which you came. People often talk about their ailments as diseases or symptoms that *run in the family,* but they don't always give credence to the depth of this statement. Understanding the ailment (e.g., breast cancer, anxiety) is important for tracking genetic heritability, but it is also crucial to understand *why* the ailment developed in the first place (e.g., emotional stress, exposure to environmental pollutants).

The fields of intergenerational family trauma and epigenetics focus on the intersection between the genes we inherit and our individual life experiences. These two influences help researchers understand how families transmit genetic, emotional, behavioral, and even spiritual patterns from one generation to the next in a thread of symptoms, patterns, and dysfunctions that can now be traced through science. When we better understand how the physical, emotional, and psychological contents of our ancestors remain alive within us like fingerprints, we can more effectively heal familial traits that do not serve us. The acknowledgment of what's *mine* vs. what's *not mine* allows us to own our place in the family chain and mindfully heal ourselves so that we avoid passing unhelpful genetic material to our descendants. It turns out we don't just leave our legacy jewelry to our children and grandchildren, but also our stories, traumas, and secrets.

LINEAGE PATTERNS, LEGACY BURDENS, AND FAMILY SECRETS

The long-debated nature vs. nurture question has inspired debate within scientific and clinical circles for decades, but I think most practitioners would agree that we are a product of both. The genetic material we are programmed with (nature) and the dynamics of our relationships and lived experiences (nurture) play a role not only in the type of person we become but also in our physical, mental, and emotional health. In the next section on epigenetics, we will discuss the *nature* component, but for now let's explore how *nurture* shapes us.

Lineage patterns are behaviors, messages, and thinking patterns linked with core beliefs and experiences that have been sustained across multiple generations in the same family. Lineage patterns can be as simple as a fear of canines, or as complex as manipulative control and power dynamics in relationships. Much of the transmission of such patterns originates in the relationship between parents and their babies through verbal, nonverbal, and implied messaging. For example, if a father was violently bitten by a dog when he was young and never had a corrective experience to rebuild feelings of safety with the animal, he would likely (unconsciously) teach his own child to fear dogs, too. The father's anxious response to dogs, combined with efforts to limit his child's exposure to the animal, would send a strong message to his child that dogs are unsafe. Although the child may not have experienced a dangerous canine firsthand, the father's energy would teach his child that dogs are dangerous and should be avoided. A pattern like this can repeat for several generations if each subsequent family member embodies the fearful energy of the initial person's experience without inquiring as to why the pattern has continued and making a direct effort to heal it.

In psychology, attachment theory helps us understand how cognitive, emotional, and behavioral patterns pass between generations. Attachment theory studies how our earliest relationships shape our emotional well-being and worldview, and it pinpoints how insecure or avoidant attachment can influence the development of physical issues as well. If parents neglect their child's needs, abuse them, or harm their delicate young psyche in any way, that child will have an increased risk for not only mental health challenges but physical disease and symptomology as well. This happens because our bodies tend to hold the intense internal energy in our musculature and tissue that our minds either cannot or will not acknowledge. If you have ever experienced a stomachache in response to anxiety or stress, that's what happened.

The emerging study of *psychosomatic disorders* focuses on the very real physical issues that seem unexplainable in their origin but likely arise in response to emotional repression and trauma. An example of a psychosomatic issue is the hives I mysteriously developed from the stress and relational trauma my wedding stirred within me. Doctors were unable to ascertain a cause from my blood tests, and the hives seemed spontaneous outside of their emotional link to the massive tension I had lived with for months. In addition to the study of psychosomatic disorders, many medical fields consider that stress and psycho-emotional suffering undeniably factor into (and even lead to) the development of cancer, heart disease, and many other physical problems much more serious than hives.

Offering: In your journal, list at least three ways your body expresses stress and trauma as physical or emotional messages to alert you to its need for care.

Returning to the topic of attachment, a large part of a baby's dynamic with their caregiver is related to the fulfillment of the baby's physical needs (touch, physical safety, being fed when hungry and changed when dirty). Additional pieces of the puzzle that determine how secure a person feels in the world are emotional connection and psychological energetics from caregivers. These are verbal and nonverbal messages conveyed from parents (or caregivers) to children that are related to the little one's worth, lovability, and value.

Such messages tend to become core operating systems for how each of us live our lives.

I firmly believe that the job of a parent is the most challenging one that exists, and because of that it's really easy to mess up. I say this with the utmost humility as a parent of two. I openly acknowledge that I am an imperfect mother who, despite my best intentions, will likely create issues within my children that I cannot foresee or protect them from. I truly believe that there are no perfect parents. Most every mother, father, and guardian does the best they can with where they're at and whatever resources are available to them.

With that being said, the perceptive and intuitive senses in the systems of young children soak everything in. Little ones don't miss a beat, and whatever they perceive becomes imprinted onto the lens through which they see the world and themselves in it. This means if a parent poorly manages their mental health or trauma, if they struggle with parenting to the point of emotional unavailability, or if they are flooded by fears of instability, insecurity, or scarcity, the child knows. When a child perceives that their parents are not happy, stable, or whole, the child makes it their personal mission to fix the problem, and/or believes that it must be their fault. Objectively, I think we can all agree that the unhealed wounds of a parent are absolutely not the fault of their child, but this is how we're built. Truthfully, we all carry the weights of early childhood in our own ways. We must choose how to relate to the internalized messages that shaped our belief systems about ourselves and our place in the world and discover whether or not our beliefs are based on truths that apply to the radiant life we so desire.

If a person decides to identify, attend to, and heal their early childhood wounding, they harness the power to provide repair within themselves and also for their descendants. This is where the word *lineage* in lineage patterns come in. Consider Jenelle, who was born to an emotionally distant and unavailable mother. Jenelle did not have the education, support, or resources to face the wounding her maternal relationship created within her, so when she became a mother herself, she unintentionally acted out the same dynamic with her child. Jenelle did not intend to repeat the emotional unavailability that was bestowed upon her, but because it was all she knew motherhood to be, it perpetuated. In a natural response, Jenelle's child perceived Jenelle to be cold and distant the way Jenelle perceived her mother before her. On and on it perpetuated through time and generations until finally someone in Jenelle's lineage looked directly at the pattern and decided to change it.

Offering: In your journal, write about a lineage pattern in your own ancestral line and how you experience this pattern in your life. If you feel safe with certain family members, consider speaking with them about their experiences with the lineage pattern.

The same thing happens with family secrets, which is why they insidiously repeat across generations. Family secrets come in many flavors, and they usually function to protect the family members from feeling pain. Sometimes family secrets also fulfill an obligation to protect something or someone within the family system, contain disbelief about a private reality only the members know about, or perpetuate denial. In general, family secrets tend to carry the energy of: *We don't talk about this because it's too painful.* When such a trend exists in a family, the constant avoidance of the issue keeps it from ever being resolved, while a giant elephant is simultaneously maintained in the middle of the family system. Such a secret ends up being fueled with implied messages about the importance of keeping the secret and perpetuating its concealment.

Offering: Write about your family secrets in your journal, and how you feel about their existence. Explore where your family secrets originated and how they live within you.

Dr. Galit Atlas aptly stated, "When things go wrong, secrets are born."[1] This happens when something painful occurs within a family, and the collective psyche of those involved consciously or unconsciously decides that they would rather lock what happened away in the *do not touch* files of the emotional family archive than face painful exposure to the experience.

A *legacy burden* is something members of a family carry within themselves that was not of their making or direct experience, and many family secrets become legacy burdens. My sister and I happened to be born right at the apex of two lineages absolutely riddled with family secrets and legacy burdens. My paternal grandmother gave birth to a baby out of wedlock when she was still a teenager—an experience for which she was harshly exiled from her nuclear family. In her shame and trauma, my grandmother gave her child up for adoption and never spoke of him again. Years later, she married my grandfather and had three more sons with him. She never mentioned the existence of her first child to her husband or her sons, so it was a real shocker when my father and his brothers received contact from their half-brother fifty-some years later. As it turns out, this man (whose existence had been kept secret for decades) underwent a genetic tracing journey inspired by his own lineage questions. His discovery began at an online website, and landed squarely in the lives of his three unsuspecting siblings. As you can imagine, the experience was both enlightening and shocking for all involved. Once my father (and potentially his siblings) had knowledge of his half-brother's existence, the shape of his world changed in accordance with the new information. His view of his mother shifted and gained complexity, and beliefs regarding familial transparency took on a new light. To say the least, the weight of his mother's legacy burden irrevocably changed the way my father experienced both his mother and his family system.

A few years later when I was in my mid-thirties, I had been a therapist for well over a decade. Thanks to my inner work journey and clinical experience, I had built a certain level of comfort with the discomfort inherent in deep healing work and difficult interpersonal conversations. I noticed that my mind frequently strayed toward thinking not only about my paternal grandmother's secret but also secrets from the other side of my lineage. I couldn't help but notice the prevalence of patterns and secrets in my family, and I chose to face one of them head on—this time on the maternal side of my lineage.

Long before I was born, my mother's brother, we'll call him Simon, lived in ongoing discord with his parents (my grandparents). This only became worse when he married his wife and they had three children together. The bottom line of the story is that Simon and his wife estranged themselves and their children from the rest of the family. But why? That was the question no one in the family ever seemed to fully answer. The narrative I grew up hearing (on the rare instances when Simon was mentioned) was that he was a horrible person, his wife was equally (if not more) abhorrent, and they broke the hearts of my grandparents and other family members when they dramatically ripped themselves and their children away. Simon and his wife were entirely to blame for what happened, we must all hate them, and that was that. *Any questions? No? Good. None allowed. Case closed.* Despite my curiosity about my uncle, aunt, and first-cousins, I never got more information about what had happened, but I sensed the depth of secrecy embedded within the story. Finally, I reached a point where I felt the need to understand Simon's estrangement more fully so as not to unintentionally perpetuate and pass down patterns of separation and secrecy to my own children.

To the dismay and anger of some in my family, I found Simon's contact information and got in touch with him to hear his side of the story. Certain family members later told me that my choice was unforgivable and felt like a massive betrayal to them, but I think it was more a betrayal to the entity that had become the secret itself. The issues that led to Simon's estrangement had nothing to do with me, so I felt confident that I would remain clear of the trigger points previous generations had felt in response to the trauma related to Simon. I had an internal sense that I could listen to Simon's story and consider his perspective without getting hooked into the charge my other family members felt, and I was right.

We spoke, and I mostly listened. Simon told me many things I had heard before, and some I had not. I maintained an understanding within myself that Simon's story was likely distorted, just as the narrative I had been told all my life must have been. As someone dear to me one once said, "There's your truth, there's my truth, and then there's the Truth." I took no sides, made no promises, and formed no judgments. At the end of the conversation, I was (and still am) glad to have talked with Simon. I was able to make more sense of the narrative about him I had grown up with and supplement it for myself with the untold story he contributed. I trust that there is still much I do not know and may never know, and I accept that fact. Hearing my uncle's experience spoken through his voice allowed me to make up my own mind and choose how I wanted to relate to our family's wounding from his generation and my own. It provided a sense of peace and intentionality to the way I related to my family members, and allowed me to release the lingering questions I had been holding.

Even after speaking with Simon, I can still sense layers of secrecy surrounding him and other family topics, but our exchange provided me palpable relief by accessing the level of honesty that was available to me on that day. Even now, certain family members still carry wounding that I ventured beyond the family secret and contacted Simon. I understand that this rupture may or may not be reparable, and I have deep compassion for their pain. Though I hope a full repair is possible in time, I am willing to mourn any relational pieces that cannot be healed and must be permanently lost. I believe that the prolonged hurt within these individuals indicates their attachment to their own experiences with Simon, and subsequently their conscious or unconscious commitment to the web of family secrets related to him. Their interpretation of my pursuit of information as a personal or familial betrayal is not my responsibility, and my actions are something I have consciously chosen to be accountable for.

Just as fish don't know they are in water, people often do not feel the legacy burdens and disruptive lineage patterns they are immersed in because the energetics have been present in their lives for as long as they can remember. I remember seeing a comic years ago where one fish swam past two other fish and said, "How's the water, boys?" The two other fish looked puzzled and one said to the other, "What the heck is he talking about?" Sometimes we are completely blind to what surrounds us because it has become our experience of *normal*, so we cannot imagine it any other way. For me, this topic brings to mind a true feeling of common humanity,[2] because if you are human, you know pain. If you have a family, you're bound to have issues in that system. If you are a person, you likely have a hard story, and if you don't, you have probably walled yourself within protective shields to avoid feeling the hard stuff. One of my favorite Brené Brown quotes says,[3] "Everybody has a story or struggle that will break your heart. And if we're really paying attention, most people have a story that will bring us to our knees."

EPIGENETICS

Now, let's move from the therapy couch to the research lab and transition from lineage inheritance to genetic inheritance. If you're a science geek like me, you are going to love nerding out with me in this next section. If not, hang in there.

Epigenetics is a thrilling branch of science that studies the interface between our genes and our environment. Scientists in this field have gleaned invaluable information about the way interactions between our DNA and the various molecules we are exposed to environmentally determine which genes express within us and which stay dormant. *Genes* are part of the DNA that make up chromosomes, and they exist in every single one of our cells. Interestingly, the scientific community cannot agree on a precise definition for what genes really are, but something we do know is that *phenotypes* (characteristics and traits) are not determined by our genome. Instead, they are the product of the many variations of a gene's interaction with its environment.[4] This is why genetically identical twins can grow to be quite different. Both started out with the same genetic material at conception, but through their separate lived experiences, each twin was exposed to diverse experiences and influences that evoked differing phenotypes between two people who initially seemed identical.

Thomas Moore, in his groundbreaking book *The Developing Genome*,[5] writes, "A gene's context always matters." This means that the specific genetic structure within a person's DNA is changeable depending on the experiences, exposures, and happenings of their life. This is exciting because we now know that simply possessing a particular gene in your DNA (for example, having a gene for Alzheimer's or bipolar disorder), does not guarantee the manifestation of that gene into your reality. The simple presence of a gene is irrelevant if that particular strand of your DNA is influenced by epigenetic processes that render it unreadable and thus not functional in your system. The genes that exist within each of us are not permanently on or off; they're not set in stone from the moment of conception onward. Genes are changeable, and it seems to be our interactions with our environments and lifestyles that change them. I like to think of the human genome as a string of tiny lights where genes can turn on and off like bulbs, depending on the influences and exchanges a person has with their environment. If you are interested in learning the nuts and bolts of epigenetics, I highly recommend both Moore's book *The Developing Genome*[6] and, for a more comprehensive scientific run-down, *Epigenetics: How Environment Shapes Our Genes*[7] by Richard C. Francis.

Though we now know our genome is changeable, it is still up for debate whether genes adhere to a binary on/off setting, or if they act more like dimmer switches that manifest on a spectrum. The knowledge that we can potentially *switch off* genetic markers for illness and disease opens a broad new horizon for modern medicine. Imagine if, with the right information and initiative, human beings could self-direct their genome toward more abundant well-being by thinking, behaving, and internalizing their experiences in new and healthier ways. At least in part, this would give the statement *live life to the fullest* a whole new meaning. As David Moore eloquently states, "Though it is true that we are born and die with the exact same sequence information in our genetic material (for the most part), the discovery of an epigenetic code that can be influenced by environmental factors—and that subsequently influences genetic activity— should alter our understanding of why each of us develops the characteristics we do."[8] Since both our phenotypes and numerous diseases arise during development, perhaps we could learn to influence development in certain ways that prevent disease before it ever begins.

A fascinating body of inquiry has developed surrounding the epigenetics of ancestral trauma, revealing a mind-blowing discovery: We are each affected by the environment and lifestyle of our ancestors from at least the two generations before us, and we will directly impact at least the next two generations after us with our environment and lifestyle choices. This phenomenon has been named *The Grandmother Effect*,[9] and it shows evidence that epigenetic effects that occur in the fetal environment can influence descendants for at least six decades.

Consider this: When your grandmother was five months pregnant with your mother, you were present in the unfertilized eggs of your mother's fetal ovaries. Before your mother was even born, your grandmother, your mother, and the earliest origins of you all shared the same body and biological setting. Additionally, the earliest origins of the sperm cells that brought you into being were present within your father's body when he gestated in his mother's womb. Science now understands that both precursor sperm and egg cells are vulnerable to be imprinted upon by life events and have strong potentiality to affect subsequent generations.[10] If your grandmother was in the Holocaust, or exposed to famine, abuse, or toxins, the effects of her experiences trickled down to your mother, and then to you.

Francis, in his book *Epigenetics: How Environment Shapes Our Genes*,[11] discusses the 1944 potato famine in the northwestern portion of the Netherlands. The Dutch Famine Birth Cohort Study showed strong epigenetic evidence for how hardship can affect subsequent generations who were not actually present for the traumatic event itself. The study looked closely at the people who were in the wombs of the women who experienced the famine firsthand. Results displayed that pregnant women who were exposed to the famine during their second and third trimesters showed a significant propensity toward obesity—close to twice more than people born before or after the famine. Additionally, the individuals who were prenatally exposed to the famine showed a significant risk for schizophrenia, affective disorders such as depression, and an increase in antisocial personality disorder among males. Many important findings were discovered, and all evidenced that the epigenetic effects of the fetal environment can extend beyond sixty years.

Another interesting study with mice from Emory University School of Medicine in 2013[12] evidenced that descendent mice in the pup and grandpup generations both reacted with avoidance and anxiety when they smelled a scent that their predecessor became electrically shocked when exposed to. This was a scent the pups and grandpups had never before experienced. Notably, when their brains were inspected, scientists observed consistent neurological changes between mice from the study and their offspring for two generations thereafter. The brains of the mouse decedents were not only wired to have sensitivity toward the scent their parents and grandparents had learned to fear, but they also possessed their very own fear response associated with the scent.

Whether you know it or not—whether you like it or not—you are a walking-talking thread of ancestral experiences, as your descendants will be, and theirs after them. This, my friends, is the power of ancestral trauma. It results not only in physical manifestations but emotional, psychological, and behavioral generational patterns as well. When therapists say *hurt people hurt people* this is what they mean. If your ancestor was exposed to painful emotional wounding, and they did not have the safety, know-how, or resources to heal it, they are exponentially more likely to pass their wound to their descendants. Sometimes such lineage patterns look eerily similar from generation to generation, such as, *my grandmother was estranged from her parents, then her child estranged himself from her, and now I feel compelled to estrange myself from my parents.* Sometimes, *hurt people hurting people* manifests in ways that do not directly mimic the wounding of prior generations but instead present in a new and equally detrimental way such as *my father's father beat him, so my father excessively drank alcohol and raged at me verbally, and now I abstain from alcohol but I compulsively spend money.* As you can see with this example, the manifestation may be different, but the avoidance of tolerating the discomfort of wounding persists. Ultimately, *we repeat what we don't repair.* Our systems always seek healing and balance, so we will be exposed to the same mirroring of our pain, generation after generation, until we heal it by engaging our inner work and doing things differently than those before us. When a brave person chooses (consciously or unconsciously) to become a pattern breaker, they engage the powerful work of healing the ancestral wound. That pattern breaker's work is so mind-bogglingly admirable because they create lasting change despite the programming in every cell in their body (literally, biologically) to dysregulate when the going gets rough. Pattern breakers are heroes because their efforts end unhealthy patterns for the future of their lineage.

If you are feeling anxious because you're recounting your family history three generations deep and noting some pretty severe stuff, fear not! Remember, your genome is changeable. If you epigenetically evolved to face the threats of your grandparents' or parents' lifetime that are no longer present in your own life, there is no need for those markers to stay turned *on.* Sometimes the simple knowledge that *the patterns you have been living out do not belong to you* is enough to bring forward the consciousness necessary to heal them. Inner work to separate your own response to life from that of your ancestors is powerful. This work can be accomplished through therapy, energy healing, and even in direct conversational processing with your family members and trusted support people. Also consider the power that your own expressive abilities such as art, writing, breathwork, and communication hold as potent avenues for processing and restoration. When you consider the phrase *we repeat what we don't repair*, it becomes clear that fostering repair within yourself, by whatever means are effective, will result in healing. Doing something is always more impactful than doing nothing, and this type of work need not happen all at once—baby steps are more than sufficient. Now let's talk in more depth about how ancestral healing is more than a growth process for yourself but also a loving gift of service for others who share your family line.

BECOMING A PATTERN BREAKER

If I know one thing for sure, it's that patterns don't break on their own. When something is stuck in a repetitive rhythm, the path of least resistance is to keep on keepin' on. But as we well know by now from this book, the path of least resistance does not lead to a radiant life. We are living, breathing, dynamic creatures, and for us, change is not only inevitable—it is essential. In the realms of ancestral trauma, legacy burdens, and epigenetics, diverting the cycle toward a new experience happens in much the same way. It's excruciatingly simple, though not so easy: *Do things differently*. If you want change within your Self, your family, or your ancestral line, you have to *be* the change.

The experience of a pattern breaker isn't always glamorous, enjoyable, or even comfortable. As many of us understand from firsthand experience or that of others, change can be really challenging. Especially when maneuvering the deep change inherent in shifting the patterns of legacy burdens, it is common to encounter resistance. The family system itself may not hop joyfully on board with the changes you're trying to create. This proved true in my experience with Simon. Some of my family members were so intricately invested in their avoidance of the pain that could be uncovered by my looking closely enough at a pattern to change it that my choice to shift the pattern was intolerable to them. Why then, if it causes such drama in a family system, would and should we break patterns? Because when you divert an unhealthy pattern that has been agonizingly alive for years, decades, or generations, you set the entire lineage free—backward and forward from yourself.

Spiritually speaking, it is my honest belief that your ancestors wait with bated breath for someone courageous enough to come along in your family line who will stand tall against the injustices, secrets, obligations, and unhealthy patterns of your lineage and do things differently. Your ancestors do not want the pain and suffering for you that generations of people endured and perpetuated before you, and they certainly do not want the same for your children and your children's children. In all likelihood they didn't want anyone in the family to suffer at all, they just didn't have the resources, skills, and strength to become a pattern breaker themselves.

In the next chapter I will talk about the part our minds and thoughts play in developing a radiant life, and I will share the profound work of Drs. Joe Dispenza and Bruce Lipton. For now, just understand that when you make a shift to the way you think and behave, the changes you make hold potential to break patterns and shift the direction of your lineage and also to heal your own physical, mental, emotional, and spiritual bodies. Working epigenetically and with legacy burdens is immensely healing on all of these dimensions because a great deal of psycho-emotional energy is stored within the physical body.

When Jordan, a third-generation victim of child abuse, decided to break his familial pattern of violence toward children, he learned to unleash his pain in a kickboxing class instead of on his daughter. In so doing, Jordan's physical body, along with his mental and spiritual systems, began to regulate their cadence differently than those of the men who came before him. Because of this, Jordan's daughter did not experience firsthand abuse from her parent as Jordan did, and thus became much less likely to experience the particular hardships her father endured, and his father, and his father before him. Jordan's daughter undoubtedly encountered different kinds of hardship in her life, but they were not the same unhealthy dynamics that polluted the generations before her. Perhaps best of all, when Jordan's daughter had a child of her own, Jordan's grandchild was more likely to avoid such trauma as well because Jordan diverted it two generations prior.

Offering: Now it's your turn. Consider what you are going to shift for the generations still yet to come in your lineage. Write out your ideas, intentions, and plans in your journal. If you are in a partnership, explore with your partner the different ways you can structure your family system to support the changes you plan to make.

Never underestimate the power you hold within your Self to shift, change, and rewrite the story of your ancestry.

It only takes the intentional, courageous act of doing things differently, and everything can change for the better. Just start. Start where you are, with what you have, and go from there. It's okay if your efforts take repetition to stick. As brilliantly stated by Mark Nepo in *The Book of Awakening*,[13] "Repetition is not failure. Ask the waves, ask the leaves, ask the wind."

CHAPTER 7

The Stories We Tell Ourselves

The world was made to be free in.
Give up all the other worlds except the one to which you
belong.

—*DAVID WHYTE, "SWEET DARKNESS"*

THE FACTOR THAT SETS HUMAN BEINGS APART FROM ALL other creatures is our advanced cognitive ability. This higher-thinking capacity results from the prefrontal cortex (PFC) in our brains, which all other known species lack. The PFC is the topmost layer of your brain, directly behind your forehead, and it is in charge of capabilities such as planning, thought analysis, timeliness, and organization. Our thinking brains are absolutely marvelous, and our world is continuously shaped and upgraded by the inventions that grow from the thoughts we produce. If we didn't have the high-level thinking abilities of the PFC, we wouldn't be seriously talking about intergalactic travel, let alone using cars to transport us or enjoying climate control in our homes. We would be more animal-like, and we would lose our distinctly human qualities.

Science has begun to research the power our thoughts have to impact, change, improve, or destroy our lives. Our thoughts are so powerful, you see, that they can work for us or against us, and we do ourselves a great service to learn to wield them with intention. Much hype has circled within different new age communities about the power of positive thinking. Instead of talking about that, I want to share the impactful works of Dr. Bruce Lipton[1] and Dr. Joe Dispenza.[2] If you are interested in the science behind our thought processes, do yourself a favor and study the incredibly illuminating work of these two doctors. What we know through both science and observable experience is that when we think, act, and behave differently, our worlds change. If you explore Dr. Dispenza's work, you will learn in detail about how he knit his spine back together with only the power of his mind after a bicycle accident left him with a medical prognosis that he would never walk again. For you skeptics out there—I see you—his entire experience is medically documented and confirmed. Dr. Dispenza's experience demonstrates how the power of massively changing thinking and behavior can lead to outcomes unimaginably better than anyone ever dreamed—results that cannot be medically explained or denied.

Here's the crux: When a person starts thinking differently, it affects their belief systems. When belief systems change, unconscious mechanisms that had been operating in accordance with those belief systems no longer sync, which leaves the brain and body available for updates and upgrades. Interpersonal relationships can alter, improve, or end when this happens. New perspectives can bring healing to trauma, mental illness, and physical disease. In fact, our very experience of the world we live in can alter perceptibly. When we open ourselves to new and different ways of being by think-ing differently, we change our neurocircuitry. This results in infinite new possibilities for how we perceive and receive our lived experience by rewiring our brains in the direction of our attention rather than defaulting to their baseline con-ditioning. Microscopes can observe that the actual structure of our cells change when we adopt and sustain new thinking patterns. This alters our physical bodies right alongside our emotional and mental systems.

The powerful human ability to think has been studied and researched for decades. Therapists and other healers have come to use the word *narratives* to describe the whirl-wind of stories, worries, opinions, and fantasies that swirl around each and every human mind. I think we have all learned through experience one way or another that we can't always trust our thoughts to be true. The shape-shifting mind is commonly referred to in Buddhist psychology as *the monkey mind* because it swings from branch to branch, tree to tree, and takes us on wild journeys that are not always grounded in reality. Interestingly enough, though we know our minds can be fickle, it can still be endlessly seductive to believe the stories they spin (the narratives) and live our lives in accordance with these partial-truths—or, in many cases, un-truths.

A challenging reason why people struggle to detach themselves from their narratives is that we tend to have an intuitive belief that our "I"—our perceived Self—lives in the mind (thus related to the brain). Because of this, it seems easiest to identify with narratives and thoughts as *me* or *mine* because they seem to stem from the organ sitting atop our neck that we have come to believe is our head-quarters. The brain has many incredible skills and functions. I'm a big fan.

With that being said, there is a difference between the organ of the brain (the physical structure of organ, blood, and neurons) and the construct of the mind (the sense of "I" resulting from neuronal firing and thought development). Even further down the rabbit hole is consciousness itself, which is the largest possible intelligence we can conceptualize as an interconnectedness between all that exists in our world and beyond. We all certainly *have* consciousness, and additionally are *a part of* a larger consciousness that fields like quantum physics study, however there is much we do not yet understand. To lump the brain, mind, and consciousness all together into head-quarters, believing that all cognitions are real and true, does us a disservice. Truthfully, our perception of our world is quite limited, fallible, influenceable, and malleable.

Offering: Write in your journal about your brain, mind, and consciousness. How do they connect, and in what ways are they different?

Remember *Magic Eye* books? Each page is filled with intricate colorful patterns that reveal a secret embedded image if you stare at them in just the right way for the perfect amount of time. *Magic Eye* is an example of how perception can change with shifted focus, allowing us to see things we missed before—visually or otherwise. Narratives work this way, too. We tell ourselves endless stories about the world we live in and our place in it. Sometimes we are the hero, sometimes the villain or victim. Occasionally a story's construct changes when we gain deeper information or notice something new, and a total shift to the way we see the picture of our life ensues. We humans also have an uncanny way of enhancing our stories with new versions of the same narrative that reinforce and affirm the original story.

Here's an example: From witnessing volatile dynamics between his parents, Jim held a childhood narrative about relational danger, believing he must defend himself against others. In adolescence, he fueled this narrative by instigating fist-fights with other boys, which only reinforced that he must continually defend himself. In adulthood, Jim was known to verbally argue with colleagues and family members, further affirming the narrative of combative relationships.

Offerings: In your journal, list and expand upon some of the narratives you unintentionally repeat.

We cannot see new dimensions of the truth when we attach to our narratives without allowing them to be fallible. The stories we tell ourselves cannot possibly capture the full picture of our lives because they are experienced only from the perspective of the *I* or the *ego* within us. Mathias De Stefano[3] teaches that the truth is a sphere. Just as you can only see the moon from your own vantage point, leaving many other parts of the sphere unknown to you, it is the same with the truth. If ten people stand in a circle surrounding a giant sphere in the center, they will each see their own perspective of that sphere. Each person's truth is only one part of the whole that exists. There is no way to understand the entire wholeness firsthand. This happens when we get stuck in our narratives as well. We see only the vantage point we have grown attached to at the deficit of all other perspectives, and in so doing we limit our ability to see the full truth of our experience and potential. The one-dimensional belief that our lens is the only one that sees the truth does not leave room for the perspectives of people you have affected or impacted, the ripples of your actions, or the fingerprints you leave behind from your work and choices.

For the most part, narratives are based on one of three perceptions: memories of the past, emotional experiences in the present, and projections of the future. For example:

A narrative built from a memory of the past: *I studied hard in my high school chemistry class, and nonetheless ended up with a C for my final grade. This means I am stupid and should never try to learn science again.*

A narrative built from an emotional experience in the present: *I am at a large social gathering, and I feel awkward and uncomfortable talking to people who seem to show very little interest in me. I am such a loser, nobody likes me.*

A narrative built from projections of the future: *If I want to become successful as a financial advisor, I need to harden my heart and think only of winning at all costs. If I am too soft or weak, I'll never make it.*

Can you see how any one of the narratives listed above can grow into a full-blown belief system? We tend to see what we are looking for, so if we narrate to ourselves that we are stupid, unlikable, or ruthless, we will find those reflections in all that we do. If I ask you to spend one day looking for pregnant women, you will likely notice that pregnant women are everywhere. Does this mean that there were no pregnant women before I asked you to look for them? Absolutely not; how silly. It means that your attention honed in to notice the specific prevalence of pregnant women because my request drew your attention to it. The exact same thing happens with narratives, just like the way Jim told himself that relationships are combative and unsafe, and he thus noticed opportunities to fight all around him.

One particular narrative that seems common in Western culture (and possibly others as well) is related to the fear of upsetting (and even losing) loved ones if you grow or change for the better. Essentially, it sounds something like: *If I grow into the next version of myself and set better boundaries, live with higher integrity, and shift dynamics in my relationships to align with my best self, my [partner, mother, friends, whomever] will get angry and/or leave me.* This corrupt narrative is based on the belief that you must remain who you have always been in order to keep what matters to you. It is important to understand that there may be truth in your fear of change. If the people in your life are invested in your self-abandonment because they benefit from your smallness or unhealed wounds, they will probably be upset if you reclaim your sovereignty. In cases like these, the misalignment in your relationships is not the problem (that issue can be resolved in various ways). Rather, your narrative about staying small instead of updating your Self for the better becomes the issues that holds your radiant life further out of your reach.

Offering: When have you kept yourself small or stunted for fear of upsetting a relationship? How did that work out for you? Explore these questions in writing, contemplation, or safe conversation.

Another harmful collective narrative is the one that compares your suffering to that of another person. *I am devastated because I lost a job I love and am now swimming in a swamp of depression and anxiety, but it's such a First World problem. There are people who have it much worse than I do. I shouldn't be as upset as I am about this.* When you judge your own distress as lesser than someone else's, and thereby ridiculous, silly, or insignificant, you betray your Self. Comparative suffering[4] is a tool of self-abandonment because it puts red tape parameters around your experience and holds you back from true contact with your life—exactly as it is, pain and all. If we were porcelain dolls without souls or individual expression, sure, you could objectively judge who has it worse and who has it better. The good news is that we are living, breathing, soulful creatures. We cannot be compared to one another. Pain is subjective, and so is suffering, joy, and all other emotional experiences in this messy complicated life. The narrative that one person's pain is more or less valid than another's is so distorted it makes my skin crawl.

Offering: If you relate to a narrative of this kind or carry any other that betrays and abandons your Self, explore it in your journal so you can learn to let it go.

LETTING GO

If there's one phrase in the English language that has both befuddled and enraged people for generations, it's *let it go*. It infuriates us because despite our deep longing to do such a thing, letting go remains elusive and always seemingly out of reach. The culprit? Our thoughts and the narratives they build within us. Letting go is incredibly difficult for two reasons: First, we tend to avoid letting go of something we have grown attached to, and many of the stories we tell ourselves are quite embedded within the picture of who we believe ourselves to be. To let go of them risks our losing sight of who we are, and that's scary. For example, let's look at the narrative *I'm a fun person! I'm always up for a good time.* Releasing this narrative would require reorienting certain relationships, community, and a socialite personal identity, which could result in loneliness or exile. Secondly, it is difficult to let go when we feel that our narrative is protecting us in some way. If our narrative serves to keep us away from heartbreak, failure, or any other such emotional demon, it could be tough to let it go. For example: *Men can't be trusted. They'll just use me and break my heart.* Letting go of this narrative means putting your heart on the line and risking the vulnerability it takes to find lasting love. If you surmount your fearful narrative, you could get hurt, and if you get hurt there's no guarantee the whole shebang would have been worth it.

Why in the world would anyone ever let anything go if it carried such risk and insecurity? I'll tell you why: Ultimately, when we don't let go of the fears, obstacles, resistance, and rigidity in our lives, we suffer more than we would have if we had never tried in the first place. This is because we are expressive creatures, and our cultivation of a radiant life includes the risk and reward that comes with vulnerability, openness, and surrender. Releasing internal dialogues that keep us stuck and complacent frees us and opens new possibilities for how we see ourselves, our world, and our place in it. When we successfully set free the narratives that hold us back and make us small, it is as though we have exchanged our colored lenses with clear ones. We can then see things as they actually are without the charge or trigger our storytelling has attached to them. In so doing, we learn to see ourselves as a part of something larger, something wildly profound and impossible to understand in singular dimension. This is akin to how the ocean must witness a wave without attaching to its form.

One teacher who speaks beautifully about the detriments of attaching to our thoughts is Eckhart Tolle, and particularly so in his book *A New Earth: Awakening to Your Life's Purpose.*[5] In his writing, Tolle explains that the most significant reason for our suffering is never the situation itself but our thoughts about the situation—our attachments, emotional reactions, assumptions, and narratives. If we open awareness to our bubbling thoughts, and separate them from the present situation, we will see that the situation itself only exists as everything always does without the attachment of narratives—neutral. Even if we get caught in a tailspin of emotions in reaction to a story about a situation, it's important to remember that emotions themselves are not bad, wrong, or negative—even the tough ones. As Tolle says,[6] "Only the emotion plus an unhappy story is unhappiness."

When we truly let go of our attachment to what happened, is happening, or could potentially happen, we are left only with what is. Such presence is the gateway to peace because it is embodied in the richness of the moment, with all its gifts. From such a perspective, we can be much clearer about whether we must take action, surrender, soften, or respond. It is a fallacy of the human mind to believe that worry and stress empower us to change the circumstances of our lives. In reality, if we have been awake to our life and taken aligned action, whatever happens next is out of our hands. I have an easier time trusting the power of such surrender when I remember this quote from the great Indian philosopher and spiritual teacher J. Krishnamurti:[7] "This is my secret. I don't mind what happens."

Knowing that detachment from our narratives is important is quite different from integrating that knowledge into lived experience. It is certainly a process, and we must be kind to ourselves when we engage this work. Especially when working with deeply embedded narratives that have grown into core beliefs, take the long view. Simply begin to notice each time you operate from a particular narrative; notice what triggers it, how you habitually respond, and any impulses connected to it. With awareness and patience, you will bring consciousness to your story and begin to shift it.

One such embedded narrative I spent much of my life believing is that I am *difficult*. The story first developed as a response to external relationships when I was a child. Over time and with repetition, I began to notice more acutely that when I showed strength, independent opinions, or inserted personal boundaries, the word *difficult* kept coming up in reaction to me. Voicing my thoughts and feelings and being strong or honest directly opposed the flow in certain relationships. These people much preferred that I shut up, fit in, and be easygoing. My adherence to the narrative that I was inherently difficult (meaning something was wrong/bad about me), taught me that I should hide my true Self away and prevent others from knowing the strength of my nature. I became hypersensitive to the relationships that preferred I remain compliant and quiet, and unintentionally disregarded those who respected and appreciated my strength. In an effort to protect myself from seeming *difficult*, I learned to play small and hide my voice. *Go with the flow* I'd say to myself. *Just deal with your discomfort. It will feel worse if you speak up and they think you're difficult.* Well, it worked until it didn't. At that point, I realized that the energy it took to hide my strength wasn't worth it anymore. With this understanding, I intentionally worked toward letting go of the narrative that didn't serve me—the one that had been a core belief about how I needed to behave in order to achieve love and belonging.

Letting go of our stories about ourselves is a process. Especially with deeply rooted narratives that have grown into belief systems, this type of release requires patience and deliberate intention. Surrender sounds like an easy process when you visualize a person allowing themselves to be carried by the current of a flowing river (this is the mental image I always have for surrender). The truth is, the river of surrender has branches and boulders scattered throughout, and it's easy to get snagged. Letting go is easiest to achieve when you get so sick of your own narrative (and the icky feeling that comes with self-abandonment and betrayal) that you just cut the cord and free yourself. It is similar to the experience of giving up, but instead of feeling defeated you feel liberated. Giving up on something you care about and truly desire comes laced with guilt and remorse, but saying goodbye to a pattern that holds you back might be one of the most healing experiences a human can have.

Offering: Explore the differences between surrendering and giving up in your journal. List three examples of surrender, and three of giving up. Then write a few sentences about the differences you notice.

If you are not at the point where you are devastatingly sick of your own garbage but you still want to work on letting go, Jill Bolte Taylor's work[8] offers a good method to help you do so. Bolte Taylor has identified four collections of cells in the human brain that are responsible for different emotional and cognitive functions. She calls them the four characters. Though Bolte Taylor recommends that you come up with your own personalized names for each character to increase their accessibility in your life, she has aptly named these brain cell clusters Character One, Character Two, Character Three, and Character Four. Characters One and Two live in the left hemisphere of the brain, and Three and Four in the right hemisphere. All of the four Characters are important and valuable, but none is complete without the others. If the characters are out of balance with one another, they create discord in your system. Here are their functions:

Character One: Responsible for logical, linear, type A thinking. This Character helps you get things done, get to appointments on time, and pay attention to what is socially correct.

I call my Character One *Efficient Eleanor.*

Character Two: Responsible for holding and tending to past emotions and traumas. This Character helps you identify and experience emotional safety, and it serves to protect you and help you learn from difficult experiences.

I call my Character Two *Sensitive Sally.*

Character Three: Responsible for your present moment experience. This Character senses the smells, tastes, colors, and temperatures all around you, and is playful and openly experiential.

I call my Character Three *Present Polly.*

Character Four: Responsible for thinking processes that occur in the present moment that foster a sense of unity and connection between yourself and everything else in the Universe. This Character is more spiritual, holistic, and open.

I call my Character Four *Metaphysical Molly.*

Similar to Internal Family Systems (IFS) parts work, Bolte Taylor's method holds the perspective that when our different internal facets work together, we can achieve peace, joy, and freedom. This relates to the tricky business of *letting go* because it requires an intricate dance between the four Characters to identify the narrative that no longer serves you, release it from your core operating system, and learn to live without the cadence of the narrative you had previously given such credence to. Character One's ability to think and analyze is important to identify the narrative that's got to go. Character Two's job is to remind you that you have certain emotional attachments to the narrative, and it feels scary to let it go. Character Three lets you know that in the present moment you are absolutely okay, and you have resources to support you as you let go. And Character Four reminds you that on the existential journey of life and growth, letting go is extremely valuable for your evolution and healing.

Whether you use the construct of Bolte Taylor's four Characters, IFS parts work, meditation and mindfulness, or any other method, do yourself a favor and kiss your outdated narratives goodbye. Just as a heavy jacket feels stifling and weighty in the heat of summer, so do the distorted and unhealthy stories we tell ourselves once we tread the path of growth and healing toward our radiant lives.

GRIEF

It's worth mentioning that you may feel grief when you shed outdated narratives and parts of yourself that no longer serve you. Like the death of a loved one, the absence of something that has become a steady psycho-emotional companion for a long time can leave a hole—even if you're better off without it. It's okay for it to feel odd, awkward, or even painful. The loss of a faulty narrative is still a loss, and sometimes what sticks to our heartstrings is unpredictable. If you find yourself experiencing grief related to your growth process, meet yourself with gentle kindness. You may not know why the particular story you released evokes grief, but if it's happening and it's important for the health and well-being of your system, so go with it.

Sometimes deeply entrenched narratives have their roots in childhood, so we cannot remember the emotional tethers they attach to in great (or any) detail. My narrative of being *difficult* had such tethers. When I processed my attachment to the story that had become a core belief, I discovered an inner child who had experienced love as being highly conditional. My young Self learned that love must be earned by being good, compliant, and easy. Releasing the narrative that I was difficult meant facing the grief surrounding my perception of myself as unlovable, as well as the experiences that had contributed to that message.

Offering: Take a moment to consider the grief experiences you have had in your life. Notice your thoughts about grief and your emotional reactions to the topic. Consider bringing your thoughts to your journal or sketchbook for deeper processing.

Dr. Brené Brown, in her book *Atlas of the Heart*,[9] writes about the three foundational elements of grief from her research: loss, longing, and feeling lost. All three of these facets of grief are profoundly relatable, and everyone feels them at some point in life. A person can experience grief related to the physical death of someone or something, the emotional experience of loss or change, and many other occurrences that integrate Dr. Brown's three elements. The

Center for Complicated Grief at Colombia developed the term *integrated grief* to explain how we can learn to live with the shades of grief that present to us. As it turns out, we can embed our grief into our lives together with the many other experiences we have lived with and through. This reminds me of Rumi's message in his poem *The Guest House*[10] to welcome whatever comes, greet it at the door laughing, and invite it in.

One of my favorite explanations that holds a similarly compassionate stance toward the experience of grief comes from the Marvel series *WandaVision*.[11] The character Vision says to his wife Wanda, "What is grief, if not love persevering." How apt to acknowledge that when we love something in any shade of attachment, necessity, dependency, or affection, we sorely miss its presence once it is gone. I like to think about this dimension of grief as a type of gratitude. Although misaligned belief systems and narratives may be unhealthy, our systems use them to support ourselves during times of need. With this awareness, let's acknowledge that we are imperfect and complex, and the maladaptive tools we pick up along the way are plugged into our internal systems with the best intentions to create and sustain health and well-being. When we are ready to release such distorted mechanisms, we can hold gratitude in our hearts for the parts of ourselves that tried desperately to protect, nurture, and care for us.

This is the process of learning and growth we all must go through. As poet Rainer Maria Rilke said, "The purpose of life is to be defeated by greater and greater things."[12] If we are living an authentic life along the path toward radiance, we actually want to let go, to fail, to be defeated. Such an experience of loss means that we have grown. If we are constantly defeated, that indicates that we are elevating by taking life on and not hiding out in the realms of comfort and numbness. Like many links on a great chain of forward movement, the portions behind us are filled with the lessons we have learned and wisdom we have earned. That's a journey worth taking for anyone.

PERFECTIONISM

Perfectionism has been addressed several times in this book as a common coping tool for managing anxiety and striving toward approval and acceptance, and now I want to explore how it relates to grief and the narratives we tell ourselves. As a gentle reminder, nobody is perfect—not even the shiny-haired woman from the gym whom you enviously admire every time you see her. Perfection is a myth, and it is rooted within our collective societal narrative as well as individual stories we tell ourselves. Many people hold the expectation for *perfection* as the standard to strive for in all they do and all they are. I could spend pages writing about how detrimental this narrative is to our collective psyche, not to mention that of our impressionable children, but I'm going to spare you my rant because I think you already know for yourself that perfectionism harms us rather than helps.

This is where grief comes in: As with anything else that purposely or unintentionally vacates our lives, letting go of perfectionism can bring up some skeletons. Especially if you have toted perfectionism in your life as a facet of your *Self-improvement* work, it's important to debunk that this mechanism is not actually about your Self at all, but actually about everyone else. One hundred percent of the lifeforce that drives perfectionism is the insecurity-fueled desperation to be liked, accepted, admired, and approved of by other people. The most insidious edge within the perfectionist parts of us is that we feel we must *earn* belonging and approval. We believe that we will not be loved and accepted if we do not pretzel ourselves into an unrecognizable version of ourselves in order to meet the standards of others. Offloading this narrative (or collection of narratives) can be really intimidating and scary. If a person can truly look their perfectionist part directly in the face and understand why it operates the way it does, I can almost guarantee that they will discover a protective mechanism that guards the fragile energy of an exile part (speaking in IFS terminology) from flooding their system with inner child wounding.

I went to my child's bake sale with my hair a mess and store-bought muffins, and now everyone thinks I am a terrible mother. Krista, the woman in this example, neglected to include in her narrative that she just finished a ten-hour overnight nursing shift in a busy hospital, went directly to the bake sale to support her daughter without a moment's rest, and tried tirelessly each day to be both a loving mother and careerwoman. Krista, however, wasn't able to see the entirety of the situation in all its complexity. She was only able to see her imperfections in comparison with the other parents who had more time to prepare for the bake sale. Little did Krista know that the unconscious factor motivating her harsh narrative was an inner child wound related to her own parents' emotional unavailability for her when she was a child. Only after months of inner work did Krista discover that her little Self was so hurt by her parents' lack of participation in her childhood that she turned herself inside out as a full-time working mother to avoid treating her daughter the way she was treated as a child. In part, Krista behaved this way because of her love for her daughter and desire to be part of her life, but she was also motivated to earn her child's love in ways her own parents did not earn hers.

Krista's is a real-life example of how narratives can be built from core wounds. These stories we tell ourselves tend to build walls and shields over time to protect our original wounds. Once Krista did the work to access and tend to her wounded inner child, she was able to grieve for the lack of emotional support her little Self endured and separate her daughter's experience from her own. As a next step in Krista's healing process, she brought curiosity back on-line and became present with the here-and-now dynamic between herself and her daughter. She learned to embrace her imperfection and to foster effective communication with her daughter that allowed space for her daughter to express her needs. As it turns out, Krista's daughter didn't care whether her mother attended the bake sale or not, but she did want Krista to pick her up from the school bus each day. Attending to the wounds that reinforced her narrative ultimately set Krista free to be an even more connected mother—and without all the stress.

Dr. Brown says, "Perfectionism kills curiosity by telling us that we have to know everything or we risk looking 'less than.' Perfectionism tells us that our mistakes and failures are personal defects."[13] This bit about *personal defects* is a piece that fuels many perfectionists. For some, the narrative of *There's something wrong with me, and I can't let anyone else know or I will be ridiculed and exiled* is what keeps people grievously apart from a radiant life. Brown calls this perfection-oriented stuckness *life paralysis.*[14] When a person becomes paralyzed in their own life, they inhibit their growth by avoiding new experiences for fear of not being perfect/good/the best at them. A narrative surrounding life paralysis might be: *I've always wanted to play the ukulele, but I would be so awful at it that I'm not even going to try.* We must be willing to fail, flail, stumble, and get back up repeatedly— and allow others to do the same. Life paralysis does no one any good.

Life is not an easy road to travel. It's hard, arduous, tricky, and unpredictable. No one will do it perfectly, and if you hold yourself back from trying because you are too afraid to fail, you will miss out sorely on the gems buried within the imperfections. As Glennon Doyle writes, "Being human is not hard because you're doing it wrong. It's hard because you're doing it right. You will never change the fact that being human is hard, so you must change your idea that it was ever supposed to be easy."[15]

Now, moving into new territory, let's inquire more deeply about the sticky little triggers, narratives, and wounds that just don't seem to go away regardless of how much inner work you do. Read on for my theory on *Sharks and Bathtubs*.

CHAPTER 8

Sharks in the Bathtub

The Tough Cookies of Your Psyche

Courage is not an absence of fear. Courage is fear walking.

—Dr. Susan David, "Emotional Agility"

SOMEWHERE IN THE MAZE OF MY EARLY TWENTIES, I found myself holding an almond milk latte and sitting across from a loved one as he talked about a medical issue with his prostate. While my friend shared his symptoms and fearful feelings about the various medical and surgical interventions that awaited him, I noticed a worried thought arising in myself: *Oh my god, how terrifying. I hope my prostate is okay.* I felt a perceptible shift in my physical body with this thought—a clenched nausea deep in my gut and a racing heart. While an explosion of fearful thoughts took root in my mind, I suddenly felt acutely aware of my urgent need to worry about something I was unaware I needed to worry about until that precise moment. The rush of heat and stress through my nervous system reminded me of a similar (though less intense) experience from high school when I suddenly realized that I was completely in the dark about an important exam that I was utterly unprepared for and doomed to fail. Fast forward to the almond milk latte and my rapidly mounting fear for my prostate: I did my best to continue listening while wrestling the increasing flood of concerns that filled my mind. Only now can I laugh about the embarrassingly long time I spent frozen in fear and dysregulation before I remembered that in my female anatomy I do not, in fact, have a prostate.

Reader, meet my shark: *health anxiety.*

Now, let's fast forward again almost twenty years to a crisp autumn morning when I felt angsty and rattled throughout my entire nervous system. On that particular Thursday, I anxiously told my friend Becca about the latest iteration of fear-tinged frustration surrounding my body's uncanny pattern of developing random and concerning physical symptoms—this time, a full-body allergic reaction for no apparent reason. As we talked, I was struck with a mental picture like a lightning bolt to the visual cortex of my brain: *sharks and bathtubs.*

I realized that whenever something goes askew with my health, I respond to the trigger as though it were a deadly shark swimming toward me; my body immediately floods with fear. It feels like my life depends on keeping the fear (shark) away, so I activate an emotional container inside myself, like an inner *bathtub* to hold the shark. Even if my containment for the shark is short lived, it encloses my building panic and gives me enough space to fend the feeling off.

Sharks are intense reactions to personal issues and sensitive triggers that repeat over time and don't seem to go away. In my case, the physical symptom of allergic hives was not the health anxiety shark. The shark was my intense fear and panic about the hives, which leapfrogged into distorted thinking about how the hives would last forever and ruin my life.

Bathtubs are the psychological mechanisms we develop over time for holding it all together and keeping ourselves from being overwhelmed. Bathtubs are essential. We need them, and it is crucial that they be in balance with the rest of our lives so we don't dip into the troublesome territory of avoidance, addiction, disembodiment, and numbing. To cope with my fear on that Thursday with Becca, I constructed a bathtub of external processing with my trusted friend, the physical movement of walking, self-compassion, and the comfort of having a scheduled appointment with my doctor. My nervous system began to soothe.

SHARKS

The hardest, most painful, and most fear-fueled experiences of life are an undeniable part of being a person. These trigger sharks by provoking the feelings of hopelessness, helplessness, and fear that threaten to drown you and eat you alive. When something is a shark, it keeps popping up regardless of your voracious efforts to eradicate it. You can go to every seminar, read every book, stuff your feelings beneath layers of food or substances, visit shamans from far reaching remote islands, or meditate on the impossibly high mountaintops of Tibet, and the shark will remain.

In this chapter you will learn about why sharks exist, how to identify yours, and how to foster a new relationship with sharks to rebalance their power over you. Similar to the Internal Family Systems (IFS) perspective that Self must regain control from the many parts that try to run your system themselves, my ultimate goal for you is to reach a place where your sharks are not driving your life—you are. Although sharks can be long-standing for years or decades, many of them, when engaged thoughtfully, can morph into tame goldfish. Some sharks will transform so dramatically that they take on a new role in your system where they no longer terrify, threaten, or disturb you. Truthfully, I have seen my clients metamorphosize sharks into downright allies with this meaningful work.

Sharks, represent your *stuff*—your emotional baggage and chronic issues. These are the particular problems you have dealt with in one form or another for years, yet they keep boomeranging back to smack you in the face every time you think you've got them nipped. Sharks are the interior parts of you that frustrate you to no end and that you most dread experiencing. They are the parts of your life that you desperately try to keep others from seeing, and you likely keep them out of your own awareness as well. This only works until a shark gets triggered and you have no choice but to deal with it in one way or another. As you read this you may be thinking, *Yikes! I have lots of sharks that repeatedly derail my happy peaceful life.* Worry not, my friend. Multiple sharks are a definite reality. They come in different shapes and sizes, and it is normal to have them.

Offering: What are some of the sharks you are aware of in your life? Think about them, write about them, or draw them.

Sharks are often referred to by therapists as *triggers*. We feel triggered when something in life activates an intense emotional reaction within us. It can take almost nothing to ignite a trigger (ahem, shark) because they tend to be incredibly sensitive and close to the surface.

Sharks are not objects, people, or experiences. They're not your migraine headaches, egotistical boss, or bottle of whiskey. Things and people such as these are the stimuli that aggravate your sharks, while sharks themselves are your reactions, responses, and attachment to them. Your shark may be the anxiety you feel about your persistent migraine, the resentment you feel toward your boss, or the shame related to your impulsive alcohol consumption. Your shark is a recurring stressor in your mind/body/heart/soul system related to fear, anxiety, depression, hopelessness, or prolonged exposure to an emotional trigger.

Here are some examples:

- Some people's sharks are related to their body weight. Deep within, they have a little nagging voice that screams, *You're enormous! Everyone is looking at you and laughing. You are gross and ugly. You will never fit in.*

- Others may feel a particular hang-up with a long-standing mental health challenge like depression, anxiety, bipolar disorder, posttraumatic stress disorder, obsessive-compulsive disorder, or another diagnosis. Their shark's inner lingo may sound like, *I'm broken, damaged, and hopeless. I am different than everyone else and will never be free from this issue. Everyone can see that I'm damaged goods.*

- In another person, the feelings of inadequacy and incompetency might be a shark. Their narrative might sound like, *You are an idiot! Nobody takes you seriously.*

You have no right to be here, and everyone knows you're an imposter. You are completely worthless.

- Someone else may recognize a shark in their nagging experience of not-enough-ness. Therapists call this *scarcity,* which manifests with an inner dialogue like, *Keep going, never stop. There isn't enough [money, love, food, whatever] for me, so I have to relentlessly forge forward and claim as much as possible so I don't end up in dire straits (e.g., alone, poor, starving).*

I shared my biggest shark with you; the one I have come to call *health anxiety.* Since very early childhood, I have felt an eerie underlying sense (simmering just beneath the surface) that something is most definitely wrong with me physically—we just don't know what it is yet. Although I have always maintained robust health, I have experienced multitudes of *flukey shit* (the nontechnical term my doctor uses to reference the various strange and unusual medical symptoms my body produces).

Some issues, such as an inflammatory eye condition called Iritis (where the eye is inundated with white blood cells that cause pain and danger to the eye), have left physicians puzzled when my blood tests return void of clarifying pathologies. I have been labeled as *idiopathic* more times than I can count, which in doctor-speak means *we have no idea where this symptom came from or why it's here, and there is no discernable root we can understand to diagnose and treat it.* Essentially, I've been labeled a medical mystery for most of my life. Doctors look at me with puzzled expressions about my bizarre symptoms. Baffled, they don't know what to do with me or how to help, and they occasionally ask if they can include me in obscure medical trials to study my strangeness.

Whether this is an insult or compliment, I'm not sure, but to say the least—it's been frustrating.

Despite the presence of various bizarre health disturbances, my physicians have never discovered the dreaded underlying medical issue I always feared must be right around the corner. Over time, the repetitive nature of my idiopathic symptoms grew into sharks loaded with anxiety and fear.

BATHTUBS

Now, onward to *bathtubs*. Your bathtubs are the adaptive (sometimes sophisticated, sometimes dodgy) inner mechanisms you call upon to contain your sharks. They are the vessels your psyche has learned to construct to keep sharks from spilling out into your life in a way that overwhelms your system and shuts you down completely. Can you imagine a life without bathtubs? I don't even want to try. It would be an existence where our deepest and most distorted, messy, disorganized inner narratives run wild without so much as a warm blanket to soothe them. I'm game for a challenge, but no thanks on that one.

Different people's bathtubs exist in varying sizes, shapes, sturdiness, and reliability, which results in some people having a better handle on their sharks than others. Depending on the construction of your bathtub, certain issues will be more contained and managed than others. Bathtubs are often built with a variety of mechanisms that may include coping skills (healthy and unhealthy), denial, avoidance, emotional numbing, expression, mindfulness and meditation, reality checking, and many, many more. Think about how you handle life's biggest stressors, and you will begin to understand what your bathtubs are made of. Maybe you go for a walk, cry hysterically alone or with a friend, reach for a substance (not all bathtubs are equally healthy), journal about your feelings, go skydiving, or distract yourself. The coping strategies are endless.

Offering: Write about or sketch your bathtubs in your journal or sketchbook.

I have drastically changed and updated my bathtub since I first met my health anxiety shark when I was three years old. At that time, life was stressful for me because my baby sister had recently been born. As such a little girl, I must have felt massive loss as the only-child attention I had grown used to expanded to encompass the new red-faced screaming human in the bassinet. I am certain my parents did their best to stretch their love and attention around both myself and my new baby sister, but little Me socked up some collateral damage regardless.

Who knows if the skin disturbances that took up residence on my forehead, chin, hands, and knees at that young age were viral, bacterial, or a psychosomatic response to my stress (the term *psychosomatic* describes a phenomenon that happens when our bodies create physical reactions to an emotional issue). Nonetheless, they existed, and despite the valiant efforts of my parents, physicians, and a smattering of holistic healers, they took many years to clear up. I was three years old when I first experienced the puzzled expression that doctors have when they don't know how to make a problematic symptom go away.

It was a pretty big deal for such a little girl to experience all of this, especially considering that my short life had amounted to three basically happy years. Sadly, such stress and helplessness within my little Self resulted in the development of my very first shark. A lasting psychological mark developed from my early experiences that flagged my body as untrustworthy, unreliable, and unsafe.

What's a little tyke to do when flooded by fear, embarrassment, uncertainty, and stress? She builds a coping system to the best of her limited ability so that she can continue playing with her toys and laughing with her friends at playgroup. Back then, my bathtub was mainly constructed from my reliance upon my parents. I relied almost exclusively on them (especially my mother) to try to fix my problem and comfort me when humiliation and shame bubbled to the surface surrounding my skin's appearance. I also incorporated a hypervigilance within myself where I frequently (mostly unconsciously) scanned my body for worrisome symptoms to try to catch them before they grew into something scary. Another element of my bathtub at this young age included a fair amount of avoidance in the form of dodging mirrors so I wouldn't have to see the icky abnormality of my own face looking back at me. Even to this day, I gently work with my protective "not looking" behavior, as it's proven over time to be a tenacious one for me. As we have discussed, fear becomes oh-so-powerful when we avoid it.

Another element of my child bathtub was the time I spent distracting myself by escaping into magical play. In the illustrious ethereal worlds I concocted, I embodied a sense of control and power over the uncertainties that challenged me. A therapist would call this coping mechanism *magical thinking*, and it was my favorite element of my bathtub at that young age (and even into adulthood).

At my first women's retreat as a young adult, the retreat leader shared her opinion that what I had always considered within myself to be deep spirituality may have instead been magical thinking. In that moment, I immediately felt defensive, triggered, and misunderstood (shark alert!). I did not understand that I had invested enormous protective energy into my perception of what I thought spirituality was, and in so doing overlooked how it created a convenient bypass for me to avoid touching into my root issues.

I have since learned that true spiritual practice does not function as an avoidance strategy in any way. John Welwood[1] developed a term called *spiritual bypassing*, which is the conscious or unconscious avoidance of necessary healing through perceived spiritual practice. *We're all ethereal beings in an impermanent world, so it isn't really important that I manage my anxiety and fear. Those are just illusions like the rest of human life. Every time I feel anxious, I'll just focus on the impermanence of life and the discomfort will fade.* But will it? This example illustrates how a person might use spiritual terminology and thought processes to avoid facing the tough realities of life. In the years before I learned about the paradigm-shifting truth of my own spiritual bypassing, I clung to the belief that if I had otherworldly powers at my disposal, I could cure anything with the wave of a wand or the expression of a wish. I just needed to become a little more magical to achieve this, and I worked at it every day.

Over the years and through different iterations of my shark over time, I was challenged to patch, replace, and rebuild aspects of my bathtub that were no longer appropriate as I outgrew preschool. I learned how to support myself rather than relying solely on the heroics of others to rescue me. I cultivated courage and practiced facing my shark head on rather than stuffing my head in the sands of avoidance. I gained skills to tolerate uncertainty, got educated on various types of healthcare and how to access them, grew more comfortable with discomfort, and learned creative expression. These days, my bathtub is not without its weak spots or vices. I still occasionally grasp for supportive tools that work against me, but overall, I must say it's pretty solid and highly adaptable as I grow and change.

Offering: Now that you've heard a slice of my story, I invite you to explore your own narratives and experiences in your journal. Please consider:

- *What happened long ago that is still alive within you, and how did you cope when it happened?*
- *How do you typically handle life stressors?*
- *What are the coping tools you employ to manage hard things when they arise?*
- *Are you using outdated tools to support yourself? Where did you learn them?*
- *Which areas in your life still feel chaotic, dysregulated, or unsupported?*

When you get curious about your bathtub, it is crucial to be honest with yourself. Hiding your vices doesn't make them disappear, so if you reach for Netflix, alcohol, the intimate company of random strangers, or your credit card to cope, gently acknowledge the truth of your maladaptive behaviors. The time for dishonesty is behind us.

The truth is, struggle exists in life no matter how you slice it. Since we've all got sharks, we all need bathtubs. As we move through existence, we (mostly unconsciously) build bathtubs to hold our sharks. Containment is essential for compartmentalization and inner support because it protects us from being constantly flooded by the scary, painful stimuli of life. Bathtubs hold our fear and suffering so that we can go to work, maintain relationships, get the grocery shopping done, put the kids to bed in one piece, and maybe even enjoy a hobby or two.

Since human beings are thrifty, we will grab whatever we can find to reinforce our bathtubs to keep our sharks safely contained. We may accumulate denial, avoidance, expression, projection, maybe even some deep breathing (all held together with chewing gum and duct tape for good measure) to keep our sharks from erupting into our lives and wreaking the havoc we greatly fear. For most of us, sharks have mistakenly or accidentally been unleashed a time or two from their safe containment, so our nervous systems remember the horror of what happens when they are on the loose. We become impulsive, reactive, and act in ways we often regret. To avoid such experiences, our systems work relentlessly to keep such seemingly dangerous inner qualities tightly locked away.

Let's use Stuart's hot temper as an example: He operated from a bathtub that contained some healthy and some unhealthy mechanisms. It was built of deep breathing, Cognitive Behavioral Therapy skills, aged bourbon, and the practice of walking away. These containment strategies kept Stuart's angsty temper at bay when it got aggravated for the most part, but occasionally his inner flames could not be restrained. When this happened, Stuart would rage at whomever was nearby: an unsuspecting neighbor, intern bank teller, or confused customer service agent at Costco. Because Stuart was familiar with the regret and guilt that historically followed the release of this particular shark, he learned to double down reinforcing his bathtub with therapy skills, breathwork, and drunken avoidance when he noticed his temper rising. As you can see, some containment strategies are healthy and helpful, others not so much.

No matter how vigilantly we avoid releasing our sharks, accidents happen, and they sometimes get loose. For the most part, however, our bathtubs effectively help us cope. They allow us to be functional humans and juggle the ridiculous number of balls it takes to operate in society. Though bathtubs are a positive and necessary part of human life; the trick is cultivating healthy containment that serves and supports us, rather than a rickety system that regularly backfires and collapses. Befriending your sharks and being mindful of your bathtubs ultimately returns you on to the lap of your authentic Self.

IT'S ALL OKAY

Human beings have sophisticated and engrained systems for coping with life's speedbumps that are hardwired into our brains and even our cellular structure. Some aspects of these systems are healthy, others are harmful and toxic, but they're always (and I mean always) adaptive. We do what we do for a reason, whether it makes sense to the rational mind or not. Our reactions and responses serve us, even if only to airlift us to psychological safety or extinguish an imaginary fire. These feedback loops were built from direct experience, meaning that you have a magical ability to adapt internally and holistically to meet the challenges of your environment, for better or worse. You are built for this life, with all its flavors, and there is always room for growth and improvement to the way you function. When you remove your sharks from the captain's chair and coexist more peacefully, you can more easily engage the plethora of human experience you came here to participate in.

The sharks/bathtubs model is about checking yourself out under the hood to discover what lies beneath. In so doing, you will understand yourself more deeply and build a life that supports and sustains all aspects of you—including your messy qualities. You will learn to dance with your seemingly unlikable and problematic inner qualities rather than aim to eradicate them. Learning about sharks and bathtubs can strengthen your inner support system and open new portals of discovery for embodiment and compassion in every season of your life.

Part of the bathtub I unconsciously built to cope with my health anxiety shark was to become hypervigilant about my physical body. I armored up with this defense mechanism to keep myself safe from my greatest fear: suffering. Nothing scares me more than the prospect of an existence of prolonged misery that diminishes my quality of life and ultimately ends with me lying six feet underground before I've gotten the chance to meet my grandchildren (cue the dramatic music). *Hypervigilance* is the constant scanning and alertness that keeps a person perched on the edge of their seat searching for danger. This protective mechanism (though not the most refined or healthy of the tools in my toolbox) has been part of my bathtub since I was very young.

The sensitivity I developed to the slightest disruption in my bodily homeostasis has honed within me the precision of a trained sniper preparing to shoot down an enemy. This is my system's adaptive tool for catching looming sharks in the water as soon as they present. Small, seemingly insignificant health flaws seem like they could potentially be the first symptom of the massive health issue I've always known was there but haven't discovered until THIS. VERY. MOMENT. In the beat of a second my field narrows, and I feel like something is threatening my life (even if it's just a passing virus or strange bodily manifestation not worth its weight in worry). This example demonstrates the power and intensity sharks carry in our psyche. Although the perceived threat is distorted in its over-reactivity, when I am caught in the energy of my sharks, the threat feels as real as the nose on my face.

My narratives can sound like, *Oh no! A red spot on my skin. This might be the first sign of a terrible disease, and soon it will be everywhere! Yikes! A sharp pain in my side. Which organ is that? There's something wrong with me. I am going to suffer because of this, and it's probably going to tank my quality of life forever.*

When something is a shark, it tends to stick around, even amid your best efforts to kick it to the curb. I can tell you from experience, my health anxiety shark has proven over time that it's here to stay—at least in some capacity. I have felt at times that I was playing a frustrating game of whack-a-mole, where every time I think I've healed the issue, it pops up again in another form I didn't foresee. This is how I know it's a shark: Regardless of my efforts to rid myself of health anxiety, shades of it remain. It's sneaky, and against all odds, I have learned to befriend it. You may be thinking, *What? Befriend it?* Yes. Stay tuned and we'll talk about how to make friends with sharks.

I want to be clear on something important: Having sharks and bathtubs does not mean something is wrong with you or that you are messed up, broken, or limited by any harmful narrative of shame you feel flooded by. Sharks and bathtubs are normal parts of being a person. Having one shark/bathtub situation does not make a person better, healthier, or more advanced than someone who has multiple shark/bathtub situations. These triggers and containment strategies are in direct response to lived experience, so different people will have varying types of sharks and bathtubs depending on the hand they were dealt in life. Josie only had one shark and bathtub duo, but it was unstable because her bathtub was akin to a twiggy nest held together with scotch tape. With such a weak containment system, Josie barely held it together, and thus experienced a life filled with painful outbursts. Mary, on the other hand, had various sharks, but she effectively held them in numerous thoughtfully crafted bathtubs. This resulted in a more stable, grounded life for Mary with healthier relationships to her trigger points.

I want you to remember that the number of sharks and bathtubs you hold within yourself is mutually exclusive from your health and stability in life. It's about how you support and manage your sharks and bathtubs that matters most, not how many you have. Read that again, and think about it every time you feel the impulse to judge yourself or someone else for having several areas of inner work on the table.

Offering: Take a breath and take a moment to thoughtfully consider your sharks and bathtubs. Take your exploration to your journal, sketchbook, therapist, or best friend for deeper processing.

Next, let's bring compassion into the picture. A common reason why we have hot buttons that either shut us down or induce lash-outs is related to this: When we have little to no awareness of our sharks and bathtubs, we are less likely to lovingly attend to our most sensitive areas. If you have ever responded irrationally to something you later realized was minimal, you either triggered an intolerable shark, or you were working with a leaky bathtub in need of TLC. Whether you encounter off-the-handle reactivity in yourself, a loved one, or even a stranger, remember the universality of sharks and bathtubs, and try to source compassion. This practice both increases your capacity for empathy and wholeheartedness and models for others how we can build a loving world rather than one based on tearing each other down when our pain gets exposed.

If you have a nose, toes, and a beating heart, sharks swimming in bathtubs exist within you in this very moment. Everyone's sharks and bathtubs present differently and need unique support, but every single person has them. Release the idea that you're an abnormal freak of nature because you have these recurrent trigger points. You are in good company with the rest of humanity.

Swimming with Sharks

If you have ever swam with living sharks—I've done this, and it's not my favorite experience—you know the eerie feeling of such an experience. Surprisingly, it isn't unnerving because there are sharks swimming around you but *because of what you believe* about sharks swimming around you. Our minds and the core beliefs we create within ourselves become powerful sculptors that shape how we see our world, and they are sometimes based on fallacy.

Through the prism of the human mind, many of us fear sharks because they are great and powerful predators, however this is only one fractal of the truth. When you consider the ocean as an intelligent ecosystem, sharks are as vital a component to the marine world as clownfish and coral. Though they hunt when hungry and attack when threatened, as nature designed, sharks are not a danger to everything that crosses their path.

In this section, you will learn how to make a change by actively shifting your perspective about your sharks. Norton Juster, in his novel *The Phantom Tollbooth*,[2] unveils an enlightening statement about the power of perspective. He writes, "From here that looks like a bucket of water. But from an ant's point of view it's a vast ocean, from an elephant's just a cool drink, and to a fish, of course, it's Home. So, you see the way you see things depends a great deal on where you look at them from."

Just as an ocean's completion results from the vast array of sea creatures and flora in its womb, human completion results from our assortment of emotions, memories, and lived experiences. Though it may be light and lovely to surf the gentle aquamarine waters of hope, happiness, and love, there is also value in navigating the stormier seas of hardship and heartbreak. Tough emotions are part of our contract with life. Though we may reject this reality, we came into human form to experience such things as rage, fear, and despair too.

The bathtubs we adaptively construct necessarily provide us breathing room from constant exposure to our sharks, but bathtubs do not have the power to do away with sharks—only to contain them for a while. Over time, repetition has taught me that the goal is not to become shark-free, but to learn to swim in peace together. An important mindset to hold while considering the possibility for peaceful coexistence lies in seeing sharks as a natural and essential part of life and crafting our reactions toward them into thoughtful responses.

Think back to Chapter 5 and Tara Brach's[3] distinction between *reacting* and *responding*. It applies directly to swimming with Sharks. As a reminder, *reacting* contains elements of control, fear, and aggression, while *responding* holds curiosity, compassion, and presence. I can certainly recall memories when I was reactive rather than responsive, surrounding myself with control and rigidity as armor. I'll be the first to admit that these situations didn't go well.

Resistance is a huge part of reactivity. This is the *make it go away* energy we tend to hold toward sharks. For many years, I exclusively related to my health anxiety shark with reactivity. Each time I noticed a health concern (no matter how small) fear and anxiety rose up in me, and I reacted by fearfully scheduling a medical appointment, sliding down the slippery slope of worst-case-scenario thinking, and implored deep resistance toward the symptom. I was consumed by my desperation to remove the discomfort so that I could return to stress-free life.

My cascade of urgency and tension worked precisely never. Instead, a continuous looping back into the same pattern as always would ensue. The shark would present and ignite fearful resistance within me, then eventually I would manage to beat the shark into remission, then time would pass, and the shark would present again in a new or familiar way. On and on it circled until one day I decided to respond instead of react.

By responding to a shark (aka a prolonged headache, full body allergic reaction, or unexplainable inflammatory response), I became familiar with Brach's[4] *attend and befriend* mantra. When I approached an ignited trigger with presence and curiosity, my sense of urgency decreased and I was able to access embodied presence and think calmly. I could ask myself questions like, *What's going on here?* or *Is there something my body is trying to tell me?* Attending to my sharks in this new way allowed me to open up to the intrinsic self-support that had always been available to me. Before I achieved this growth, I had not seen the extent of my own interior strength because of my entrenchment in outdated patterns. From a perspective of curiosity, I more easily listened to my body, met arising needs I had not previously noticed, and calmly soothed my stress response.

If I realized there was nothing to be done after I attended to a shark, I could befriend my experience by remaining embodied in the present moment and counteracting my habitual loop toward fear. *Yes, this sucks. It's really painful and mysterious. I've done all I can do for now, and I am still basically okay in this moment. I am breathing, I have the warmth of my mug of tea to comfort me, and gravity still holds me to the planet. When the time comes to take action, I trust I will. For now I acknowledge that I am okay.* When there's nothing to be done to eradicate my shark, the best thing I can do is befriend it and try to learn more about why it presented.

The befriending of sharks involves offering a loving presence toward the most terrifying, triggering experiences of life, so I understand you might feel squirmy about it at first. Still, I invite you to consider it. When there is no obvious solution, no external rescuer, and no magical wand to make the discomfort disappear, you have two choices: You can resist and react, or you can respond and soften. In my experience, dizzying myself in a whirlpool of anxiety is unproductive and only makes matters worse. It takes practice and patience, but with time, a befriending response toward sharks ultimately builds respectful internal relationships that can guide you deeper into your healing.

In large part, befriending sharks involves being here and now in the present moment. Eckhart Tolle has been at the forefront of this work with his books *The Power of Now* and *A New Earth*. Tolle, Brach, and other mindfulness practitioners teach about the incredible strength and freedom derived from holding mindful presence with our stressors, looking them squarely in the eyes, and accepting that peace comes from being present in the eternal Now. When we achieve presence, we see that Now is all we ever really have. The knife edge of the moment is where freedom exists, and its spaciousness allows for the backward and forward extensions of time to dissipate.

Martha Beck, in her book *The Way of Integrity*,[5] speaks to the experience of mindful presence when she says, "You are already coping with it right now, and right now is the only thing you'll ever have to cope with."

Offering: Herein lies your opportunity to make a shift. Slow down and reel yourself back from catastrophic future worries or traumatic past memories—land squarely in the eternal Now. Use your breathing as a vehicle into the present by simply noticing the cadence of your inhalation and exhalation. Simply observe and share space with your sharks as they present to you, and notice that you are still breathing—still basically okay— even in their presence. You may notice bathtubs jumping in to diminish the intensity of the sharks: "Grab a drink! Buy some stuff online! Yell at someone!" Just thank them kindly for doing what they know how to do to minimize your pain, then ask them to step back. Allow your bathtub to see your strength and courage, and that your survival is not presently threatened. Then enhance your curiosity of the sharks even more. Notice their rubbery skin and razor teeth. Remember, your sharks are not the symptom, not your physical pain, or emotional rage, or alcoholic craving. They are the way you feel about the symptom, which manifests as reactivity, self-judgment, or fear. Simply be with your sharks and remind yourself that in this moment, regardless of the presence of sharks, you are basically okay—maybe even better than you previously thought. Your heart is beating, blood is flowing, breeze is blowing. It may not be the most comfortable moment of your life, but you're okay. Perfect? No. Basically alright? Yes. Now write about it in your journal.

AN ODE TO INNER WORK

One of my favorite Elizabeth Gilbert quotes states, "Surely something wonderful is sheltered inside of you. The universe buries strange jewels deep within us all, and then stands back to see if we can find them." I certainly have discovered numerous strange jewels on my healing journey that have become priceless treasures in my everyday life—one of which being the gift of my health anxiety shark.

Over my more than twenty-five years of intentional psycho-spiritual work, my health anxiety shark has become much less menacing, as have other issues that are tethered to it. Even so, I suspect there will always be more layers of work to be done. Now when I spot the threat of a sneaky dorsal fin in the distance, I am well-equipped to notice, observe, and work with my shark rather than get completely flooded by its energy.

It is my intention to share what I have learned about my sharks to help you learn to swim with yours. You may be a therapy-regular yourself, or this book might be your first introduction to self-help. Either way, the healing path is a journey worth taking. I've never met a person who started the quest of inner work and found it to be a waste of time.

I strongly encourage that anyone interested in this depth of work find a licensed and trained therapist to accompany them on their journey. The objective reflection and support of an experienced professional is an invaluable resource.

You will discover with inner work that sharks may endure and scare the very breath from your lungs, but over time they shift. With intentional work, sharks tend to appear tamer, smaller, and more manageable than before. You may even notice that your sharks are not as horrifying as you originally thought they were, and a space of compassion or even appreciation for your sharks may open within you. I can promise you it's possible because I've seen it with my own eyes in the experiences of inspiring clients whom I have worked with and in the work I've done myself. You now know that we all have tricky inner business that needs tending: our *sharks in the bathtubs*. You're far from alone.

One of my favorite oceanic mental pictures was inspired by the wisdom of Vietnamese Buddhist monk, peace activist, and writer Thich Nhat Hanh, who said, "Enlightenment for a wave is the moment the wave realizes it is the water. At that moment, all fear of death disappears."[6] Humans are made of salt and water, and we are each an ocean of our own being. We are massive in our abilities to hold the complexities of human experience. Everything that jolts, charges, and upsets us in life are simply waves moving through our interior ocean—ebbing, flowing, crashing, and shifting within the structure of our existence. Regardless of a wave's size and magnitude, it does not consume its container. The ocean is never threatened by the passage of its waves, nor is it overwhelmed by their existence. The ocean can hold any arising swell within its boundless shape, and so can we.

Ocean wisdom understands that sooner or later all waves crest, fall, and rejoin the eternal tides of the body of water to which they belong. Similarly, we are capable of immense holding for the shifting currents within our bodies and our lives. We hold within ourselves boundless capability for healing and growth. The more we consciously access awareness and awe in the process of living, the more our lives fill with meaning, aliveness, and empowerment. Your radiant life welcomes all aspects of you—even, and perhaps especially, your sharks and bathtubs.

CHAPTER 9

Integrity and Alignment

Our Relationship with the Truth

The truth can scare you half to death, but it's never as destructive as deception.

—*MARTHA BECK*

AUTHENTICITY ASKS: WHAT IS REAL?
INTEGRITY ASKS: WHAT IS TRUE?

This blissfully simple delineation is how I have come to think about authenticity and integrity. Much overlap exists between living authentically and living with integrity, and I do believe a heaping dose of both is required for a radiant life. Even with the similarities between these two concepts, there are subtle differences that allow for authenticity and integrity to mingle well and enhance one another's effect in the world like partnered friends.

The best explanation of integrity I have found comes from Martha Beck's *The Way of Integrity*.[1] I recommend this wonderful book to anyone who will listen—in fact, I think it should be required reading in every high school. In her vivid explanation, Beck creates a juxtaposition between humans and airplanes.[2] She discusses the importance of an airplane being in *good integrity* before it takes flight with the lives of hundreds of precious souls inside. This means that the entire airplane is in good working order, operating as it should be, with every little part doing its job and working in harmony with all other parts of the plane for wholeness and unity in the system. When good working integrity is achieved on an airplane, it is most likely to successfully blast through the air and land safely at its destination.

If you thought you were very different from an airplane, think again. An airplane needs to be in good integrity for it to take off, fly, and land in one piece, and so do you. Granted, our integrity looks more like honest relationships, meaningful work, and genuine values than engines, pipelines, and propellers, but on a basic level it's the same.

When I define integrity as *what is true*, I mean that it is the consistent living of our lives in congruity with the full battery of the truth encoded within our numerous inner systems (e.g., values, interests, desires, driving purpose). These inner mechanisms join together with the realness of authenticity to make up our sophisticated and unique human identities. Though we can flex and adapt, each person has the True North compass we discussed in Chapter 1 that guides them toward what is real and true within their inner landscape. When we stray from integrity and act in discord with what is true for us in any or all of these arenas, our larger system tries to compensate, deviate, or shunt energy to stay afloat. When this happens, our authentic engagement with life from true Self gets bumped off course, which greatly diminishes our freedom and joy.

I'll stick with Beck's airplane example to paint you a picture: Imagine you are gliding 30,000 feet above Earth, squished in your uncomfortable airplane seat, when you simultaneously feel and hear a bang. The pilot's voice carries across the intercom saying that one of the airplane's jet engines has just gone kaput. Does the airplane take a drastic nosedive toward its imminent demise? Not necessarily, which is lucky for you and your in-flight neighbors. The other jet engine(s) can struggle along for a short while to keep the plane flying (though at decreased speed and power) until your skillful pilot can bring her down safely.

The same thing happens with us; however, we don't often hear/feel a bang to notify us that one of our systems has gone down. Instead, we often ride along with compromised integrity for a lot longer than we should. Most often, the loss of integrity is a subtle experience of self-abandonment, socialization, or mis-attunement that moves us directly apart from a radiant life. It shows up for most of us not dramatically as a loud explosion, but more like saying yes when we really want to say no. Or accepting a job we can't stand because of its high salary. Or meeting a friend for lunch (again) when we decidedly do not enjoy said friend's company. This is the way the integrity system of a modern person gets derailed, and you can bet it's an experience everyone is familiar with to some extent or another.

TRUE YES AND TRUE NO

My friend Nola adores Loki, the god of mischief from Norse mythology (alright, I'll admit, I like him too, just not as much as Nola). Loki is an interesting character when you perceive him through the lens of integrity because he demonstrates how discerning true authentic integrity isn't always straightforward. Loki constantly shape-shifts, lies, and conjures up deeply twisted plans in his misguided pursuit of mutiny and power. On one hand, Loki could be considered to have the least authentic integrity of all beings, due to his chameleon nature and deceptiveness. Or does he, perhaps, act authentically when he embraces and embodies his changeable qualities of Self? This question points to an important distinction: *Who we are* and *what we do* belong to two wildly different realms outside the land of authenticity, but resonate the same when within it. Perhaps Loki exists completely embodied in his authentic Self and is simply following his True North by honoring his chameleon nature. In this case, Loki simply appears fickle and unsteady only to those who do not truly know him. Conversely, if Loki were not living in integrity, he would flip-flop, shape-shift, and transform before your eyes in various mischievous acts of confusing mayhem without a tether to his true Self. Only Loki himself can say which is true, but notice how it can go both ways depending on a person's congruity with integrity. For Loki (as well as the rest of us mere mortals) it is only when *who we are* and *what we do* align that the result is authentic integrity. Otherwise, it's simply feigning a persona while remaining untethered from resonant congruence to Self. This is where *True YES* and *True NO* come in as an internal experience only you can sense for yourself.

Throughout my personal healing journey, I was taught by mentors and therapists how to discern my own True YES and True NO. This concept is so important that I am shocked that it is not a fundamental teaching for every kindergartener before they even learn to read or write, but it will have to suffice that we learn it better late than never.

True YES and True NO are *embodiment practices.* This means they are felt and sensed within our bodies, not brainstormed in the ever-righteous monkey mind. Though our minds can participate in asking questions, our bodies are necessary for discerning true answers. You see, our minds are fickle and changeable and, therefore, can provide many different answers that may or may not be entirely truthful. Human minds can be easily swayed, influenced, and confused by other people and stories. Because of this malleability, it is crucial that we learn to listen to our minds solely as informants, not as messengers of absolute truth. Our bodies, on the other hand, don't know how to lie. Bodies just share what they know and communicate their truth through feelings and sensations because they don't have words.

To practice accessing embodied discernment, we'll start by working with a question—something easy. By the way, not all questions need to be asked verbally; they can also be posed to the Self as imagery, a memory, or a quality of experience. I often ask my clients to visualize a movie screen or performance stage where they can envision a person, thing, experience, or option, and I'll ask you to do the same.

Offering: Let's start with your favorite food. Close your eyes and visualize your favorite food on your interior movie screen, and simply notice how your body responds. Assuming you were correct in your preference for this food, you may notice a lightness in your body, a tingling in your mouth, a warmth, or surge of energy. You may notice other sensations as well—there's no right or wrong here, it's all very personal. This is your True YES feeling. Now, try the same exercise with a food you simply detest. Speak its name and/or visualize it on your movie screen, and notice the way your body tenses, twists, feels weighty or squirmy. This is your body saying True NO. As you get more comfortable with this exercise, try increasingly complex questions like "Is it time to leave my unhappy marriage?" Or "Do I trust myself being alone with this person for international travel?" If you're listening to your body (not your silly monkey mind) you will notice the same True YES and True NO sensations you felt toward basic food preferences. Write about this visualization experience in your journal.

The key to this process—and when I say key, I mean absolute key—is that you actually listen to your True YES and True NO. If you notice your mind and body entering a bidding war for which to trust, just remember that your body never lies. You may not like the gut feeling you're getting or the true answer to your question, but that doesn't make it any less true. I can't begin to tell you how many therapy sessions go something like this:

Client: *I don't know why I am so unhappy.*

Therapist: *How do you experience your job/relationship/etc.*

Client: *Well, I know my job/relationship/etc. is terrible, but I stay in it because I feel like I have to and I am afraid to leave.*

Therapist: *So your body is screaming NO and your mind is screaming YES, and you're listening to your mind?*

Client: *Pretty much. I'm afraid to make less money/be alone/etc. so I just stay.*

Therapist: *How's that working out for you?*

Client (Back to the way this whole thing started): *Well, I'm unhappy.*

Next comes the empowering process of learning to trust the messages from your body and put your mind in the back seat for a hot minute. Once you start being honest with yourself about where in your life you are ignoring True YES and True NO sensations, you open the portal of possibility to make aligned changes in your life based on your authentic preferences and desires. In the long run, staying in an unhealthy job, relationship, or any other situation never pans out. So why not shift the scales toward integrity sooner rather than later and reclaim your birthright to live a wildly radiant life?

WHAT MISALIGNED INTEGRITY LOOKS LIKE

One example of a disguised type of poor-integrity living is a person who doesn't walk their talk or actively show up to live the life before them. We can safely assume that it's easier to give advice than receive it, and even living in coherence with our own good advice can be a real challenge. The know-it-all person who barks directives for how others should be living their lives while standing atop their proverbial ivory tower is a prime example of low-integrity living. Call me crazy, but I have always respected and appreciated people who expose honest vulnerability about their pitfalls and missteps in life—for better or worse. I intrinsically trust such people more because I know they're down in the weeds with me, learning and pursuing growth right alongside me, instead of feigning enlightenment. As the writer and poet Mark Nepo says,[3] "Life, it seems, reveals itself through those willing to live. Anything else, no matter how beautiful, is just advertising." Can we agree, here and now, to stop false-advertising to one another and simply live our lives with integrity and authenticity?

I like examples, so here's another one for misaligned integrity: the *tortured artist* persona. Elizabeth Gilbert speaks about this phenomenon in her work,[4] and I'd like to build on it. I spent a large part of my formal education in art school, which rendered me intimately familiar with many people who subscribed to the tortured artist identity. Cue the slideshow: Van Gogh who cut off his own ear, Kurt Cobain who tragically died by suicide, and other artists who use their own (or someone else's) blood and snot to make viscerally poignant artwork. Sure, some artists may be emotionally tortured. There may also be psychologically inflamed accountants, anesthesiologists, and parking lot attendants.

A frequent misunderstanding, both by practicing artists and the patrons who appreciate their craft, is that the sensitivity so often found in artists must be based on suffering. It is true that many artists possess the bittersweet gift of sensitivity, and some can even transmute unfathomable emotional depth within those who bear witness to their art. This does not automatically equate to the artist being psychologically gnarled, unstable, misguided, or even dangerous. By nature, artists tend to channel emotional depth and sensitization, and some of the best artists can articulate these profundities in their work. The gift of an artist's access to emotional experience is mutually exclusive from their identity of being agonized, tortured, or tormented—even if they do, in fact, tap into such suffering while channeling their expressive work.

What I know from treating clients with severe depression and mental illness is that a person in the throes of major depression, inciting rage, or paralyzing agony has immense difficulty uncovering their creativity. Instead, it is those who are able to process emotional experiences enough to effectively funnel their grief, rage, or bliss into a meaningful creative process who make art therapy such an effective healing modality. Almost always, after directing emotional content into creative manifestation, layers of pain and suffering shift and often alleviate for the artist. This is the process of *sublimation* we discussed in Chapter 3. The perceived agony of a creator cannot be an ongoing state or it becomes too incapacitating to reap much of anything—let alone produce highbrow art.

What does all of this have to do with integrity? The tortured artist example demonstrates a process of self-abandonment and misalignment that can happen when a person mistakenly believes it is *necessary* to be tortured to create anything of real meaning. An artist who buys into misunderstanding their creativity in this way believes that beauty and agony are inextricably linked, and that art must be filled with anguish to be legitimate. This person intentionally nurtures their suffering (and even acts to enhance it) because they hold dear an erroneous belief that without pain they cannot create anything of significance or value. I am reminded of the lyrics of the 1994 song by The Offspring called "Self-Esteem": "The more you suffer, the more it shows you really care." Look, I identify as an artist, and still, I'll be the first to vote myself off the island of *no pain, no gain*, thank you very much.

My client Penny was another example of living misaligned with integrity. She was a new mother with highly unrealistic perfectionist standards. The magazine and billboard images of white-toothed mothers with expertly designed messy buns only reinforced the picture-perfect social media photos of her friends. While Penny's Instagram feed overflowed with blissful images of do-it-all supermoms and their cooing babies, she had no way of knowing that the same mothers likely felt inadequate and flawed when off-camera, from the bags under their concealer-covered eyes down to the Spanx that obscured their stretch marks. These women experienced the same stressful hustle of motherhood as Penny, yet everyone felt isolated within the cage of their own beliefs that they were alone in the experience. Penny, because of societal messaging surrounding the reality of motherhood and because she did not have a community of high-integrity friends, harshly limited and judged herself. She could not allow herself to weep or leave dirty dishes in the sink because she was flooded by the fear that without a flawless façade, she had no worth as a mother or woman (ahem, see *Patriarchy* in Chapter 2).

SECRETS AND LIES

Though the loss of integrity shows up in our relationships, the most sorrowful transgression we can make against integrity is when we are dishonest with ourselves. A misstep of this kind can present in various magnitudes. One seemingly small degree of misalignment is saying *yes* when every cell of your being screams *no* to traveling cross-country to help a friend move homes. On the other (more insidious) end of the spectrum, it can show up as living a completely misguided life based on values that are not your own, acting in ways that are not congruent with who you truly are, and basing your life's momentum upon an ideal that is untrue for you. In the world we live in, I think we can all agree that there are many ways (both seemingly harmless and overtly dangerous) to manipulate, confuse, betray, and blatantly lie to ourselves.

A popular Alcoholics Anonymous slogan states, *You're only as sick as your secrets.* I think this is poignant, and I want to deepen it another layer by asking you to consider the secrets you keep from yourself and the lies you tell inwardly. Dig deep for this next offering with the understanding that inner dishonesty never serves you for long. The sooner you engage your fear about facing the secrets and lies you tell yourself, the sooner you can move beyond them toward your radiant life.

Offering: Write about the secrets you keep from yourself and lies you tell yourself. Then write about why you keep secrets from yourself and tell lies to yourself. If you notice any type of discomfort while engaging this process, note that it is normal to feel a bit squirmy when exploring such a deep degree of honesty with yourself—especially if you have been dishonest or secretive with yourself for a long time. It's okay to move through this process in baby steps; give yourself space when the discomfort grows too large.

The human brain and mind have evolved to such an extent that secrets and lies have become grouped into the territory of omission, manipulation, avoidance, propaganda, and projection. All of these transgressions exist directly alongside more overt forms of deceit such as blatant dishonesty, falsehood, and fabrication.

Beck, in her book *The Way of Integrity,*[5] referenced a study that was conducted with gay men who had all tested positive for HIV. Researchers found that the more the men in the study hid their true sexuality, the faster the HIV infiltrated through their bodies and caused negative effects. This is a direct example of how living out of integrity by keeping internal secrets can impact real damage within a person—in the case of the study's men, affecting dire consequences to their health.

PEOPLE PLEASING

Sometimes secret-keeping can piggyback on the tendency to people please, which is another dangerous effect of low integrity living. *People pleasing* is when you override your own desires, feelings, and truth to behave in a manner you believe will satisfy another person. Not only is people pleasing a behavior most (or even all) people engage in to varying degrees, it is culturally advertised as the pathway to good relationships.

Here's the deal: People pleasing does work to gain relationships. Let's face it—people like being pleased. It just doesn't work if you're trying to cultivate the kind of connection that is based on integrity. Here's why: When a relationship is formed upon or sustained by dishing out behaviors, responses, and participation you think an external person wants (at the expense of honoring your own needs and desires), it builds an unstable dynamic. A house built upon a faulty foundation has the same issue, and it can easily blow away with a stiff breeze. The truth is that nothing secure can be constructed on top of a shaky baseline. When a relationship is dependent upon people pleasing, it does not allow for its participants to be their authentic Selves.

The whole point of connection in this jungle of life is to journey with the love, support, and partnership from relationships that meaningfully contribute to your existence. If you are so busy keeping the other person happy by being who you think they want or need you to be in order to meet their needs, the relationship will lack the integrity to be truly fulfilling. If our relationships are more work and stress than benefit to us, what's the point? Popularity for popularity's sake results only in a heap of conditional love, not the true support and connection that comes with aligned relationships.

Conditional love is a tough pill to swallow. This is especially loaded for a person who believes that they must be all the things to all the people to earn love (*earn* being the operative word). If someone cares for you only when you show certain parts of yourself, cater to their needs, or behave in ways they prescribe as acceptable, their affection is illegitimate. Coming to grips with this realization can bring up the ugly monsters of rejection, failure, and abandonment, but please just look those creatures in the face and take your power back from them. Although parts of you want to believe that performing for love is normal and necessary, true connection does not require you to abandon your Self— it requires you to *be* your Self. The parts of you that believe in such fallacies most likely developed when you were small. They likely learned that love is something you must earn by being good, compliant, uncomplicated, and easy.

Offering: See if you can observe the wounded parts of yourself as young children. Visualize grouping them into a great big bear hug with your adult Self. In the embrace of true Self, your inner child parts will begin to feel the resonance of unconditional love—maybe for the first time in their existence. Draw or write about it if you feel so inclined.

Over time, with conscious care and effort, you can teach your wounded parts that true care is given freely and whole-heartedly; it doesn't come with strings attached. You have the power to provide young parts of yourself the corrective experience of unconditional love they so yearn for.

For a strong example of high-integrity unconditional love, I'm going to point to Glennon Doyle's book *Untamed* [6] where she includes a bit of dialogue between herself and her twelve-year-old daughter, Tish:

> Glennon: *Every time you're given a choice between disappointing someone else and disappointing yourself, your duty is to disappoint that someone else. Your job, throughout your entire life, is to disappoint as many people as it takes to avoid disappointing yourself.*
>
> Tish: *Even you, Mom?*
>
> Glennon: *Especially me.*

HOW WE UNCONSCIOUSLY SELL OURSELVES

A big component of people pleasing is related to the archetype of the prostitute. Before I lose you with the charge and implications of the word *prostitute,* just hear me out. In Jungian psychology,[7] an *archetype* is defined as being a universal symbol or quality that we collectively possess. Many archetypes have been developed into literary and movie characters—the *hero,* the *villain,* the *victim,* or the *crone* to name a few. Somewhere deep inside each of our psyches, we all hold the capacity to experience life through the lens and vehicle of archetypes. One archetype that is intimately related to people pleasing is the *prostitute.*[8] This particular archetype is part of the *shadow* of our psyches, meaning that it is a quality we perceive as being unlikable and distasteful, and we would rather banish it to a dark corner of our mind than admit it is a part of us. Just like exile parts in Internal Family Systems (IFS), the shadow archetypes that we hold under lock and key within ourselves do not cease to exist; they only go into repression for a while until something (usually unintentionally) triggers them and brings their existence into conscious awareness.

Returning to the prostitute, this is the archetype within us all that gives things away that we don't really want to give; the part that pimps itself out for far less than it's worth in order to survive. People pleasing is one of the many behaviors of the prostitute archetype—maybe the most common—but the prostitute can also be seen in the behaviors of selling yourself short, giving in to a plan or agreement you don't really believe in, manipulating yourself into believing that you are worth very little, and doing things you don't truly want to do in order to meet someone else's standard. If you take away the label of *prostitute*, I'm sure we can all relate to behaving in these ways.

I mentioned earlier that the prostitute archetype behaves how it does in an effort toward *survival*. This is worth a second glance because it lends new depth to the people pleasing behaviors you may have previously thought were harmless. If you consider the core needs of a human, being loved and offering love in return are pretty high on the priority list for most of us. Along with love comes the safety, security, and companionship we so need and desire.

When the creatures of Earth were put on this planet, some were given fur to keep them warm, shells to retreat into, or claws and teeth to protect themselves. Humans, however, were not granted any of those gifts. Human beings were given big brains, opposable thumbs, and each other. With such invaluable gifts, the human race grew into the sophisticated species we are today. In large part, it is because of our communities and connections with one another that we have survived. Without our relationships with other people, we would not be able to find food, keep ourselves warm, nurture our young, remain safe, or build cities. Let's face it: We need each other. Because we so desperately need other human beings to survive, our brains have developed to do whatever it takes to secure and maintain interpersonal connections. In many cases this looks like self-abandonment, which can take the shape of the prostitute archetype.

As we discussed earlier, self-abandonment is a pretty functional tool if all you need are people at any cost (hey, sometimes a person just needs another warm body beside them). If you don't have the luxury to be picky and choose your connections with emotional congruity in mind, feel free to go ahead and just take whatever you can get. It does seem, however, that in our present world, most of us have a great deal of choices when it comes to whom we invite into our lives. If you open your mind and walk down a busy street in a big city, you will be amazed at the smattering of different personalities, temperaments, styles, and types of people you will encounter. I truly believe that there is someone for everyone out there—and probably more than just one.

The key to finding your people is to drop self-abandonment and make high-integrity choices. Step one: Throw people pleasing into the dumpster and move your fine Self forward. Meet new aligned people and engage authentically with the connections you already have; say *yes* when you mean *yes* and *no* when you mean *no*. Don't pretend to be into Star Wars if you're not, and order whatever you want for dinner (even if it doesn't seem like your companion would approve). Ask inquisitive questions to learn about who other people truly are, and show them the weirdness in you. Do *you* in the most authentic way possible, and you will attract people who can jive with your style and flow congruently in relationship with you. As an added bonus, you won't have to do stuff you don't want to do anymore.

Offering: In your journal, list at least three qualities/preferences that are uniquely You. Next, list three self-abandoning behaviors you will stop doing right now (or ASAP).

REPAIRING YOUR INTEGRITY

The road to high-integrity living is a winding one that requires patience, so please be gentle with yourself as you navigate this work. Living in a society that prizes inauthenticity and self-abandonment has embedded messages into our collective consciousness that we should not think of our own integrity first. Instead, we have been groomed to think first about what other people want or need from us. Rewiring these neuropathways will take some repetition. It may feel a bit uncomfortable at first to prioritize integrity practices in your life, but believe me when I say it is well worth it.

When you commit to your Self first and foremost above all else, you do not become a narcissist, as society would have you believe. In fact, you become shades brighter in your ability to love, care for, and relate to other people because you connect with others from a resourced state of being rather than a depleted one. When our cups are full, we can pour into the cups of others with our overflow. When you trade the momentum of a low-integrity lifestyle for one that holds healthy boundaries, lives honestly, and tends to the needs of your inner system, you become a holistically healthier person. Radiance such as this results in a more generous threshold toward other people, as well as a calmer nervous system and clearer mind and heart.

MIRRORS, NEURONS, AND EMPATHIC ATTUNEMENT

One of the built-in mechanisms for connection that sometimes gets in the way of high-integrity relationships is our mirror neuron system. *Mirror neurons* are certain brain cells that have been discovered in the brains of humans and monkeys. These special neurons help us relate to one another and share social experiences.[9] When we talk about "reading people," the clusters of mirror neurons in our brains are the system that do so. Mirror neurons help us read faces, micro-expressions, and even seemingly imperceptible energetics to help us understand the experiences of other people. They even aid in our ability to predict another person's actions based on their mental states. Not only does our brain's mirroring system read the intentions and feelings of others for the purpose of keeping us safe, it also enhances empathic attunement and interpersonal connection.

Consider watching someone else experience something (maybe enjoying a decadent ice cream cone, or tripping over a rock and nose diving into the mud). Perhaps you salivate at the thought of ice cream or cringe at the thought of stumbling face-first into the mud. Watching sappy romantic comedies has the same effect when you feel warmth in your heart in response to two charmingly awkward actors falling in love. Thanks to your mirror neurons, an on-screen romance can activate feelings of love within you, too. In the same way, witnessing a car accident can result in your own elevated blood pressure and stress response. These internal reactions derive from your mirror neurons, and they activate a sense of vicarious experience within you in response to the happenings of others. Though such relatability is best felt in real time, visualization, memory, and characters from books or movies can all elicit powerful mirror neuron responses.

Mirror neurons allow us to notice if the person we are talking to enjoys our company, seems distracted, or wants to bolt. They support our discernment about whether a person is trustworthy or compatible. Perhaps one of the greatest gifts of mirror neurons is that they help us experience empathy and compassion that lead to strong social bonding, and even guide our behavior to enhance connection and intimacy. Mirror neurons are undoubtedly valuable for social belonging and deep connection, but there's a dark side too. When our mirror neurons perceive that certain relationships require actions, behaviors, belief systems, or forms of connection that feel incongruous with our personal integrity, an inner dilemma can develop.

Consider this example: Jean spent a week gossiping cruelly to anyone who would listen about a neighbor who embarrassingly cried about her divorce during the ladies' weekly mahjong game. When Jean bumped into Emily at her mailbox and started gossiping about their neighbor's emotional meltdown, Emily's mirror neurons responded by sending the message: *Jean is warm and friendly when we gossip together, so I should gossip with her so that she will like me and I'll earn continued belonging with her.* Meanwhile, Emily's high-integrity heart space sent her the message: *Gossiping is out of alignment with my values, and when I gossip I self-abandon. My relationship with Jean is conditional upon behaviors like gossip, and therefore not a true friendship.* What's a girl to do when one system says one thing and another says something different? Well, it depends. If Emily had committed to high-integrity living, she would respond by not participating in gossip, and gently shifting the topic of conversation. If Emily had not begun inner work on integrity, she very well might listen to her mirror neurons and later notice an icky feeling within herself resulting from abandoning her values.

Offering: Write about an experience where your mirror neurons took precedence over your heart space and you behaved out of alignment with your integrity for social acceptance.

Next, write about an experience when you overrode your mirror neurons with your high-integrity heart space and behaved in accordance with your values despite the possibility of social rejection.

Mirror neurons grant humans (and monkeys) the profound ability to attune to one another. This includes feeling compassion, empathy, and sympathy. It is possible to live in integrity with these mechanisms by learning to access such heart-centered relational perspectives without losing ourselves in them and abandoning our True North. Due to the inter-related nature of empathy, compassion, and sympathy, I want to offer my definitions for each in response to a friend who lost her son to suicide:

Empathy is your ability to feel what you imagine another person feels. An empathic response to your friend's loss might be to feel the heartbreak and pain within your own body that you imagine your friend must feel, possibly to the extent of being overwhelmed. This includes not only emotional pain and grief, but also physical responses such as decreased appetite, lethargy, tearfulness, etc.

Compassion is feeling warmth and openheartedness toward another person without drowning in the feelings you imagine they must feel. Compassion includes the emotional resonance of empathy, but with added mindfulness to remember that the experience you are witnessing is not happening to you. A compassionate response to your friend would be a caring swell of your heart, an experience of softness and sadness for her, and an offering of whatever support you can give without self-abandoning.

Sympathy is a detached experience toward the pain and suffering of another person that acknowledges their hardship as exclusively theirs and does not open your heart to them in any real way. Where empathy says *I feel what you feel,* and compassion says, *I witness your experience and honor it with love,* sympathy says, *I feel badly for you from a distance.* A sympathetic response to your friend would be saying that you are sorry for her loss, and then moving along.

Though sympathy offers a detached response to another person's pain, please understand that you don't need to settle for sympathy in order to maintain high-integrity boundaries with another person. You can feel compassionate warmth toward a person who is not a perfect fit for you integrity-wise by remaining mindful of the difference between their experience and yours. It is my goal to access compassion for all humans on Earth, regardless of their shortcomings and wrongdoings (I'm still working on this). The heart is a bold and resilient organ, and it can emit expansive love, even if you choose not to develop a close relationship with every person in your orbit. Practice feeling softness when you witness another person, even if you do not build a friendship with them or swoop in to rescue them from a sticky situation (this isn't your job anyway).

As human beings, we were gifted complex emotional systems (including mirror neurons) because attunement is an important part of being a person. Let yourself feel the relatability of this complex human experience without feeling obligated to nurture relationships with every person you feel compassion for. Practice feeling joy for the person who got the job promotion you wanted but were unqualified for. See if you can feel compassion for your son's friend whose grades declined because of his learning disability. Recognizing the interconnectedness of all human experience, and then discerning which relationships to invest further emotional energy into is a healthy practice. Holding such boundaries with yourself will give you more energy and internal resources to further develop the relationships that do feel aligned for you—most importantly, your relationship with your Self. High-integrity living requires that you understand the tipping point between compassionate attunement and inauthenticity based on compulsive caregiving, emotional codependency, and chaotic emotional regulation. If you witness a person navigating difficult emotional territory, and you are clear that they are not an aligned person for you to be in deep relationship with, send them a love bubble from your heart, and move on. Do not remain stuck in unhealthy dynamics with other people because your mirror neurons relate to their suffering.

Offering: If you have ever experienced this type of relational dynamic influenced by mirror neurons, jot some notes about it in your journal.

In the same ballpark as mirror neurons is my *mirror theory of relationships*, which assumes that all people are made of the same stuff (psycho-emotionally speaking). Despite our unique experiences, we all operate from the same basic ingredients, so we will inevitably see ourselves in one another—for better or worse. I teach my clients that relationships are like mirrors, and the world is a giant mirror room that constantly reflects qualities of ourselves back toward us depending on whom and what we are exposed to. If you react negatively toward someone else, it means that they display a trait or behavior you recognize and have identified within yourself as undesirable. When you feel attraction or resonance with another person, it is because they reflect qualities you enjoy about yourself or want more of in your life. Here are a few examples of how this can look:

A person who prizes creativity and innovation (and sees these qualities as desirable) might react to an artistic person like this: *I love that person's creativity! Their expansive mind! Their patience to learn and develop creative skills!*

A person who believes they must always be selfless in order to earn love, and thus gives externally to the point of depletion, might react to a person who prioritizes their own needs like this: *That person is so selfish! Who do they think they are? Don't they ever think of anyone but themselves?*

A person consumed by loneliness and the longing to be loved might react to an available (though misaligned) romantic date like this: *They're not perfect, but I can find things to love about them. I'll make this work. More important than whether I like them is whether they like me.*

Your reactions and responses about other people offer valuable information about your own internal state. In truth, when you feel triggered by another person, it isn't them who triggers you—it is your association with the quality or trait they are embodying *as it lives within you* that feels intolerable. If you were familiar with your disdain for that irritating quality within yourself, you would have no reason to reject it in another. When you live in awareness of the unhealed, yearning, and bias parts of yourself that are reflected back to you by others, you can more easily take accountability for the projections you subscribe to your relationships. By taking ownership of your patterns, wounds, and favoritisms with this work, authentic relationships become both more appealing and more accessible. You can release the expectation for your relationships to mirror back ideal reflections of yourself and open the door for more diversity and integrity in your life. When you free your relationships from needing to reinforce your limited beliefs of your own worth and value, you allow them to nurture and contribute to your life in beneficial ways.

Offering: In your journal, write a list of at least three of your biggest relational triggers.

Next, explore through writing how these triggers say more about YOU than about THEM.

Now that we have discussed the sovereignty and joy linked with high-integrity living, I feel compelled to issue one gentle caution: There is a price to pay for the freedom granted by living with high integrity—sometimes a large price, depending on how misaligned your life has become. When you align with integrity, you truly open yourself to all that you could dream of and desire, but the facets of your life that are incongruous with your integrity cannot join you. Martha Beck says[10] *burn everything but the truth,* and it can be quite devastating to do so. But that doesn't mean you shouldn't do it. If you are truly on board for deep integrity work, you must enter into it with your eyes wide open. You must be willing to stir things up and say goodbye to aspects of your life—including people, communities, career paths, belief systems, and behavioral habits—that do not support the truth of who you are. This is going to be uncomfortable for a while because misaligned aspects of life do not appreciate the tectonic shift that comes from realigning with integrity. You must be willing to hold your self-commitment in your heart as your highest priority while the storm of angry people, accusing voices, judgmental systems, and rickety belief structures collapse around you.

Don't worry—you will undoubtedly survive the hurricane, and you will discover rich potential for rebuilding without false structures looming around you and blotting out your light. Just know that there is a phoenix rising period inherent with this work, and it is absolutely and completely worth it.

CHAPTER 10

Making Stuff

What Creativity's Got to Do With It

We will not starve for lack of wonders
but for lack of wonder.
—*HARRY MCQUEEN, "SUPERNOVA"*

WHAT DOES CREATIVITY HAVE TO DO WITH LIVING A RADI-
ant life? Lots. Why, you may be wondering? (Specifically
those of you self-proclaimed non-creatives back there in the
corner—I'm talking directly to you). Creativity is absolutely
essential because it is one of the main ingredients in a truly
authentic life, and authenticity is the main ingredient in a
radiant one. If creativity is not part of your life, you're not
living authentically or radiantly. Period. For every single one
of us. How do I know? Because creativity is built into our
genome and always has been since our earliest ancestors
made stuff with whatever mud, blood, sticks, or bones they
had access to.

Most people who identify as *non-creative* simply forgot
their creativity, along with their lunchboxes, somewhere in

the realm of grade school. Early childhood is the time when many people shut down their precious creative pipeline and buy into whatever they think will earn them what they most want at that time. Friends? Safety? Belonging? Money? You name it.

Offering: How do you feel about creativity and yourself as a creative person? Thoughtfully consider this, or write about it in your journal.

As a board-certified art therapist, I inherently believe in our ability to heal through art and other creative processes. The field of art therapy is based on this belief, and it has now been confirmed by science[1] that creative expression heals our brains and nervous systems. In art therapy, a person can move their internal energy, feelings, and expressions outwardly through a creative endeavor (with art materials of all kinds) that allows for release and repair. Both the process of creating art and the product we make hold immense power to reflect insight, provide safe containment, and foster emotional healing. In addition to art therapy, other creative therapies include dance and movement therapy, music therapy, play therapy, and wilderness therapy. These methodologies provide similar benefits of healing, repair, processing, and introspection through their various tools and teachings.

When I studied art therapy in graduate school, I learned that people's art ability stalls at the point in time when they stop engaging it.[2] If Tom stops painting pictures of zoo animals at age ten, this is where it stops for him—well, until it starts again. If he stops painting in fifth grade, maybe in humiliated reaction to some awful art teacher's judgment (you wouldn't believe how many people have early memories of painful experiences with art teachers), when he picks up a paint brush in his thirties, he'll be right at that same developmental level of creativity he was at when he was ten and expressed in that particular way.

It makes sense, doesn't it? What else would you expect to happen when you don't use a muscle. In fact, we're lucky our creative muscles simply pause and lie hibernating in wait until we return to them rather than atrophying completely. Bottom line, we're all creative on some level of our being, and it's a massive disservice to your authentic expression of Self to shut creativity down. Part of stepping into a radiant life is shaking awake the dormant creature of your creative mind, body, and soul and calling it back to you. *Hello, old creative friend. Yawn and stretch, dust yourself off, and let's get you back on board!*

When I talk about creativity, I am speaking about the infinite library of creative pursuits available to all of us, not only those that use the traditional art supplies from your local supermarket (though these certainly count as creative tools if they light you up). Painting or drawing, collage, playing music, singing, dancing, building business models, brainstorming travel itineraries, gardening, and cooking are some common creative modalities, but there are endless ways to be creative. Consider the creativity it takes to craft a new algorithm, the inspiration required to construct a company, or even the ingenuity needed to devise an organizational system for your socks and underwear in their impossibly tiny drawer. Creative potential surrounds you on all sides, if only you allow yourself to see it and remember how to access it. Then it's like the old adage of riding a bike. You always knew how to be creative, you just forgot that you knew.

A client of mine, Josephine, continually declined my creative therapeutic offerings, proclaiming that she was not an artist. For two sessions while we sat and talked, and I became increasingly aware that Josephine was deeply creative—just not in a sense she had initially defined as so. Each session Josephine spoke (almost unconsciously) about the elaborate cakes and cupcakes she made for her children. Josephine embodied such delight when she talked about baking that her face lit up and her voice seemed to sing while she recalled the vibrant colors and imagery of her decadent desserts. It was obvious to me that Josephine had developed an effective creative outlet with her baking, but when I reflected this observation to Josephine, she initially shot it down. *Oh no, my baking is just for fun. Those aren't serious artistic endeavors. They are just silly cakes.* It took only a few more sessions for Josephine to recognize and take ownership of the unique way her creativity manifested. Once she was able to do so, Josephine enjoyed even more fulfillment from her baking because she recognized it as the imaginative expressive process it truly had been all along.

Offering: Jot down at least five creative methods you already use or are willing to try. Think outside the box, and get expansive in your imaginings of creativity.

My two elementary-aged children constantly remind me of the natural flowing channel of creativity in childhood. It's astounding and unbelievable how many pieces of artwork they bring home from school. There are not enough shoeboxes and folders in an Office Depot store to house all the creative makings of a child. Some of what comes home in my kids' backpacks are well developed pieces of artwork, while many others are creative projects that were abandoned halfway through. Still others boast squiggles and sequins from creative friends who were conveniently seated next to my kids.

The point is this: Kids create naturally, abundantly, and without consideration of limits or judgments. They are not attached to final products, nor do they stress unduly over comparisons between one another. If they like what they made, they bring it home to show it off. If they kinda-sorta like their creation, they toss it into their backpack too, for good measure. When kids make something they don't like, they brush it aside and move along. Little ones create this way because it feels good, because it feels right to move energy through themselves in an expressive way. That's it. No need to attach and judge every piece, or even keep it. They create for the simple act of creation, and you can, too.

Elizabeth Gilbert, in her book *Big Magic,* writes about the musician Tom Waits and what he believes to be true about his creative process. She writes how Waits reportedly thinks of songwriting as making jewelry for the inside of other peoples' minds—a kind of decoration for the imagination. When I first read this, I stopped in my tracks and reread it a few more times. I love the visual of bedazzling the interior of our minds with our creative pursuits. Even if you're only decorating your own mind and no one else's, this is the magic of creativity.

When you allow yourself to come into resonance with your creative process, regardless if it is underwater basket weaving or devising magic tricks with paper doves from your pockets, you become more yourself. A radiant life includes the integration of the creativity within you that has always been there and desperately longs to be set free into your life.

It can be a hobby or pastime that you enjoy for no other purpose than the expression it offers you. It doesn't have to be your vocation or career path, though every career can and does most certainly benefit from an infusion of creativity. In any way you can, by whatever means possible, just create. If you think of creative engagement as decorating your imagination, or extending bedazzlement into the imaginations of others, it can take any shape, form, feeling, passion, action, message, or expression you like. As my neighbor Joe says, "There's an ass for every seat." The same applies to creativity. Whomever you may be, there's at least one form of creative expression (likely more than one) that will fit for you and light you up. It doesn't matter what you create, who you create for, or even if you create for anyone outside yourself. In the realm of creativity, not much matters in terms of what/how/why/how much/how fancy. Just make stuff—with your hands, your mind, your heart.

ART AS THERAPY

I have been making stuff for as long as I can remember. My creative drive may have been influenced by my Dad's skillful ability to sculpt stone or my grandmother's love of color and floral painting, but artistic expression was one of my earliest passions. Somewhere along the way, making art became more than just the development of a pretty picture. I learned firsthand about the therapeutic effects of artmaking long before I pursued a career as a board-certified art therapist, so that made it a no-brainer career path when the time came to choose. From quite a young age, stacks of black sticker-covered sketchbooks lined the shelves of my bedroom, and one was always on my person wherever I roamed. These days, whether you find yourself in the dentist's waiting room or on the evening commuter train, most people can be seen in deep engagement with some absorbing app or email on their smart phone. I was exactly like that, but instead of a screen, I had my face buried in one of my sketchbooks. My medium of choice for sketchbook art was black rollerball pens, which I fondly called *juicy pens* in tribute to their luxuriously smooth yet precise ink tip. At the rate and frequency I drew, I probably went through at least a pen per week. I'm sure juicy pens were an anticipated and accounted-for budget item in my household. Unlike my friends and fellow art students, I didn't draw pictures of people, animals, landscapes, media icons, or fantasy scenes. I had my own particular style of design I lovingly called *professional doodles*, because there really wasn't another way to describe them. I was a master of patterns, and I had an uncanny ability to uniquely puzzle together intricate lines, shapes, and design systems in ways that amounted to one-of-a-kind abstract images (see figure 10.1). Over time, I played with adding bits of collage paper, wisps of accent color, and even sewing golden thread into my images to add dimensionality, but it was black lines and patterns for a very long time.

I always understood that my doodles were a bit strange and definitely uncommon, but there was a specific feeling I experienced in my body and soul when I made them that I needed at that time. They felt authentic to where I was on my journey, even before I knew what authentic meant. When my various art teachers in high school, college, and graduate school required me to sketch a portrait, paint a landscape, or use charcoal for a figure drawing, I obligingly complied before returning to my sketchbook doodles as soon as class was dismissed. My drawings were intimately important to me in ways I was unaware of until well into

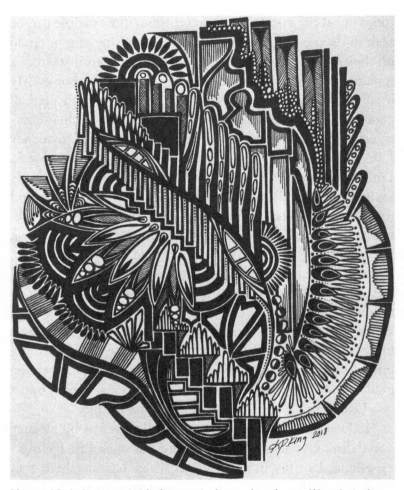

Figure 10.1. I created this image during a time in my life when the world seemed quite black and white, and I was in need of the type of rigidity and structure it provided for my psyche. At that time, the clearly defined structure and form of images like this felt compartmentalized and contained, while simultaneously expressing my felt-need to keep things organized and in their proper places for my own safety.[3] Kate King, *Untitled*, 2018, pen and ink on paper, 8.5 x 11 in., Denver, Colorado.

Figure 10.2. This image was created during a time in my life when I had healed many of the deep childhood wounds and patterns that previously required strict containment and rigidity in my psyche. Notice the softness of lines and colors, as well as the flowing nature of this image. The image reflects my psychological comfort with softening and expanding my perception, and displays psycho-emotional safety.[4] Kate King, *Celestial Goddess*, 2021, gouache on paper, 9 x 12 in., Denver, Colorado.

young-adulthood when they spontaneously changed. I cannot pinpoint an exact date, but at some juncture I just stopped drawing my doodles and started making something new. I first explored with loose juicy pen lines across brilliantly colored backgrounds, then began creating vividly colorful images of animals, mystical creatures, and portraits. My new creative expressions morphed and changed over time, mostly exploring the realms of colored pencil and watercolor paints, and leaving the rigidity of black patterns behind (see figure 10.2).

Notice how different the two images above are: Image 1 reflects rigidity and containment with its limited color, tightly organized lines, and exquisite attention to detail. Figure 10.2 displays freer expression, softness, and blending. Being an art therapist, I understand that the visual transformation of my art through the years mirrors the metamorphosis I moved through in my life. My art reflects my healing and growth through time. As I courageously navigated powerful layers of introspection, inner exploration, and trauma healing within myself, old habituated parts of me loosened and became more free—and so did my line quality and imagery. The world did not seem quite so black and white anymore, and I felt definitively less compelled to depict it that way through my drawing. My healing had unwound decades of repressed emotions and psychological patterns that had been stowed away in the pages of my sketchbooks and the basement of my psyche. It suddenly became evident that the perfection, organization, and rigidity of my doodles had served as a sophisticated coping mechanism that helped me hold it all together within myself and remain stable and coherent. For the longest time, I was so terrified of my own lived experiences and psychological layers that I kept them under lock and key within me; but like all energy, they had to come out somehow.

I will always remember a particular day when I was twenty-eight years old and in my third trimester of pregnancy with my first child. I sat on the carpeted floor of my home surrounded by stacks of black sketchbooks from years of doodling, and could do nothing but cry as I flipped through their seemingly endless pages. I had finally reached a level of healing at that point where I was able to see my sketchbook expression for what it was: a trauma response. My expansive awareness of the emotional repression and desperate coping that had been channeled into those bound sketchbooks nearly broke my heart. On the other hand, my containment process for the emotional burdens and pain I had carried struck me as quite magical—mystical, even. There was a definite awe to the way my sketchbooks had provided a safe holding space for the unhealed parts of myself to safely dwell until I was ready to heal them. My authentic Self had been wisely guiding my pen to take care of me at the level I could tolerate. Drawing like this provided the essential structure and containment I undeniably required during those many challenging years. The type of art therapy I had unknowingly practiced for all those years is what art therapists call *Art as Therapy*. This is the branch of art therapy that believes the process of creating art (with no other therapeutic interventions) is healing. *Art as Therapy* is distinctly different from *Art as Psychotherapy*, which is a branch of art therapy that combines creative expression and therapeutic intervention such as analysis, processing, and intentional inner-work to access psychotherapeutic healing and growth.

In time, I grew into an *Art as Psychotherapy* approach with my creative expression. Using art therapy and other methodologies, I followed the healing path of my inner journey and came into closer contact with the wounded parts of myself that had yearned for healing. I met strong and resilient aspects of my authentic Self that I had no idea were available to me. With each layer of healing, I came to know my true essence more intimately, and I learned to trust my process of healing in ways that had been previously unimaginable. I am eternally grateful for those voluminous black pebble-textured sketchbooks and the space they held for me to support myself through creative expression. I cannot imagine who I might have become, what I might have done with my pain and trauma, or where I might have turned for coping without them. I am certain they saved my life.

ART AS PSYCHOTHERAPY—A PARTS PERSPECTIVE

As you know from previous chapters, my work is influenced by the Internal Family Systems (IFS) model, and it has also influenced the way I use art therapy. I have devised a creative process that incorporates parts work in methodology that is not affiliated with IFS. I call this process *Parts Cards*. Parts Cards are circular pieces of cardstock (or any shape the creator prefers—I prefer circles) about the size of an outstretched hand that have imagery on one side and writing on the other. Both sides of a card process a person's perception of and experience of a particular part of themselves. On the side with imagery, creative materials such as magazine cutouts, different colored papers, or drawing/painting are used to depict the visual sense of a part. If the part feels cold, distant, and harsh, the imagery might reflect such experiences with icy colors, jagged lines, and photo depictions of icebergs or affectless faces. Below are two examples of my own Parts Cards that display my personal depiction of two of my parts: *The Judge*[5] and *The Cocoon*.[6]

On the reverse side of each Parts Card, writing is used to bring words to the description of the part. For the example above about a cold, distant, harsh part, the written portion might say, *I am ice and stone. My heart is covered by a frozen layer that cannot be punctured. Do not come near me or you will freeze alongside me. I have been here for so long, I cannot remember how my circumstances originated.* On the written side of my personal Parts Cards shared above (*The Judge* and *The Cocoon*), I developed the following character descriptions of my parts. Keep in mind that these are my individual descriptions of these parts, and if you experience such parts within yourself, you may relate to them in similar or different ways. The beauty of Parts Cards is that we can each creatively express our own perceptions, relationships, and experiences with our parts. This allows for infinite descriptions, depictions, and expressive potential. Here are mine:

The Judge: The Judge prides himself on his decision-making abilities. He has an impeccable sense of right and wrong, and he could find True North with his eyes closed. Growing up in a family with eight children fostered a sense of chaos and disorganization that often left him in the pickle of having a pair of socks that didn't match in color or size. When he was old enough to move out and get a job, The Judge committed himself to a life of organization and clarity. One by one he removed all colors from his life, and then set to work on each shade of gray. Now The Judge takes solace in his black and white world, always finding that

Figure 10.3. This Parts Card represents *The Judge.* Kate King, *The Judge*, 2021, collage on paper, 5 in. round, Denver, Colorado.

Figure 10.4. This Parts Card represents *The Cocoon*. Kate King, *The Cocoon*, 2021, collage on paper, 5 in. round, Denver, Colorado.

things can be understood when they are compartmentalized. Each pair of socks is properly matched when black and white are the only options. The Judge sometimes visits with his siblings, who cannot seem to find anything to talk to him about. Friendships are much the same, ending quickly after they begin. Even so, The Judge is mostly content in his world and pleased with the ease of binary thinking.

The Cocoon: I am your haven. Your safe, cozy nest. It is my joy to cradle you in my soft feathery warmth. You can rest and revitalize in my embrace, and no one can hurt you. There is no need for walls with me; you need no façade. Come into my arms exactly as you are, in whatever state you're in, and I will hold you. With me, there is no pressure to stay, no expiration date by which time you must leave. You decide how long you remain in my soft embrace. When you do not need me to hold you, I stand behind you. I am here to provide you with the buffer you need, the containment you seek, and the solace you crave. With me, you are both held and free. I am always with you.

By using both visual imagery and writing, Parts Cards combine two powerful creative methods to bring the presentation, voice, intentions, and wounding of a part to the forefront for our observation and attention. It is evident from my examples that all parts have their functions, as well as their extremes. When I witness my parts from the perspective of Self, I can honor their role in my system and understand their efforts to protect and care for me. I can witness each part with curiosity and compassion, and intentionally make necessary shifts to the understanding my parts hold about their roles in my system.

My personal collection of Parts Cards extends far beyond fifty different cards that each explore unique parts of myself. Some of my Parts Cards identify archetypes that exist within the collective unconscious of all of us, as Carl Jung taught.[7] These include: the wounded child, the martyr, the mother, and the villain. Other Parts Cards are qualities of myself that may be less universal, such as: the scientist, the introvert, the lineage, the teenager, the performer, and so on. New Parts Cards can be created any time you recognize aspects of yourself that you wish to work with in more depth. There is no wrong way to do this creative work. I continue to regularly create new Parts Cards when I encounter new layers of myself, and I enjoy integrating them with the parts I have been long familiar with. I have gained immeasurable insight and healing through this process, and my clients have expressed similar benefit from their own engagements with this process.

Offering: Think about three parts you would like to create Parts Cards about. Then create them!

Once you begin working with Parts Cards, it becomes easier to unblend and form healthy internal relationships between Self and parts in the service of healing, repair, and growth. The physical depiction of Parts Cards will help you remember that you are more than your parts, even if their energy strongly courses through you at times. You are an entire universe of embodied human life. Recognizing your parts can help you understand that they are only elements of you, not all of who you are. With this perspective, you will not become over-identified and attached to any particular part (or parts). You will learn to see your parts as participants in the complexity of your human experience. When you return to Self by witnessing a part through the objective, compassionate process of making Parts Cards, you open limitless possibility for the development of your psyche, soul, and consciousness.

The Parts Cards directive also provides an opportunity to use your physical cards as tangible points of reference when engaging inner work. For example, Phillip used this process in his work with perfectionism. He created a perfectionist card, as well as two other Parts Cards that functioned in dynamic with his perfectionist part: fear and insecurity. Phillip used the tangibility of his Parts Cards to illustrate the dynamic between parts by placing the cards on a table in physical relationship to one another. Phillip's perfectionist part served to manage his fear part by covering it up so that his insecure part could feel safe. To demonstrate this visually, Philip placed the perfectionist card on top of the fear card to obscure it, and then placed the insecurity card close beside the perfectionist card for safety. This allowed Phillip to visually experience the relationship of these three parts to understand how his system functioned to protect him. Phillip was then able to work with each part and better understand why it carried the energy it did. Using the visual imagery, written description, and physical expression of his Parts Cards, Phillip was able to gain clarity and work toward creating more harmony in his system.

CREATE YOUR WORLD
Just like my sketchbooks did for me, Parts Cards can serve as a powerful container to both hold and explore the energetics of wounding, resistance, healing, and growth. Creative methods like these can set a process of inner-alchemy in

motion that helps us navigate our journeys toward evolution, expansion, and radiance. In the ancient scientific art of alchemy, practitioners purportedly discovered scientific mechanisms that successfully turned lead into gold. When applied to our emotional landscape, alchemy represents a powerful metaphor for the way creativity (of all kinds) can transform the dullness and inefficiency within us into something vibrant and alive. Even when it doesn't appear to be, stagnation is a choice. Human beings are not meant to remain unfulfilled, clouded, and musty; we have magnificent souls, and we are meant to shine. To achieve the splendor our authentic Selves understand to be our birthright, we must take action. Whether by means of the tiniest nudge or the most billowing sweep, we can invoke alchemy in our lived experiences by using our creative potential to fuel and propel us toward vitality, congruence, and brilliance in our participation with life.

No other person can wield your path for you. Despite your potential yearning for such an experience, or tempting advertisements that sell gravy trains, you must create your own adventure. Your incarnation here on Earth is entirely and completely your own. This is true even if you have effortfully imitated the life of someone you admire, or if you feel your life has been shaped and affected by the forceful sculpting of some powerful external force or person. No matter how you slice it, when you get down to the essential question of *Who am I and what have I come here to do?* you inevitably discover that no one but yourself can answer that question. For better or worse, you are the only one inside yourself. This means you are actively (either consciously or unconsciously) creating the life you are living. If that's not creativity, I don't know what is.

Breath by breath, cell by tiny cell, your body, mind, and life are created by you and only you. Luckily for us, there are guides and helpers along the way like authenticity and integrity that can steer us back into contact with our essential creative power when we drift aimlessly apart from its source energy. The fact that creative energy exists palpably and undeniably within each living being on Earth brings me to my next point: Yes, you create your lived experience, and in addition to the large-scale creation of your life, you are also given personalized flavors of creativity that manifest in various expressions. This is where the artmaking, writing, meaningful movement, musical creation, theatrical expression, synergy with nature, and playful splashing in mud puddles comes in.

THE CREATIVITY/SPIRITUALITY CONNECTION

As the vibrant and expansive human beings we are, we embody many facets of creative expression. One such facet is spirituality. For the purpose of this book, when I discuss *spirituality,* I'm not talking about religion. Though religion can hold spiritual qualities depending on how it is practiced, the essence of spirituality I am speaking about is nondenominational and inherent within every human being regardless of their religious affiliation. The joining together of creativity and spirituality acts as another type of compass that returns us to our radiant lives and helps guide our lived experiences toward the anchor of our unique potential. Spirituality is integral in our personal navigation system as we move through life, and it is also an essential aspect of how we connect with nature and forces larger than ourselves.

I will always remember an impactful teaching I received during the year I was a freshman in college. That year, three

Tibetan monks visited the theology school on my campus to construct a massive sand mandala. It took the three monks several weeks of pouring tiny grains of colored sand through small metal straws into strategically placed sections within the giant mandala circle before they finally completed a strikingly detailed and colorful masterpiece. If you have never seen a sand mandala, take a moment to search for it online so that you understand the skill and mastery required to execute such a project. At the end of their weeks of creative work, I imagined the monks would pour resin over the sand to make it into a durable item they could keep, sell, or hang on an enormous wall as art—but they did no such thing. Without even taking so much as a photograph of their work, the monks promptly acquired small brooms and dustpans and got to work sweeping their beautiful design away. What was exquisite artwork only moments prior quickly became a large pile of colored dust to be thrown in the garbage. But why? Impermanence, that's why.

The monks modeled an important spiritual lesson with their creativity in those weeks: nothing lasts. No matter how beautiful they may be, and how hard we worked to create them, all things eventually return to dust. I appreciate the monks' teachings about impermanence through creativity because it allows for color, art, beauty, and heartfelt expression to be the vehicle for experiencing life rather than an end product that requires our attachment. Creativity for the sake of creativity is the point, not creativity for the sake of a frameable piece of artwork. And the same is true for spirituality: our connection within, through, and beyond ourselves to the soul of life and the energies around us does not have an end goal. It is about our practice and presence while we engage with it.

In Buddhist teachings, the word *metta* means *loving kindness*. In spiritual pop culture, the word *meta* means taking an expansive view beyond the limited Self to encompass all that is. I like to piggyback *metta* and *meta* to demonstrate the potential our creative capacity has to offer loving kindness on a large scale that reaches far beyond ourselves. When we make stuff—be it a sand mandala, musical record, or website—we dip into an infinite well of creativity that holds massive potential to express, connect, evoke, and share. If connecting our Selves to the collective is not one of the main purposes for life on Earth, I don't know what is. And the melding of spirituality with creativity is one potent method for engaging that most crucial work.

Offering: Write about at least three components of both spirituality and creativity in your journal. Then explore how spirituality and creativity can coexist in your life.

One beautiful reality I know to be true that always heartens me when I feel lost and uninspired is that creativity is not something that can be lost. Its energetic language is embedded in our cells, and has been since the inception of humankind. Our great ancestors did not paint on cave walls, sculpt from tree branches and bone, dance, drum, and chant for nothing. They were divinely called to these mechanisms of creative expression because it was an undeniable expression of their very being on a soul level. It was the outward presentation of the energetic pulse of life that coursed within them. Subsequent generations have moved farther away from the origins of human creativity, but the cellular memory epigenetically shared between generations remembers.

You see, creativity is never lost. We simply forget about its presence, and thus drift into the waters of rigidity, conformity, and the dull monotony of a life without creativity's active inclusion. Back to those of you who identify as non-creatives, I invite you now to courageously explore the well of creativity lying in wait within you; discover the reservoir waiting for your return into alignment with it, and activate its gifts in your life. Your potential may hold a simple series of lines to be jotted on paper, or even a masterpiece waiting to be born. Regardless of the shape your unique creativity takes, it is nonetheless undeniably present. It may have rested dormant beneath the layers of your conditioning while you meandered the surface above trying desperately to fit the mold you believed you needed to fit in your world. You may have spent years or decades constructing the life you hoped would bring you to that illusive place you thought you wanted to be. Only upon reflection of your series of conquests might you realize that something crucial was missing: The color. The breath of vitality. The hum of resonance. The spark that is creativity.

If you find yourself solemnly nodding your head in recognition, you have just discovered one of the main culprits in your life's misalignment. Congratulations! Now you can begin to intentionally lay the necessary stepping stones toward your radiant life. Creativity has been the missing ingredient. Once you return its influence to your life, you will be mystified that you ever lived without it.

Wholeness and Self-Led Living

Making the Shift

I HAVE ALWAYS THOUGHT OF CURIOSITY AS AUTHENTICITY'S wingman. Curiosity is the little glow in the corner of your system that asks small questions (the unassuming kind) and tends to lead toward unexpected realizations and insights. As poet and philosopher David Whyte said,[1] "Asking beautiful questions shapes a beautiful mind." Inquiry such as this forms your identity as much by asking the question as it does by having it answered. This is because questions tend to elicit answers in their likeness. When we investigate new territory with our questions, we often find ourselves learning and developing in unfathomable ways. Curiosity's magic lies in its lightheartedness.

Curiosity is like a smirking quiet person in the background, always watching and observing details, but staying far away from drama. Curiosity laughs quietly to itself and moves through the world with a certain buoyancy. It is perceptive and nimble, and it's an underrated ally you may not even know you have. Open your mind, be light, and bring the soft interested energy of curiosity closer to your consciousness. Notice more expansively who you are beneath all the white noise of expectation and conditioning. Allow a new depth of your authenticity to float to the surface and reveal itself in the warm glow of your curiosity. No pressure cooker or rigid checked boxes are necessary when playing with curiosity—just safe, fun, spacious wonderment that notices what you may not have previously recognized as You.

Offering: Close your eyes and activate curiosity. Scan your mind, body, and heart. What do you notice? Write or draw about your experience if it tickles your fancy.

Elizabeth Gilbert, in her book *Big Magic,* talks about following curiosity like a clue in a scavenger hunt. I like to think of it more as the pursuit of a thread of fairy lights where each small leap of curiosity brings you to a gleaming new insight or discovery about who you are. As you continue along the illuminated thread, you will undoubtedly notice endless additional glimmers yet to be discovered in the facets that make you so uniquely and undeniably yourself.

Curiosity holds a certain quiet strength that can powerfully initiate you into the realms of authentic Self-discovery. In the therapeutic modality of Internal Family Systems (IFS),[2] what is simply called *Self* is the IFS term for what I have been calling the *authentic Self* or *essential Self.* IFS founder Richard Schwartz talks about a group of eight core qualities that he defines as the *8 C's of Self Energy.* Can you guess what's on that list? You betcha: curiosity. Alongside curiosity are the qualities of compassion, creativity, clarity, connectedness, courage, calm, and confidence. There are five additional attributes to Self in IFS as well, called *the 5 P's*: playfulness, patience, presence, perspective, and persistence.

The point of these numerous C's and P's is to highlight the most engrained and fundamental qualities of who we are at our most essential level. Beyond the collective existence of such qualities within all people, what makes each individual authentic in relationship to these C's and P's are the dynamic ways they manifest inside every unique Self. My expression of compassion is not the same as your expression of compassion, or perspective, or curiosity. We each harness and channel our authentic Selves in the way we shine our C's and P's out into the world. It is key to understand that these qualities are not lying in wait within a one-size-fits-all super buffet. They are not monotonous ingredients that lifelessly contribute to a supreme math equation defining how to know yourself. C's and P's are more like guidelines that point each of us toward closer investigation of our unique expression of living. Just as flower genes can be intermingled and merged in countless ways to create new hybrid versions of that blossom, so it goes with the inimitable mixture of C's and P's that exist within each of our authentic Selves. The more we tap into our special flavor of authentic expression, the richer, more diverse, and more colorful our communities grow from the diversity we express within them.

YOUR PERSONAL GENIUS

Philosopher and civil rights leader Howard Thurman said, "Don't ask what the world needs. Ask what makes you come alive, and go do it. Because what the world needs is people who have come alive." The thing that makes each of us come alive is so specific, profound, and brilliant, it cannot be duplicated. Nobody can tell you what alights your soul. The desperate callings of our hurting world cannot direct the mechanism through which you activate your spark. Each of the billions of souls on Earth possesses a unique magic that has the capacity to light them up from deep within and expand their potent energy outward as their exceptional individual gift.

If you're reading this thinking, *This is absolute hogwash! I don't have a gift. There's absolutely nothing exceptional and unique about me.* Think again, and go ahead and label that narrative a limiting belief. It is my deep knowing, beyond a shadow of a doubt, that each person has a particular *gift* or *genius* that uniquely drives and sustains them. Ancient Romans called this powerful aspect of Self *daimon*. No matter what you call it, this is your special sauce, your brilliance, the thing that probably comes easily to you and seems fun and inspiring while you're doing it. It's yours and yours alone, completely one of a kind. When you're present in your gift, you feel the undeniable ease of life flowing congruently through you. It's okay if you haven't finely honed in on what yours is yet. The beautiful pace of life allows for plenty of time to sense and notice all that exists within you.

One hang-up many people have when I invite them to start getting curious about their gift is a fear related to dipping into the scandalous territory of selfishness (or even narcissism) if they dare to speak a kind or complimentary word about themselves. This thought process loops back to the acculturated belief that we must ignore (and even degrade) ourselves while calling it "humility." In reality, this type of thinking blatantly avoids the loving embrace of our authentic Selves. A tipping point most certainly exists between owning your genius and inflating yourself with undeniable arrogance. Let's be clear about one thing: Speaking kindly about your talents and the qualities of your soul that bring joy, peace, healing, creativity, magic, and ingenuity into the world is not arrogant. Themes such as arrogance, selfishness, or narcissism come into play when a person hangs their talent over the heads of others; boasts their genius in a closed-minded manner without regard for its limitations or blind spots; uses their gifts to harm, demean, or manipulate others; or touts themselves as superior in an effort to hide their own perceived inadequacies. In such cases, narcissism and arrogance are not enemy forces; they simply shine light on areas within a person that still require healing.

Confidence is often a term that gets thrown into the pot with selfishness, arrogance, and narcissism, and, like all qualities, it exists on a spectrum. True confidence is a variation of this quality that each person can and should learn as they navigate *The Radiant Life Project* because it will become a great ally to you. True confidence is not linked to success or largeness, and it does not deflate when you fail or flail. Instead, true confidence is the deep commitment to Self that always remains in support of You and the goals and dreams you hold dear. This unwavering kind of self-love means that you always have your own back, and you do not give up on yourself when challenges arise. True confidence allows you to pivot, rebuild, reconsider, and continue moving toward a radiant life with such unconditional self-support that you feel a sense of both reliability and steadiness within your Self.

Integrating true confidence as you become familiar with your gifts, talents, or genius can help you navigate the discomfort that sometimes presents when you engage the wildly unfamiliar experience of bravely illuminating your brightest qualities of Self. For a person who has grown used to the dark, the light can feel startling and uncomfortable at first. So feel free to tiptoe into it if that makes you feel more at ease.

Offering: Start by noticing what you are good at. What do you do well? What comes easily to you? What have others told you you're good at, or admired about you? Ask yourself when you feel the unmistakable sensation of being in flow³ or in the zone. Write about what you come up with in your journal.

It's okay if your exploration is simple; you can get more specific and granular as you continue building familiarity with your gifts. Reflect on the impactful moments of your life and recall experiences where you felt energized, joyful, and peaceful. I remember playing as a child in the willows outside of my home and feeling a deep sense of connection to nature and magical play. Maybe for you there's a sensation of flow as you remember your place on your high school hockey team. Perhaps it's a certain zing you notice related to your ease with problem solving or creating algorithms. Let it come to you slowly, and take notes so you can build a list of the qualities embedded in your gift.

The *qualities embedded in your gift* are the components that join together to create the wholeness of your genius. Your gift is flexible and adaptable, and does not require adherence to a single career, activity, experience, or time of life. For example, the high school hockey player mentioned above might notice that some of the qualities of their gift include athletic ability, quick thinking, strategic planning, and group participation. When applied outside the rink, these qualities could shine brightly in business, coaching, or teaching. Also, please know that your gift is not set in stone and immobile. It is a living, ethereal aspect of you that grows and adapts throughout your life. So don't feel pressure to find the one-time definition of your genius on the spot and live with it forevermore. Let your gift show itself to you in its current definition, then give it plenty of space to stretch and grow in brilliantly unexpected ways.

When I got curious about my gift, this is what I discovered: Remember the kids' game that provides several different heads, bodies, and feet for the child to mix and match together to make different unique combinations? When I'm embodied in my gift, I'm able to do something similar in the service of healing. I can thoughtfully and effectively channel helpful and supportive resources through my mind/ soul when I am in contact with someone. I have immediate access to what I experience as an endless portal of resources, teachings, creative directives, tools, reflections, stories, inspirations, and healing methodologies stored inside myself, which I fondly call my *living library*. I also house a deep well of compassion combined with an ability to read between the lines, which allows me to see and sense what may not be obvious or spoken. I process information very quickly in the living library, and then intuitively funnel and organize on-point resources both verbally and energetically in the space of a heartbeat. I creatively assemble these collections into uniquely personalized mash-ups that can aid in a person's awareness, growth, and healing if they choose to integrate them.

For each person, learning to own their gifts and genius is a revolving door that tends to incorporate great variety and depth of insight. Due to the fact that human beings are not born with an instruction manual or preprogramming to activate their gifts for easy propulsion through life, the more we learn through direct experience, the greater our relationships with our gifts and genius grows to be. Sometimes the integration of a gift happens through easeful synchronicity; other paths of self-discovery are lined with potholes and landmines. This is where locks and keys come into play.

LOCKS AND KEYS

Locks need keys to open them, and they don't only exist in the physical world. Certain experiences, exposures, realizations, or insights can act as the necessary key to unlock layers of the Self that had remained undiscovered until that very moment. I call these *healing keys.* If you are reading this and conjuring a mental image of a shiny golden key perfectly aligning within a clearly discernable lock in your imagination, go ahead and erase that visual. The healing keys I'm speaking about may occasionally arrive in glossy packaging, but more often than not they present as deeply uncomfortable, inconvenient, awkward, and even painfully unwelcome visitors.

I've had several crucial healing keys that unlocked layers of my Self for release, introspection, and healing throughout my life thus far; the latest one being my infection with Covid-19 in 2022. Let me paint you a picture of the woman I was before contracting Covid: Throughout the entire pandemic, mine was one of the families on the super-bubbled end of the spectrum. My kids were in a *learning pod* with the children of another family, and my husband and I shut down all in-person contact with our businesses, families, and communities. We basically lived in an insulated little fear bubble that turned out to be quite cozy for my naturally introverted nature. I'm pretty sure my husband thought the safety measures we took were a little extreme, and I am grateful for the grace and compassion he offered me during a time when my triggers were highly ignited. Our safety bubble lasted for quite a while beyond the point where many families returned to in-person life, which intimately linked with the *health anxiety shark* I discussed in Chapter 8. Finally, we decided to reemerge into a lifestyle of in-person contact again, and just as I was starting to feel safe and sound behind the protection of my vaccines and the seemingly low case count reported by the Centers for Disease Control and Prevention, I got Covid.

Interestingly, my Covid infection coincided precisely with the last week of my private practice before I departed onto sabbatical, and the severity of my symptoms made it impossible for me to work until my predetermined end date. Sadly, I closed my doors a few days earlier than expected, and was not able to achieve closure with each of my clients as I had planned. I felt like I had crash landed into sabbatical in an inconvenient nose-dive aimed directly under my covers. Every molecule of my being understood that the powers that be, whomever they may be (I have absolutely no clue), pulled the plug in such a nonnegotiable way that I had absolutely no choice but to put a strong and sturdy halt to all things in my life—immediately. I needed a force field to collapse around me to finally give in and let go. You might think the interesting part of the experience ended there, but it did not.

Days into my illness, I found myself swaddled in a blanket and doused in my own tears as I surfed the highly uncomfortable waves of the deepest grief and heartbreak I have ever experienced. The crashing and swelling currents within me had nothing to do with my present illness, but instead carried long-past and far-forgotten imprints from my early years. Contracting Covid, after staving it off for so long, acted as an inconvenient healing key I didn't know I needed. My illness had provided the perfect ingredient to unlock a portal within me that had remained unknown until that moment. It was through this meaningful inner-entrance that I was able to tend to deep layers of my Self with the healing awareness I so desperately needed. Strange as it may sound, I do not believe I could gain access to those raw and vulnerable shades of my wounding until Covid unlocked them for me. Once the barrier I had so arduously held around myself crumbled, ripe and willing energies flooded through me like a river.

I share this with you in true and humble testament to the longevity and infinite journey that deep inner work truly is. It does not end; even when years, decades, and mountains of repair have been achieved. Healing keys have a funny way of showing up like powerful unexpected gusts of wind that unlock doors leading to more doors—thus uncovering new healing keys that lead to endless more doors in the process of deep spiritual healing and growth.

I am grateful for the generous support of my intimate family and friends, as well as the many privileged circumstances that contributed to my healing. With those resources within and around me, I was able to move through the doorway my experience had unlocked. I discovered inner child wounds I thought I had long ago healed related to feeling lovable and worthy of care. I came face to face with shades of health anxiety (some familiar, and others I had never before encountered), and I tenderly embraced and soothed them. I moved through portals of such radical self-honesty about my professional identity and career that my heart swelled to the surface of my chest like a balloon. I traversed deeply uncomfortable territory for a period, but ultimately the distress and discovery that paired with my unlocking was a gift. I was reminded that all flavors of living carry wisdom and growth opportunities—always and without exception.

My experience reminded me of the Sanskrit phrase *Upa Guru,*[4] which means *the teacher that is next to you at any moment.* Some spiritual circles refer to this phenomenon as *The School of Life* or *Earth School,* meaning that every challenge we face was placed on our path for the learning and evolution of our souls and consciousness. Hardship has a way of inducing massive elevation in the human psyche, consciousness, and spirit. It may not always be comfortable or easy, but surrendering to healing keys and the doors they unlock is always fruitful.

Offering: Take a moment to consider and write about some of your Upa Guru experiences.

RECOGNIZING HEALING KEYS AS SUCH

Not only do psychological and spiritual healing keys often lack shiny gloss, it can sometimes be difficult to grasp or even recognize them as the helpers they truly are. Frequently, keys of this kind seem like missteps; accidental mistakes, wrong decisions, hurtful experiences, or profound resistance. All of this is part of the genius embedded in the function of healing keys. If we recognize them at face value, the journey of learning from their wisdom is sorely diminished. Much of the benefit healing keys offer is derived from learning that the object of your greatest avoidance is actually a helpful aspect of your process. Difficult people, experiences, revelations, and encounters are not just teachers, they are entrances. Your job as a human being is to cultivate the courage to see them as such and seize the healing key despite your own resistance. You must reach through and beyond the mucky darkness and grasp the golden thread that leads toward your spiritual evolution to understand the prize you have unearthed. At first it may feel risky and uncertain, but when you stay the course, the experience will transform into one of clarity and confidence. You may sense an *a-ha!* associated with the discovery of your healing key, or it might resonate in your heart as a calm sense of knowing. Recognizing your experience as a healing key does not necessarily diminish the discomfort of opening the door—in my experience the swells of grief were massive and resounding despite my awareness that they were a meaningful portal—but understanding that you are navigating a key/portal experience allows for deeper trust that there is a meaningful purpose for your pain. These experiences bring the radiant life you deeply yearn for ever closer.

PARACHUTES

Similar to a key that opens doors for inner healing, parachutes are a powerful metaphor for navigating the sometimes-bumpy journey toward fully embracing your radiant life. I don't know about you, but change isn't my favorite thing. The realm of the known is familiar, comfortable, routine, and predictable. If you agree, you'll likely concur that the cold-turkey method of boldly stepping into the brand spankin' new frontier of uncharted territory evokes an impulse to swiftly curl into the fetal position and stay there forever. This is where parachutes come in.

The kind of *parachute* I am referring to is a mechanism you intentionally activate in your life to bridge the gap from *here* to *there*. Such a tool facilitates a gentle landing in the realm of your mysterious future. Parachutes are gracious helpers that keep you from violently smashing into the vast unknown by providing a transitory holding space. From the buoyant half-cocoon of your parachute, you can ensure that you are still in one piece after leaving where you were, source the necessary repair and nourishment to return to optimal functioning, and safely eyeball your landing. This can all happen while you continue the purposeful movement toward whatever comes next without getting stuck in the tenacious territory of stagnation.

Whether your necessary shift toward higher integrity and alignment involves changing jobs, ending a toxic relationship (or several toxic relationships), embracing your authentic identity as a radiant being of light within a corrupt culture, or even adding a dash of cerulean blue to your hair, it can be a relief to understand that your transformation need not equate to a binary on/off switch. You can change your life (or your hair) in baby steps that slowly and safely transform your experience from one shade to the next. Martha Beck[5] talks about making big life modifications in one-degree turns, like a giant yacht changing directions in the ocean. Life as you know it has accrued a huge amount of momentum on the trajectory you have been following, so it makes sense that a swift hairpin turn may not be possible— let alone enjoyable.

There is no one-size-fits-all parachute, so give yourself some grace while you explore what aligns best for you. You'll know when you uncover a resonant parachute because it will feel both safe and active. Therapists often refer to this magical synergy as the process of expansion and contraction. *Expansion* is the growth experience of becoming large in your sense of Self, and healing your limiting wounds so that you can elevate your consciousness. Although lovely and gratifying, we cannot remain in a state of expansion forever (kind of like a rubber band). This is where *contraction* comes in to offer us reprieve and space to integrate the changes that took place during our expansion. The beauty of the expansion/contraction process is this: The growth you integrate during expansion becomes retained when you move into contraction, so you will not contract as tightly as before. For example, imagine tightly contracted fists opening into soft hands with expansion, then contracting into gently closed (rather than tightly closed) fists. When you are ready for another expansion, your baseline will have enhanced so that your next evolution process initiates with increased capacity. Each of these growth cycles, like long-term stock market trends, only grows with every new iteration. Sticking with our metaphor, with each expansion, the hands open more fully, and with each contraction they close less than before so that over time they become increasingly more and more open.

Once you implement an individualized parachute that fits, it will take residency within the gentle movement of one-degree turns, like a woven net of support existing securely between the lines of your every breath and heartbeat. It can be simple or elaborate, with as much action, reflection, or pacing as you need. Some examples of parachutes include (but are in no way limited to):

- Regularly repeating an affirmation or mantra that reminds you to trust the process you are in. *I trust the process I am in* or *I safely surrender to the unknown.*
- Writing about your journey, perhaps with the addition of sketching or collage for a more dynamic process that includes visual elements.

- Engaging in a thoughtfully crafted project such as creating a series of paintings, redesigning a room in your home, or planning an event. A project occupies your mind with a productive outlet while also serving as a container to thoughtfully attend to variables as they arise.

- Removing yourself from autopilot by taking a vacation, adventure, or even a sabbatical. Get out of your daily rhythm and provide yourself space to clarify your values and priorities and to recapture your desires and dreams.

- Creating or joining a community of supportive people to provide help, guidance, and reflections as you navigate your transition. Such a group can come in the form of supportive friends, a yoga circle, a therapeutic community, an interest group, or any other forum that includes the caring presence of others.

- Working one-on-one with a trusted therapist, certified coach, or mentor to help you clarify your transition with skillful reflections, questions, and insights.

- Pursuing a fun or educational class, experience, or interest you have been curious about but never felt you had the space to pursue. Learn a new language, take Aikido classes, explore Moroccan cuisine, travel around your city sampling the best craft beers—whatever ignites your interest!

Offering: In your journal, jot down your prior experience with parachutes. Consider what kinds of parachutes you might like to implement in the future.

Enjoy the experience of parachuting toward your next chapter in life, but please remember that a parachute is a temporary mechanism. Just as you can get stuck in nonaction, it is also possible to become stuck in the limbo of transition. Remember that the parachute is not your destination, but the vehicle toward that chosen landing place. Even if the location where your parachute sets you down does not have the satisfying resonance of your ideal next chapter, trust that you have been placed upon a valuable stepping stone toward it. Always continue moving ever-forward toward the pull of your radiant life. In our human lives, by divine design, the prospect of going backward is impossible. Even if you find yourself in a dizzying round-about or take a surprising U-turn, you are not reversing. You are simply revisiting sights you have already seen with new eyes. Your deviations serve the valuable function of allowing you to experience your path anew, learn from the teachers and guides along the way, and ride the winds of change with enhanced perspective. You don't have to know how, but keep faith that in some way, as long as you keep voyaging, you will eventually find yourself someplace that feels like home for your next chapter.

THE TRAP OF THE SELF-HELP JUNKIE

Early on in my sabbatical, I told my husband about a podcast[6] I had listened to about a 375-million-year-old fish species called *Tiktaalik rosae*. A fish paleontologist named Neil Shubin made the incredible discovery of this evolutionary species when his work uncovered fossils that displayed evidence of arm, leg, hand, foot, and even neck bones within the fins and body of the fish. Shubin's work is exciting because it provides evidence for the evolution from water creatures to land creatures, which ultimately lead to humans. The interesting takeaway for my husband, however, was not the huge scientific breakthrough of the *Taktaalik rosae*. He was far more interested in the earth-shattering evidence that I had listened to a podcast having absolutely nothing to do with neuroscience, human behavior, or any other psychology-related topic typical to my podcast playlist—and let me tell you, podcasting is a way of life for me. He was thrilled that I filled my headspace with something unrelated to the genre of my professional and inner-work sphere, and lovingly(ish) disclosed that he thought I had edged precariously close to self-help junkiedom. Why he never addressed this concern with me before my sabbatical, I have no idea—but hey, that's how communication goes sometimes.

For those of you who are not obsessed with inner work to the exclusion of 99 percent of all else, you may not know what a self-help junkie is, so I'll go ahead and give you my definition here: A *self-help junkie* is a person who has inundated their system with so much personal growth, inner child healing, emotional resourcing and regulation, and psychological human behavior learning that they effectively trained their brain to deposit a pleasurable dopamine hit whenever they listen, read, conceptualize, learn, or therapeutically process anything related to self-help. This means self-help junkies crave resources and tools for inner work similarly to how drug addicts crave their substance (or substances) of choice. Granted, being a self-help junkie is monumentally less dangerous and detrimental than being a drug addict, but it's still something to be aware of if you fit this description. Our brilliant and complex human minds can get addicted to anything if we have a void within us that yearns to be filled. The self-help and personal growth realms certainly possess a delicious kind of satisfaction that can hook you into an endless loop of more, newer, and progressively deeper degrees of inner work.

I want to make a distinction between the kind of person who navigates their spiritual and personal growth in a healthy way and one who has become stuck in the sticky swamp of junkiedom. Moving through life with an open heart, open mind, and curious willingness to learn more about yourself and your world is not problematic. The problem becomes when you crave the intake of knowledge or information and yearn to be inspired and gratified from a place of lack or dependency. If you feel you would be lost without your self-help literature, or if you feel empty and hollow inside because you haven't gotten your hit of stimulating information lately, that's the slippery slope of the self-help junkie. If this sounds like you, pop open the hood and check it out. Take this concept to a therapist or a coffee date with a trusted friend, delve into it on the pages of your journal, and get honest with yourself about the void your self-help interest may be filling within you.

If you wonder why a person might fall into self-help junkiedom, there could be many reasons. Remember, we can become habitually dependent or reliant upon anything that serves as a band-aid for something unhealed within ourselves. For some, it may be the strong drive toward the perfection-oriented goal of a meaningful life that gets them tangled. Many among us operate from a core belief that if we can only achieve the enlightened, completely healed (imaginary) destination where we have it all figured out, then all will be a-okay in our world. Another person may discover their dependency on self-help material is related to avoidance of discomfort. These individuals may use self-help resources, and even therapy, to cast a rosy glow around their issues and feel that they can effectively check the box of *Yep! I know all about that topic. I've read the literature and done that work already* (when truly, they've only read the book). Regardless of the reason for the unhealthy pursuit of self-help, the irony of the self-help junkie is that the basis for seeking inner-growth is derived from a core wound that will never be satisfied by the constant consumption of learning. Such healing occurs only through embodied change to a large enough degree that we actually engage life differently. True growth of this kind provides healing in an integrated sense, not just a cognitive conceptualization of well-being that comes via words alone. As the saying goes: The proof is in the pudding.

I think many people have had the experience of reading a book, listening to a podcast, or attending a seminar or therapy session where they thought to themselves, *Wow this is really incredible! I am learning so much, and this information will help me grow in so many powerful ways.* Then they return to normal life, and promptly forget 90 percent of the information they just claimed was life-changing. What was the missing piece? Let me tell you: These people walked straight out of the seminar or therapy room, closed the book, or ended the podcast, and returned right back to their regular lives without integrating and practicing what they learned. They may have even leapfrogged directly into another podcast or book without so much as a deep breath to pause and reflect on the last one. Remember, it takes huge repetition in the brain for a new skill or insight to become an integrated part of who you are. Allowing impactful information to wash over you one time before fading it into history will never accomplish the growth and healing you originally hoped for when you sought out the resource in the first place. This is what happens ad nauseum with self-help junkies. They listen to podcast after podcast, read book after book, attend class after inspiring class, and get the brief dopamine hit where they tell themselves, *This is exactly what I need to learn to change my life for the better!* But it doesn't stick.

The same cycle can ignite with therapy, too, when a person finds themselves hashing and rehashing the same or different versions of their interior baggage decade after decade, year after year, week after week. They may temporarily feel better between sessions, but soon find themselves facing the magnetic pull back onto the therapy couch for another hit. Though a lucrative business plan for clinicians, this kind of therapy is not my jam. I want my clients to experience life without therapy as a long-term crutch. My goal is not for each of my clients to become problem-free, but to help them cultivate a reliable, strong, and safe relationship within themselves where they can build an effective interior toolbox to confidently meet and work with whatever presents in their lives without therapy.

FROM JUNKIE TO SELF

I realize all of this talk about putting aside your self-help materials and anchoring into your healing journey through lived experience may seem counterintuitive given the self-help book you currently hold in your hands. Stick with me and hear me out on this one because it's a subtlety that can take some maneuvering to grasp. Resources and helpers are valuable, but only to an extent. Be it podcasts or psychoanalysis, when we don't do the legwork it takes to weave our learnings into who we are and then settle into the enough-ness of that integrated space, the craving will only return. The loop will ensue, leaving us squirmy and voracious as ever, only to be satisfied once again by another podcast, book, or therapy session. Round and round we go in absolute dizziness.

Here's the crux: We need the cerebral learning that comes with tools and information as a vehicle toward higher and deeper layers of ourselves, but it will never be a direct healing balm for our wounds. Your therapy sessions, books, and podcasts are immensely valuable, but only if you see them as a tool—not as the healing agent itself.

Offering: Write about the loops you have previously found (or currently find) yourself caught in. This is a fun one to explore artistically, if you wish. Use any art materials of your liking to display and represent the loops, as well as yourself caught in them.

The real secret is that the only healing agent that has ever existed for any person lies within their abundantly capable and brilliant Self. Guides and signposts can point the arrow, but only from Self can you gain the full and complete radiant state of being that is your birthright. Self is a powerful aspect of your being to return to the limelight as you become inquisitive about your place in the scheme of all things. When you are in self-help junkie mode, Self is not driving the bus—the wounded part of you that keeps you striving toward that idealized perfection of glowy healing is driving. Though the part flooding you with its energy is well-intentioned, it is misguided. As long as a part of you is in charge (any part that is not true Self), you can bet the bus will be following a road diametrically opposite from the True North of a radiant life.

Offering: I cordially invite you to stop and internalize the message from this page directly into your embodied lived experience. Travel inward, beyond the capacity of your incredible brain, and come into contact with the You who is your essential Self. Breathe into the truth that you have been whole and complete this entire time, and perhaps you simply got lost or forgot a few things. Take a moment to forgive and feel compassion toward the confused parts of you that unintentionally make things harder instead of easier. Remember, most of our parts are like small children, and it is healthy for them to be safely buckled into the passenger seats of the bus.

The purpose of this book has been to remind you of the loose ends or unanswered questions you hold about yourself, and perhaps offer a few new tools for you to spend time with in the coming days. Try them on for size, be they IFS parts work, Tara Brach's RAIN (Recognize, Allow, Investigate, Nurture) process, or perhaps your new awareness of a few sophisticated Sharks and Bathtubs within yourself. Simply and lovingly hold these concepts in your awareness and allow them to remain present until you are able to personalize and integrate them in your own unique way. With repeated practice, the threads you choose to follow will become part of the indestructible fibers of your inner support system. These magnificent structures will pave your way directly toward an unimaginably radiant life.

Epilogue

Just simply being here is so much.
                                    —*Rainer Maria Rilke*

In the introduction I wrote about my deeply unfashionable decision to take a four-month sabbatical from my private practice, but I didn't tell you how it all shook out for me. This is what happened:

Contracting Covid-19 was an unexpected diversion from my oh-so-thoughtfully-crafted sabbatical launch plan. With great resistance and disbelief, I honored the reality that I had to put a hard stop to all things and surrender. That's real life; sometimes it doesn't obey the calendar.

I gifted myself the deep rest and loving nurturance my twitchy nervous system desperately needed after more than fifteen years as a clinical therapist and profound burn-out. It took me a while to navigate the new rhythm of sabbatical, because rest hadn't exactly been a real thing for me before, let alone *deep rest*. I danced with lingering Covid affects for longer than I would have liked. I meditated, stretched, walked, and went to the movies (a lot). I spotted flowers I had never noticed before on my familiar neighborhood walking trails. I observed my impulse to rush, to be productive, and to fill up my calendar (which was akin to another arm or an additional spleen in the magnitude of my dependency on it).

To the beckoning invitations of urgency and obligation, I humbly declined—repeatedly. I experienced energy healing, business coaching, and self-discovery of many flavors. I also stepped outside the self-help junkie box. I spent unrushed, enjoyable time with my husband and children, and sipped tea with a few long-lost friends. I traveled, but I also homebodied (I made that word up, and I must say, I quite like it). I spent time with myself—the real kind of quality time so many of us know only as a mystical creature we vaguely remember from fairy tales—and I befriended myself in a whole new way. I was sometimes bored, and I tried not to overthink it. I thought about painting a new phenomenal body of work, but it didn't happen. I wrote to myself, to you, and brought this book into being. I explored and excavated the layers of my own confusion, sometimes getting lost, other times finding myself found. I thought about my clients, and reflected on the future of my clinical practice. My heart swelled with pride for all I had the privilege to witness and experience in my work, and also grieved for the loss and change I knew awaited me. I learned that I would emerge from sabbatical anew, authentic to the season of life I had found myself in, and ever-the-more radiant. I began to manifest a magical platter of fresh, inspired offerings for my work, my loved ones, and myself, which is now *The Radiant Life Project* platform. Profoundly and courageously, I dove deeply within and sourced from a well of implicit trust that a new chapter of meaningful work would develop along the way. And so it has.

At the end of my sabbatical, I had some things figured out, while others remained open-ended. While I healed my mind, body, and soul, I realized that an essential component of self-nurturance at that juncture was to radically transform my life and business, and ultimately birth *The Radiant Life Project* into being.

Throughout my sabbatical, it became vividly clear to me that the ripple effect is a very real phenomenon—and one we must each be thoughtful about. When we engage with the world from anything other than our truest, most aligned, most brilliant and flawed authentic Selves, we send ripples out into the world that resonate like a mistuned instrument. We teach each other with our own inauthenticity that realness isn't where it's at, and we participate in the perpetuity of mask-wearing with ourselves, one another, and society at large. We spread the rumor among ourselves that radiance is unattainable, though it most certainly is not.

Because of the ripple effect, it is exceedingly important to ensure that whatever extends outwardly from ourselves originates from the eternally sacred and inherently whole fountain of realness we are each capable of accessing. When we engage with our world and one another authentically, we are much more likely to receive the same in return. And that, my friends, is how together we not only build a radiant life for every one of us, but also a radiant world.

Thank you for joining me on this profoundly meaningful journey of inner growth and healing. For more information about *The Radiant Life Project* and its programs, retreats, and talks, please visit www.TheRadiantLifeProject.com.

Sending you absolute love and radiance until we meet again.

Kate

NOTES

CHAPTER 1

1. David Dobbs, "The Science of Success," *The Atlantic*, December 1, 2009. https://www.theatlantic.com/magazine/archive/2009/12/the -science-of-success/307761/.

2. Ellis, Bruce J., W. Thomas Boyce, Jay Belsky, Marian J. Baker-mans-Kranenburg, and Marinus H. van Ijzendoorn. "Differential Susceptibility to the Environment: An Evolutionary-Neurodevelopmental Theory." *Development and Psychopathology* 23, no. 1 (2011): 7–28. doi: 10.1017/S0954579410000611.

3. Ellis, Bruce J., W. Thomas Boyce, Jay Belsky, Marian J. Baker-mans-Kranenburg, and Marinus H. van Ijzendoorn. "Differential Susceptibility to the Environment: An Evolutionary-Neurodevelopmental Theory." *Development and Psychopathology* 23, no. 1 (2011): 7–28. doi: 10.1017/S0954579410000611.

CHAPTER 2

1. Bethany Webster, *Discovering the Inner Mother: A Guide to Healing the Mother Wound and Claiming Your Personal Power* (New York: William Morrow, 2021).

2. Andrew Huberman, "Erasing Fears & Traumas Based on the Modern Neuroscience of Fear. Episode 49." *The Huberman Lab* (podcast), December 6, 2021. https://open.spotify.com/episode /0I1kiY8IbFrl36WQjjeGek.

3. *The Devil Wears Prada*, directed by David Frankel (Fox 2000 Pictures, 2006).

4. Pema Chodron, *Welcoming the Unwelcome: Wholehearted Living in a Brokenhearted World* (Boulder: Shambhala, 2019).

5. *Encanto*, directed by Byron Howard and Jared Bush (Walt Disney Pictures, 2022), 34:21.

6. The myth of Sisyphus comes from Greek Mythology. Due to cheating death twice, Sisyphus was punished by Zeus by being forced to roll a boulder up a hill only for it to roll back down each time, and he was doomed to this cycle for eternity.

CHAPTER 3

1. Terry Real, *Us: Getting Past You and Me to Build a More Loving Relationship* (New York: Goop Press/Rosedale, 2022).

2. Deb Dana, *Anchored: How to Befriend Your Nervous System Using Polyvagal Theory* (Boulder: Sounds True, 2021).

3. Dana, *Anchored*.

4. Andrew Huberman, "The Science of Gratitude & How to Build a Gratitude Practice. Episode 47." *The Huberman Lab* (podcast), November 22, 2021. https://open.spotify.com/episode/5GYvrvQmFQmD77vpsiMn59.

5. Huberman, "The Science of Gratitude." 56:15.

6. Glenn R. Fox, Jonas Kaplan, Hanna Damasio, and Antonio Damasio, "Neural Correlates of Gratitude," *Frontiers in Psychology* (September 30, 2015).

7. Tara Brach, *Radical Acceptance: Embracing Your Life with the Heart of a Buddha* (New York: Bantam Books, 2016).

8. Brené Brown, "The Anatomy of Trust." *Brené Solo* (podcast). November 4, 2021. https://brenebrown.com/podcast/the-anatomy-of-trust/.

9. Kristin Neff, *Self-Compassion: The Proven Power of Being Kind to Yourself* (New York: Harper Collins, 2011).

10. Galit Atlas, *Emotional Inheritance: A Therapist, Her Patients, and the Legacy of Trauma* (Boston: Little, Brown Spark, 2022).

11. Harriet Lerner, "An Unforgettable Tale About Forgiveness," *Psychology Today*, September 11, 2016.

CHAPTER 4

1. Richard Schwartz, *No Bad Parts: Healing Trauma and Restoring Wholeness with the Internal Family Systems Model* (Boulder: Sounds True, 2021).

2. Terry Real, *Us: Getting Past You and Me to Build a More Loving Relationship* (New York: Goop Press/Rosedale, 2022).

3. M. P. Gilbey and K. M. Spyer, "Essential Organization of the Sympathetic Nervous System." *Bailliere's Clinical Endocrinology and Metabolism* (April 7, 1993): 259–78, doi: 10.1016/s0950-351x(05)80177-6. PMID: 8098208. https://www.sciencedirect.com/science/article/abs/pii/S0950351X05801776?via%3Dihub.

4. This is only a tidbit of the massive body of work and research that is The Polyvagal theory. For more in-depth learning about this topic please pursue further reading by Stephen Porges and others. Stephen W. Porges, *The Pocket Guide to The Polyvagal Theory: The Transformative Power of Feeling Safe* (New York: W. W. Norton & Company, 2017).

5. "SAMHSA's Concept of Trauma and Guidance for a Trauma-Informed Approach." Substance Abuse and Mental Health Services Administration. HHS Publication No. (SMA) 14–4884 (Rockville, MD: Substance Abuse and Mental Health Services Administration, 2014). https://ncsacw.acf.hhs.gov/userfiles/files/SAMHSA_Trauma.pdf.

6. Bruce D. Perry and Oprah Winfrey, *What Happened to You? Conversations on Trauma, Resilience, and Healing* (New York: Flatiron Books, 2021).

7. Dr. Kristin Neff has a brilliant website with incredible resources (https://self-compassion.org).

8. Kristin Neff, *Self-Compassion: The Proven Power of Being Kind to Yourself* (New York: Harper Collins, 2011).

9. Aura Glaser, "Into the Demon's Mouth," *Tricycle: The Buddhist Review*, Spring 2012. https://tricycle.org/magazine/demons-mouth/.

10. Peter Levine, *Waking the Tiger: Healing Trauma* (Berkeley: North Atlantic Books, 1997).

CHAPTER 5

1. Jill Bolte Taylor, *My Stroke of Insight: A Brain Scientist's Personal Journey* (New York: Penguin Books, 2009).

2. Mark Nepo, *The Book of Awakening: Having the Life You Want by Being Present to the Life You Have* (Newburyport, MA: Red Wheel/Weiser, 2020), 14.

3. Tara Brach, *Radical Acceptance: Embracing Your Life with the Heart of a Buddha* (New York: Bantam Books, 2016).

4. Brach, *Radical Acceptance*.

5. Katherine May, *Wintering: The Power of Rest and Retreat in Difficult Times* (New York: Riverhead Books, 2020).

6. Nepo, *The Book of Awakening*, 93.

7. Brené Brown, *Atlas of the Heart: Mapping Meaningful Connection and the Language of Human Experience* (New York: Harper Collins, 2021).

CHAPTER 6

1. Galit Atlas, *Emotional Inheritance: A Therapist, Her Patients, and the Legacy of Trauma* (Boston: Little, Brown Spark, 2022).

2. "Common humanity" is a term coined by Dr. Kristin Neff from her self-compassion work. Kristin Neff, *Self-Compassion: The Proven Power of Being Kind to Yourself* (New York: Harper Collins, 2011).

3. Brené Brown, "Everyone Has a Story," June 7, 2018, accessed June 13, 2022. https://brenebrown.com/articles/2018/06/07/everyone-has-a -story/.

4. David S. Moore, *The Developing Genome: An Introduction to Behavioral Epigenetics* (New York: Oxford University Press, 2015).

5. Moore, *The Developing Genome.*

6. Moore, *The Developing Genome.*

7. Richard C. Francis, *Epigenetics: How Environment Shapes Our Genes* (New York: W. W. Norton & Company, 2011).

8. Moore, *The Developing Genome.*

9. Francis, *Epigenetics.*

10. Mark Wolynn, *It Didn't Start With You: How Inherited Family Trauma Shapes Who We Are and How to End the Cycle* (New York: Penguin Books: 2016).

11. Francis, *Epigenetics.*

12. Wolynn, *It Didn't Start With You.*

13. Mark Nepo, *The Book of Awakening: Having the Life You Want by Being Present to the Life You Have* (Newburyport, MA: Red Wheel/ Weiser, 2020).

CHAPTER 7

1. Bruce Lipton, *The Biology of Belief 10th Anniversary Edition: Unleashing the Power of Consciousness, Matter & Miracles* (Carlsbad, CA: Hay House, Inc., 2016).

2. Books by Dr. Joe Dispenza include *Becoming Supernatural: How Common People Are Doing the Uncommon, Breaking the Habit of Being Yourself: How to Lose Your Mind and Create a New One,* and *You Are the*

Placebo: Making Your Mind Matter. Dr. Dispenza also has a series on Gaia TV called *Rewired,* and he has various interviews on many platforms.

3. Mathias De Stefano, https://www.matiasdestefano.org/. He also has a wonderful show on Gaia TV called *Initiation.*

4. "Comparative suffering" is a term from Brené Brown, *Atlas of the Heart: Mapping Meaningful Connection and the Language of Human Experience* (New York: Harper Collins, 2021), 130–31.

5. Eckhart Tolle, *A New Earth: Awakening to Your Life's Purpose* (New York: Penguin Books, 2008).

6. Tolle, *A New Earth.*

7. Eckhart Tolle, "Not Minding What Happens," *Awakin.org,* accessed on June 21, 2022. https://www.awakin.org/v2/read/view.php?tid=2089.

8. Jill Bolte Taylor, *Whole Brain Living: The Anatomy of Choice and the Four Characters That Drive Our Life* (Carlsbad, CA: Hay House, Inc., 2021).

9. Brown, *Atlas of the Heart: Mapping Meaningful Connection and the Language of Human Experience* (New York: Harper Collins, 2021).

10. Jalauddin Rumi, "The Guest House," *All Poetry,* Rumi, J. Translated by Coleman Barks, accessed on May 22, 2022. https://allpoetry.com/poem/8534703-The-Guest-House-by-Mewlana-Jalaluddin-Rumi.

11. *WandaVision,* Season 1, episode 8, "Previously On," directed by Matt Shakman, aired February 26, 2021, on Disney+ (Marvel Studios, 2021), 24:50. https://www.disneyplus.com/video/ebaaf404-b012-4a35-a4bd-0d5d4f32ccd0.

12. Excellence Reporter. "Rainer Maria Rilke: On the Wisdom and the Purpose of Life." June 17, 2019. Accessed on June 1, 2023. https://excellencereporter.com/2019/06/17/rainer-maria-rilke-on-the-wisdom-and-the-purpose-of-life/.

13. Brown, *Atlas of the Heart.*

14. Brown, *Atlas of the Heart.*

15. Glennon Doyle, *Untamed* (New York: The Dial Press, 2020).

C<small>HAPTER</small> 8

1. John Welwood, *Ordinary Magic: Everyday Life as Spiritual Path* (Boulder, CO: Shambhala, 1992).

2. Norton Juster, *The Phantom Tollbooth* (New York: Yearling, an Imprint of Random House Children's Books, 1961).

3. Tara Brach, *Radical Acceptance: Embracing Your Life with the Heart of a Buddha* (New York: Bantam Books, 2016).

4. Brach, *Radical Acceptance*.

5. Martha Beck, *The Way of Integrity: Finding the Path to Your True Self* (New York: Penguin Life, 2021).

6. Mark Nepo, *The Book of Awakening: Having the Life You Want by Being Present to the Life You Have* (Newburyport, MA: Red Wheel/Weiser, 2020).

CHAPTER 9

1. Martha Beck, *The Way of Integrity: Finding the Path to Your True Self* (New York: Penguin Life, 2021).

2. Beck, *The Way of Integrity*.

3. Mark Nepo, *The Book of Awakening: Having the Life You Want by Being Present to the Life You Have* (Newburyport, MA: Red Wheel/Weiser, 2020).

4. Elizabeth Gilbert, *Big Magic: Creative Living Beyond Fear* (New York: Riverhead Books, 2015).

5. Beck, *The Way of Integrity*.

6. Glennon Doyle, *Untamed* (New York: The Dial Press, 2020), 173.

7. Carl G. Jung, *Memories, Dreams, Reflections* (New York: Vintage Books, 1989).

8. Stacey Couch, "The Prostitute: Living in Integrity," *Wild Gratitude*, 2021. https://www.wildgratitude.com.

9. Chris D. Frith, "The Social Brain?" *Philosophical Transactions of the Royal Society of London. Series B, Biological Sciences*, 362(1480), 671–78 (2007). https://doi.org/10.1098/rstb.2006.2003.

10. Beck, *The Way of Integrity*.

CHAPTER 10

1. Noah Hass-Cohen and Richard Carr, *Art Therapy and Clinical Neuroscience* (London: Jessica Kingsley Publishers, 2008).

2. Judith A. Rubin, *Child Art Therapy* (Hoboken, NJ: John Wiley & Sons, Inc., 2005).

3. Kate King, *Untitled*, 2018, pen and ink on paper, 8.5 x 11 in., Denver, Colorado.

4. King, *Celestial Goddess*, 2021, watercolor on paper, 9 x 12 in., Denver, Colorado.

5. King, *The Judge*, 2021, collage on paper, 5 in. round, Denver, Colorado.

6. King, *The Cocoon*, 2021, collage on paper, 5 in. round, Denver, Colorado.

7. Carl G. Jung, *Memories, Dreams, Reflections* (New York: Vintage Books, 1989).

CHAPTER 11

1. Krista Tippett hosts "David Whyte—Seeking Language Large Enough." *OnBeing with Krista Tippett* (podcast), May 26, 2022, accessed August 10, 2022 (42:10). https://open.spotify.com/episode /5ifznyLW4WRWbPQowEzuV3.

2. Richard Schwartz, *No Bad Parts: Healing Trauma and Restoring Wholeness with the Internal Family Systems Model* (Boulder, CO: Sounds True, 2021).

3. Mihaly Csikszentmihalyi, *Flow: The Psychology of Optimal Experience* (New York: Harper Perennial Modern Classics, 2008).

4. Ram Dass, "The Need for a Guru," 2022, Ram Dass Love Serve Remember Foundation. https://www.ramdass.org/need-guru/.

5. Martha Beck, *The Way of Integrity: Finding the Path to Your True Self* (New York: Penguin Life, 2021).

6. Keith Miller, host, "Neil Shubin: Your Inner Fish." *The Soul of Life* (podcast), October 14, 2021, accessed May 11, 2022. https://open.spotify .com/episode/5R38tfgaYUQxAbBHNy20Do.

BIBLIOGRAPHY

Atlas, G. *Emotional Inheritance: A Therapist, Her Patients, and the Legacy of Trauma.* Boston: Little, Brown Spark, 2022.

Beck, Martha. *Finding Your Own North Star: Claiming the Life You Were Meant to Live.* New York: Harmony, 2002.

Beck, Martha. *The Way of Integrity: Finding the Path to Your True Self.* New York: Penguin Life, 2021.

Bolte Taylor, Jill. *My Stroke of Insight: A Brain Scientist's Personal Journey.* New York Penguin Books, 2009.

Bolte Taylor, Jill. *Whole Brain Living: The Anatomy of Choice and the Four Characters That Drive Our Life.* Carlsbad, CA: Hay House, Inc., 2021.

Brach, Tara. *Radical Acceptance: Embracing Your Life with the Heart of a Buddha.* New York: Bantam Books, 2016.

Brown, Brené. *Atlas of the Heart: Mapping Meaningful Connection and the Language of Human Experience.* New York: Harper Collins, 2021.

Brown, Brené. "Everyone Has a Story." June 7, 2018. Retrieved June 13, 2022. https://brenebrown.com/articles/2018/06/07 /everyone-has-a-story/.

Brown, Brené. "The Anatomy of Trust." *Brené Solo* (podcast). November 4, 2021. https://brenebrown.com/podcast/the -anatomy-of-trust/.

Cambridge English Dictionary. (n.d.). "Radiant." Retrieved May 10, 2022. https://dictionary.cambridge.org/us/dictionary/ english/radiant.

Chodron, Pema. *Welcoming the Unwelcome: Wholehearted Living in a Brokenhearted World.* Boulder, CO: Shambhala, 2019.

Couch, Stacey. "The Prostitute: Living in Integrity." *Wild Gratitude*. 2021. Accessed August 2022. https://www.wildgratitude.com.

Csikszentmihalyi, Mihaly. *Flow: The Psychology of Optimal Experience*. New York: Harper Perennial Modern Classics, 2008.

Dana, Deb. *Anchored: How to Befriend Your Nervous System Using Polyvagal Theory*. Boulder, CO: Sounds True, 2021.

Dass, Ram. "The Need for a Guru." 2022. Ram Dass Love Serve Remember Foundation. https://www.ramdass.org/need-guru/.

De Stefano, Mathias. (n.d.). https://www.matiasdestefano.org/.

Dispenza, Joe. *Becoming Supernatural: How Common People Are Doing the Uncommon*. Carlsbad, CA: Hay House, Inc., 2019.

Dispenza, Joe. *Breaking the Habit of Being Yourself: How to Lose Your Mind and Create a New One*. Carlsbad, CA: Hay House, Inc., 2013.

Dispenza, Joe. *You Are the Placebo: Making Your Mind Matter*. Carlsbad, CA: Hay House, Inc., 2015.

Dobbs, David. "The Science of Success." *The Atlantic*, December 1, 2009. https://www.theatlantic.com/magazine/archive/2009/12/the-science-of-success/307761/.

Doyle, Glennon. *Untamed*. New York: The Dial Press, 2020.

Ellis, Bruce J., W. Thomas Boyce, Jay Belsky, Marian J. Bakermans-Kranenburg, and Marinus H. van Ijzendoorn. "Differential Susceptibility to the Environment: An Evolutionary-Neurodevelopmental Theory." *Development and Psychopathology* 23, no. 1 (2011): 7–28. doi: 10.1017/S0954579410000611.

Excellence Reporter. "Rainer Maria Rilke: On the Wisdom and the Purpose of Life." June 17, 2019. Accessed on June 1, 2023. https://excellencereporter.com/2019/06/17/rainer-maria-rilke-on-the-wisdom-and-the-purpose-of-life/.

Fox, Jonas, Glenn Kaplan, Hannah Damasio, and Antonio Damasio. "Neural Correlates of Gratitude." *Frontiers in Psychology*, September 30, 2015. https://doi.org/10.3389/fpsyg.2015.01491.

Francis, Richard C. *Epigenetics: How Environment Shapes Our Genes.* New York: W. W. Norton & Company, 2011.

Frankel, David, director. *The Devil Wears Prada.* Fox 2000 Pictures, 2006.

Frith, Chris D. "The Social Brain?" *Philosophical Transactions of the Royal Society of London. Series B, Biological Sciences, 362*(1480), 671–78, (2007). https://doi.org/10.1098/rstb.2006.2003.

Gilbert, Elizabeth. *Big Magic: Creative Living Beyond Fear.* New York: Riverhead Books, 2015.

Gilbey, M. P., and K. M. Spyer. "Essential Organization of the Sympathetic Nervous System." *Baillieres Clinical Endocrinology and Metabolism* (April 7, 1993): 259–78, doi: 10.1016/s0950-351x(05)80177-6. PMID: 8098208. https://www.sciencedirect.com/science/article/abs/pii/S0950351X05801776?via%3Dihub.

Glaser, Aura. "Into the Demon's Mouth." *Tricycle: The Buddhist Review,* Spring 2012, accessed July 11, 2022. https://tricycle.org/magazine/demons-mouth/.

Hass-Cohen, Noah, and Richard Carr. *Art Therapy and Clinical Neuroscience.* London: Jessica Kingsley Publishers, 2008.

Howard, Byron, and Jared Bush, directors. *Encanto.* Walt Disney Pictures, 2022. 34:21.

Huberman, Andrew, host. "The Science of Gratitude & How to Build a Gratitude Practice. Episode 47." *The Huberman Lab* (podcast). November 22, 2021. Accessed November 30, 2022. 56:15. https://open.spotify.com/episode/5GYvrvQmFQmD77vpsiMn59.

Huberman, Andrew. "Erasing Fears & Traumas Based on the Modern Neuroscience of Fear. Episode 49." *The Huberman Lab* (podcast), December 6, 2021. https://open.spotify.com/episode/0I1kiY8IbFrl36WQjjeGek.

Jung, Carl G. *Memories, Dreams, Reflections.* New York: Vintage Books, 1989.

Juster, Norton. *The Phantom Tollbooth.* New York: Yearling, an Imprint of Random House Children's Books, 1961.

King, Kate. *Celestial Goddess,* watercolor on paper, 2021, 9 x 12 in., Denver, CO.

King, Kate. *The Cocoon*, collage on paper, 2021, 5 in. round, Denver, CO.

King, Kate. *The Judge*, collage on paper, 2021, 5 in. round, Denver, CO.

King, Kate. *Untitled*, pen and ink on paper, 2018, 8.5 x 11 in., Denver, CO.

Lerner, Harriet. "An Unforgettable Tale About Forgiveness," *Psychology Today*, September 11, 2016.

Levine, Peter. *Walking the Tiger: Healing Trauma*. Berkeley, CA: North Atlantic Books, 1997.

Lipton, Bruce. *The Biology of Belief 10th Anniversary Edition: Unleashing the Power of Consciousness, Matter, & Miracles*. Carlsbad, CA: Hay House, Inc., 2016.

May, Katherine. *Wintering: The Power of Rest and Retreat in Difficult Times*. New York: Riverhead Books, 2020.

Merriam-Webster. (n.d.). "Radiant." Accessed May 10, 2022. https://www.merriam- webster.com/dictionary/radiant.

Miller, Keith, host. "Neil Shubin: Your Inner Fish." *The Soul of Life* (podcast). October 14, 2021. Accessed May 11, 2022. https://open.spotify.com/episode/5R38tfgaYUQxAbBHNy20Do.

Moore, David S. *The Developing Genome: An Introduction to Behavioral Epigenetics*. New York: Oxford University Press, 2015.

Nagoski, Emily. *Burnout: The Secret to Unlocking the Stress Cycle*. New York: Random House Publishing, 2020.

Neff, Kristin. *Self-Compassion: The Proven Power of Being Kind to Yourself*. New York: Harper Collins, 2011.

Nepo, Mark. *The Book of Awakening: Having the Life You Want by Being Present to the Life You Have*. Newburyport, MA: Red Wheel/Weiser, 2021.

Perry, Bruce D., and Winfrey, Oprah. *What Happened to You? Conversations on Trauma, Resilience, and Healing*. New York: Flatiron Books, 2021.

Porges, Stephen W. *The Pocket Guide to The Polyvagal Theory: The Transformative Power of Feeling Safe*. New York: W. W. Norton & Company, 2017.

Real, Terry. *Us: Getting Past You and Me to Build a More Loving Relationship*. New York: Goop Press/Rodale Books, 2022.

Reed, Peyton, director. *The Break-Up.* Universal Pictures, 2006. https://play.hbomax.com/page/urn:hbo:page: GYgboSQtlcJ3CwgEAAAAJ:type:feature.

Rubin, Judith A. *Child Art Therapy.* Hoboken, NJ: John Wiley & Sons, Inc., 2005.

Rumi, Jalaluddin. Translated by Coleman Barks. "The Guest House," All Poetry. Accessed May 22, 2022. https://allpoetry .com/poem/8534703-The-Guest-House-by-Mewlana-Jalaluddin-Rumi.

Schwartz, Richard. *No Bad Parts: Healing Trauma and Restoring Wholeness with the Internal Family Systems Model.* Boulder, CO: Sounds True, 2021.

Substance Abuse and Mental Health Services Administration. "SAMHSA's Concept of Trauma and Guidance for a Trauma-Informed Approach." HHS Publication No. (SMA) 14–4884. Rockville, MD: Substance Abuse and Mental Health Services Administration, 2014. Accessed March 13, 2022. https://ncsacw.acf.hhs.gov/userfiles/files/SAMHSA _Trauma.pdf.

Tippett, Krista. "David Whyte—Seeking Language Large Enough." *OnBeing with Krista Tippett* (podcast). May 26, 2022, 42:10. Accessed August 10, 2022. https://open.spotify .com/episode/5ifznyLW4WRWbPQowEzuV3.

Tolle, Eckhart. *A New Earth: Awakening to Your Life's Purpose.* New York: Penguin Books, 2008.

Tolle, Eckhart. "Not Minding What Happens." *Awakin.org.* Accessed on June 21, 2022. https://www.awakin.org/v2/read /view.php?tid=2089.

Tolle, Eckhart. *The Power of Now: A Guide to Spiritual Enlightenment.* Novato, California: New World Library, 2004.

WandaVision. Season 1, episode 8, "Previously On." Directed by Matt Shakman, aired February 26, 2021, on Disney+ (Marvel Studios, 2021). 24:50. https://www.disneyplus.com/video /ebaaf404-b012-4a35-a4bd-0d5d4f32ccd0.

Webster, Bethany. *Discovering the Inner Mother: A Guide to Healing the Mother Wound and Claiming Your Personal Power.* New York: William Morrow, 2021.

Welwood, John. *Ordinary Magic: Everyday Life as Spiritual Path.* Boulder, CO: Shambhala, 1992.

Wikipedia, Wikimedia Foundation, Inc. "Sisyphus." Last modified November 7, 2022. Accessed June 30, 2022. https://en.wikipedia.org/wiki/Sisyphus.

Wolynn, Mark. *It Didn't Start With You: How Inherited Family Trauma Shapes Who We Are and How to End the Cycle.* New York: Penguin Books, 2016.

INDEX

Page references for figures are italicized.

accountability, 16–17, 69, 109–10
adopted children, 121–22
adversity, 19–20, 21, 37–38
affirmations, 28, 44, 242
airplane integrity, 180, 181
alchemy, 222–23
Alcoholics Anonymous, 189
alignment, 182
Allow, in RAIN practice, 60
anatomy of trust, 62
ancestral trauma, 127–31
anchoring, 7–8
anger, 75–76, 94–95, 166
ANS (autonomic nervous system), 39–42, 77
anxiety, 90–91, 99. *See also* health anxiety shark
apologies, 17, 69–70
archetypes, 192–94, 220
arrogance, 232–33

Art as Psychotherapy, 215–17, *217, 218,* 219–22
Art as Therapy, 210–11, *212,* 213, *214,* 215
artist, tortured (persona), 186–87
art therapy, 5–6, 85, 206
Atlas, Galit, 65–66, 121
Atlas of the Heart (Brown), 149
attachment theory, 117–18, 118–19
"attend and befriend" mantra, 173–74
attunement, 198, 199–200
authenticity: creativity and, 205; giving from, 105–8; in gratitude, 56–57; importance of, xxii–xxiii; integrity *vs.*, 179; kindness and, 14–17; meaning/purpose and, 24–25; orchid hypothesis, 1–4; ripple effect and,

253; Self, layers of, 4–8; True North, finding, 8–14

authenticity answer, xxiii

autonomic nervous system (ANS), 39–42, 77

Bakermans-Kranenburg, Marian, 1

bake sale scenario, 152–53

baking, as creative outlet, 208

balance, 43–44

bathtubs: as coping mechanism, 167; defined, 157; described, 161–62; examples of, 162–65, 166–67; for health anxiety shark, 162–63, 168–69, 173–74; honesty about, 165; hypervigilance about physical body, 163, 168–69; magical play, 163–64; mirrors, avoidance of, 163; need for, 165–66; parents, reliance on, 163; for skin disturbances, 162–63. *See also* sharks/bathtubs model

bean dip exercise, 93–95, 97

Beck, Martha, 8, 175, 179–80, 181, 189–90, 202, 241

benefit of the doubt, giving, 17

betrayal, feelings of, 123, 124–25

Big Magic (Gilbert), 209, 230

binary thinking, 35–36

body weight, 94–95, 159

Bolte Taylor, Jill, 92–93, 146–48

The Book of Awakening (Nepo), 97, 105–6, 134

books, 247, 249

boundaries, 52–53

Boyce, W. Thomas, 1–2

Brach, Tara, 59–61, 99–100, 102, 173, 175

brain: brainstem, 82–83; cortex, 83; creativity, healing through, 206; diencephalon/reptilian, 82–83; gratitude and, 57–58; limbic/mammalian, 83; narratives and, 137–38; prefrontal cortex, 57, 135; trauma and, 82–84

BRAVING framework, 62

The Break Up, 57

Brown, Brené, 11, 62, 112, 125, 149, 153
bubbles, pandemic, 236–37
Buddhism, 107, 137, 224–25
burdens, legacy, 121–25
burning someone's house down, 15–16, 17
burnout, xvii–xix, 30, 31, 32
Burnout (Nagosaki & Nagosaki), 36
bus driver metaphor, 73, 77, 249–50

canines, fear of, 117
car accident, as trauma, 81
caregivers, 46, 105–8
Celestial Goddess (King), 213, *214*
Center for Complicated Grief, 150
challenges, 19–20, 21, 37–38
change: fear and, 141; recognizing need for, xxv–xxvi; resistance to, 240; slow and safe, 241; timing for, xxiii
Character One, 147, 148
Character Two, 147, 148
Character Three, 147, 148
Character Four, 147, 148
chess players, master, 21

child abuse, 133
children: adopted, 121–22; creativity in, 208–9; dandelion, 1, 3; as impressionable, 119; narratives and, 145, 149, 152–53; orchid, 1–2, 3–4; suicide of, 198–99
Chinese proverb, xxiii
Chodron, Pema, 28
The Cocoon (King), *218*, 220
combative relationships narrative, 139
common humanity, 25–26, 28–29, 84, 103–4, 125
communication, high-integrity, 16–17
community of supportive people, 243
comparison, 26, 28, 141–42
compassion, 28, 65, 84–85, 103–4, 170–71, 199
competition, 28
conditional love, 191
confidence, 233–34
connection, 25–26, 147, 148
consciousness, 138
contraction, 242
contrast, importance of, 20
core emotional experience, 94–95
core values, 12

cortex, 83
Covid-19 infection, 237–38, 251
Covid-19 pandemic, xvii–xviii, xxi, 20, 236–38
creativity, 205–27; Art as Psychotherapy, 215–17, *217*, *218*, 219–22; Art as Therapy, 210–11, *212*, 213, *214*, 215; authenticity and, 205; in childhood, 208–9; exploring, 226–27; healing through, 206; importance of, 205, 207; loss of, 205–6, 226–27; loving kindness and, 225–26; origins of, 226; spirituality and, 224–26; stalling of, 206–7; types of, 207–8, 209–10; world, creating your, 222–24
C's of Self Energy, 230, 231
culture: hustle, 30–33, 44–45; messages from, 33–36; patriarchal, 35–36, 46–47; Western, 19, 35, 37, 46–47, 141
curiosity, 229–31

daimon. *See* gifts
dandelion children, 1, 3

David, Susan, 155
deep rest. *See* nurturance and deep rest
defects, personal, 153
Demasio, Antonio, 58
De Stefano, Mathias, 139–40
detaching from narratives, 137, 143–45
The Developing Genome (Moore), 126, 127
The Devil Wears Prada, 27
diencephalon brain, 82–83
difficult, belief that one is, 145, 149
discomfort, avoidance of, 247
Discovering the Inner Mother (Webster), 22
dishonesty, 188–89
Dispenza, Joe, 136
Dobbs, David, 1
dogs, fear of, 117
dolls, Russian nesting, 5–6
doodling, 211, *212*, 213, 215
dorsal vagal system, 40–41, 42, 78
doubt, giving benefit of the, 17
Doyle, Glennon, 55, 154, 192
dress rehearsing tragedy, 113

driver of the bus metaphor, 73, 77, 249–50
Dutch Family Birth Cohort Study, 128–29

Earth School, 239
ebb and flow, 30
effects, in trauma definition, 81
8 C's of Self Energy, 230, 231
Ellis, Bruce, 1–2
embedded narratives, 142–43, 145, 149
embodiment practices, 183
Emory University School of Medicine, 129
"Emotional Agility" (David), 155
emotional generosity, 62–65
emotions: attachments to, 147, 148; bean dip exercise, 93–95, 97; equanimity, 99–100; exile parts and, 95–96; experience, core, 94–95; experience, present, 140; importance of, 98; Internal Family Systems, 95–98; as multidimensional, 97–98; naming and visualizing,

98–99; 90-second rule, 92–93; protector parts and, 95–96; reaction vs. response, 99–100
empathy, 198, 199–200
Encanto, 32–33
epigenetics: about, 116, 125–27; ancestral trauma, 127–31; pattern breakers, 130–34
Epigenetics (Francis), 127, 128–29
equanimity, 99–100
E's, in trauma definition, 81
estrangement from family, 122–24
event, in trauma definition, 81
evolutionary species, 244–45
exile parts, 74–76, 95–96, 111–12
expansion/contraction process, 241–42
experience: core emotional, 94–95; present emotional, 140; present moment, 147, 148; in trauma definition, 81
expression, 65–68
extrovert/introvert spectrum, xviii, 13–14, 48, 90–91

false summit, 102–3
family, estrangement from, 122–24
family history, medical, 115
family secrets, 120–22
famine, potato, 128–29
fawn behavior, 78–79
fear: about, 109, 113–14; change and, 141; of dogs, 117; exile parts and, 111–12; Parts Cards and, 222; protector parts and, 110, 111–12; of sharks, 171–72. *See also* sharks/ bathtubs model
feminine qualities, 35–36, 46–47, 49
fight/flight response, 40, 77–78
Finding Your Own North Star (Beck), 8
firefighter protector parts, 74
fist expanding/ contracting, 242
5 P's, in Internal Family Systems, 230–31
flame blower-outers, 10–11
foreboding joy, 112–13
forgiveness, 68–70
four characters framework, 146–48

Francis, Richard C., 127, 128–29
freeze, 78
future, projections of, 140

gaslighting, 79
gay men with HIV, 189–90
generosity, emotional, 62–65
genes, 115, 126
genetic vulnerability model, 2
genius. *See* gifts
genome, 126–27, 130
genuineness. *See* authenticity
ghosts, hungry, 107
gifts, 231–36; about, 231–32; changing nature of, 234–35; confidence and, 233–34; hang-ups about, 232–33; learning to own, 235–36; living library and, 235; qualities embedded in, 234
Gilbert, Elizabeth, 176, 186, 209, 230
giver trap, 45–47
giving from authenticity *vs.* giving with an agenda, 105–8
giving up *vs.* surrender, 146
gossip, 197–98

The Grandmother Effect, 128
gratitude, 55–59
grief, 148–51
grit, 37–38
groupthink, 13
growth, meaningful, 89–114; caregiver distortion, 105–8; emotions, 92–100; fear, 109–12, 113–14; joy, 112–13; seasons of life, 104–5; stacked bricks and spirals, 101–3; "who you are" *vs.* "where you're at", 89–92
The Guest House (Rumi), 100, 150

hardship, 19–20, 21, 37–38
healing: creativity for, 206; Internal Family Systems, 73–77; spiral perspective of, 101–3. *See also* trauma
healing keys, 236–40
health anxiety shark: about, 155–56, 157, 160–61, 176; bathtubs for, 162–63, 168–69, 173–74
HIV, gay men with, 189–90
hives, 118, 156, 157, 162–63
homeostasis, 30

honesty, 52, 165, 188–89
house plant analogy, 51–52
Huberman, Andrew, 56–57
human connection, 25–26, 147, 148
human genome, 126–27, 130
humanity, common, 25–26, 28–29, 84, 103–4, 125
human kindness, 14–17, 25–26, 52, 103–4, 225–26
humility, 232
hungry ghosts, 107
"hurt people hurt people," 34, 129–30
hustle culture, 30–33, 44–45
hypervigilance, 80, 83, 163, 168–69

idiopathic symptoms, 160–61
IFS. *See* Internal Family Systems
impermanence, 225
inadequacy/incompetency, feelings of, 159–60
inauthenticity. *See* authenticity
inner work, 176–78. *See also* growth, meaningful
insecurity, 222
integrated grief, 150

integrity, 179–203; airplane example, 180, 181; alignment and, 182; attunement and, 198, 199–200; authenticity *vs.*, 179; caution about, 202–3; compassion and, 199; defined, 180; empathy and, 198, 199–200; lies and, 188–89; Loki (god of mischief), 181–82; mirror neurons and, 196–98; mirror theory of relationships and, 200–202; misaligned, 185–88; people pleasing and, 190–92, 193; prostitute archetype and, 192–94; repairing, 195–96; secrets and, 189–90; self-abandonment and, 187, 194–96; sympathy and, 199; True YES and True NO, 182–85

intentionality, 13, 56–57

Internal Family Systems (IFS): described, 73–77; 8 C's of Self Energy, 230, 231; emotions, 95–98; fear, 110–12; 5 P's, 230–31; sharks/bathtubs

model compared to, 157–58

introvert/extrovert spectrum, xviii, 13–14, 48, 90–91

Investigate, in RAIN practice, 60

I-statements, 16

Jewish Hasidic parable, 69–70

joy, 112–13

The Judge (King), *217,* 219–20

juicy pens, 211

Jung, Carl, 220

Juster, Norton, 172

"just like me" (affirmation), 28

keys, healing, 236–40

kindness, 14–17, 25–26, 52, 103–4, 225–26

King, Kate: burnout, xvii–xix; *Celestial Goddess,* 213, *214; The Cocoon, 218,* 220; Covid-19 infection, 237–38, 251; *The Judge, 217,* 219–20; marriage, 55, 118; mother, conversations with, 15–17; pandemic practices, 236–38;

sabbatical, xviii–xx, 35, 251–53; self-perception, 145, 149; *Untitled*, 211, *212*, 213

Krishnamurti, J., 144

layers of Self, 4–8
learning process, 21, 247–48, 249, 250
legacy burdens, 121–25
letting go of narratives, 142–48; difficulty of, 142–43; four characters framework, 146–48; as process, 144–46
Levine, Peter, 87
library, living, 235
library of personal values, 12
lies, 188–89
life, seasons of, 104–5
"Life is about the journey, not the destination," 102
life paralysis, 153–54
limbic brain, 83
lineage patterns, 116–17, 120, 129–30
Lipton, Bruce, 136
living library, 235
logical thinking, 147, 148
Loki (god of mischief), 181–82
loneliness, 201

love: conditional, 191; longing for, 201; self-love, 47–50, 107–8, 233–34; sharks, befriending, and, 174; unconditional, 46, 85, 191–92
loving kindness, 225–26

magical play, 163–64
magical thinking, 163–64
Magic Eye books, 138
mammalian brain, 83
manager protector parts, 74
mandalas, sand, 224–25
mantras, 173–74, 242
masculine qualities, 35–36, 46–47
matryoshka dolls, 5–6
May, Katherine, 105
McQueen, Harry, 205
meaning and purpose, 19–20, 23–25
meditation, 6–7
memories of past, 140
mental health challenges, 159
meta (all that is), 225–26
metta (loving kindness), 225–26
microaggressions, 79
middle prefrontal cortex, 57

Milarepa (Tibetan saint),
86–87
mind, 137, 138, 183
mindfulness, 175–76
mindset, unconscious, 13
mirror neurons, 196–98
mirrors, avoidance of, 163
mirror theory of
relationships, 200–202
modeling, xx
monkey mind, 137, 183
monkeys, mirror neurons in,
196, 198
monks, Tibetan, 224–25
Moore, David, 127
Moore, Thomas, 126, 127
Morgenstern, Erin, xvii
mothers, xviii, 15–17, 120,
187–88, 198–99
motivation, hopeful, 63–64
mourning, 65–66

Nagosaki, Amelia, 36
Nagosaki, Emily, 36
narcissism, 232–33
narratives: brain and, 137–
38; changing, 138–39;
childhood roots of, 145,
149, 152–53; combative
relationship, 139; defined,
137; detaching from, 137,
143–45; difficult, belief
that one is, 145, 149;
embedded, 142–43, 145,
149; fear of upsetting
others, 141; future
projections and, 140;
letting go of, 142–48;
memories of past and,
140; power of, 58; present
emotional experience
and, 140; as protective,
143; sharks/bathtubs
model and, 169; suffering,
comparative, 141–42;
wounds and, 152–53
nature anchor, 7
nature vs. nurture question,
116. See also epigenetics;
family secrets; legacy
burdens; lineage patterns
necklace as totem, 9
Neff, Kristin, 84
neocortex, 83
Nepo, Mark, 97, 105–6, 134,
185–86
nervous system: autonomic,
39–42, 77; creativity,
healing through, 206;
parasympathetic, 40–41,
43, 67, 78; sympathetic,
40, 41–42, 43, 67, 77–80
Netherlands potato famine,
128–29

neural network, pro-social, 57
neuromodulators, 56
A New Earth (Tolle), 143–44, 175
Nhat Hanh, Thich, 177
90-second rule, 92–93
NO, True, 182–85
Norse mythology, 181–82
North Star (Stella Polaris), 8–9
North Star necklace as totem, 9
"no," saying, 54
not-enough-ness, 160
nourishment in relationships, 50–55
numbness, 31, 41
nurturance and deep rest, 39–71; autonomic nervous system, 39–42; expression, 65–68; forgiveness, 68–70; giver trap, 45–47; gratitude, 55–59; nourishment in relationships, 50–55; nurturance, 42–45, 55; RAIN practice, 59–61; self-love, 47–50; trust and generosity, 61–65
Nurture, in RAIN practice, 60

Occelli, Cynthia, 89
ocean wisdom, 177–78
offerings, about, xxii
The Offspring, 187
Oliver, Mary, 19
openness, xxv–xxvi
orchid children, 1–2, 3–4
orchid hypothesis, 1–4
over-giving, 105–8

pandemic, Covid-19, xvii–xviii, xxi, 20, 236–38
parable, Jewish Hasidic, 69–70
parachutes, 240–44
parasympathetic nervous system (PNS), 40–41, 43, 67, 78
parents, 119, 163. *See also* mothers
parts: about, 73–77; exile, 74–76, 95–96, 111–12; firefighter protector, 74; manager protector, 74; protector, 74–76, 95–96, 97–98, 110, 111–12
Parts Cards, 216–17, *217, 218,* 219–22
parts work: Internal Family Systems, 75–76, 97–98; Parts Cards, 216–17, *217, 218,* 219–22

past, memories of, 140
patriarchal culture, 35–36,
  46–47
pattern breakers, 130–34
pens, juicy, 211
people pleasing, 190–
  92, 193
perception, changing,
  138–39
perfectionism, 26–27, 95,
  151–54, 187–88, 222,
  246–47
permanence, lack of, 225
Perry, Bruce, 82
"personal defects," 153
personal genius. *See* gifts
perspective, power of, 172
The Phantom Tollbooth
  (Juster), 172
phenotypes, 126
Plato, 103, 104
play, magical, 163–64
PNS (parasympathetic
  nervous system), 40–41,
  43, 67, 78
podcasts, 244–45, 247, 249
polarization, 35–36
Polyvagal theory, 40
Porges, Stephen, 40
posttraumatic stress disorder
  (PTSD), 80, 81
potato famine, 128–29

The Power of Now
  (Tolle), 175
prefrontal cortex, 57, 135
present emotional
  experience, 140
present moment experience,
  147, 148
procrastination, 44
professional doodles, 211,
  212, 213, 215
projections of future, 140
pro-social neural
  network, 57
prostate health fears, 155–
  56
prostitute archetype, 192–94
protector parts, 74–76,
  95–96, 97–98, 110,
  111–12
proverb, Chinese, xxiii
P's, in Internal Family
  Systems, 230–31
psychosomatic
  disorders, 118
Psychotherapy, Art as,
  215–17, *217*, *218*, 219–22
PTSD (posttraumatic stress
  disorder), 80, 81
purpose and meaning,
  19–20, 23–25

quarrel between king and son, parable of, 69–70

radiant, definitions of, xi–xii
The Radiant Life Project, xix, 252
RAIN practice, 59–61
reacting *vs.* responding, 99–100, 173–74
Recognize, in RAIN practice, 59–60
relationships: challenging, 20; combative, 139; dissatisfaction in, 5–6; mirror theory of, 200–202; nourishment in, 50–55; survival and, 194
repair, 62, 130, 131, 195–96
repression, 65
reptilian brain, 82–83
resiliency, 37–38
resistance, 49–50, 173
respect, 52
responding *vs.* reacting, 99–100, 173–74
rest, 22, 35. *See also* nurturance and deep rest
retirement, 31, 32
Rilke, Rainer Maria, 73, 150, 251
ripple effect, 253
Roosevelt, Theodore, 115

Roshi, Suzuki, 39
Rumi, Mewlana Jalaluddin, 100, 150
rupture and repair, 62
Russian nesting dolls, 5–6

sabbaticals, xviii–xx, 35, 243, 251–53
safety bubbles, pandemic, 236–37
sand mandalas, 224–25
scarcity, 160
The School of Life, 239
Schwartz, Richard, 73, 75, 230
Schwartz, Robert, 1
The Science of Success (Dobbs), 1
screaming at someone, 67–68
seasons of life, 104–5
secrets, 120–22, 189–90
Self: authentic *vs.* "where you're at," 89–92; in Internal Family Systems, 73–77; layers of, 4–8
self-abandonment, 187, 194–96
self-care. *See* nurturance and deep rest
self-compassion, 84–85
self-criticism, 63–64

Self Energy, 8 C's of, 230, 231
"Self-Esteem," 187
self-health junkies, 245–50, 252
selfishness, 232–33
self-knowledge, lack of, xxi
selflessness, 201
self-love, 47–50, 107–8, 233–34
self-pity, 84
self-understanding, 168
seminars, 247
serotonin, 56
sexuality, keeping secret, 189–90
shadow archetypes, 192–93
shadow side, 2, 37, 67
sharks: befriending, 169, 172–76, 177; body weight as, 159; defined, 156–57; described, 157–58; examples of, 159–60; fear of, 171–72; health anxiety, 155–56, 157, 160–61, 176; inadequacy/ incompetency feelings, 159–60; love and, 174; mental health challenges as, 159; mindfulness and, 175–76; scarcity as, 160; as triggers, 158–59.

See also sharks/bathtubs model
sharks/bathtubs model: adaptive nature of, 167–68; compassion and, 170–71; inner work and, 176–78; Internal Family Systems, compared to, 157–58; narratives and, 169; as normal, 169–70; self-understanding and, 168; therapy and, 176–77. See also bathtubs; sharks
Shubin, Neil, 244–45
sketchbooks, 210–11, 212, 213, 214, 215
skin disturbances, 118, 156, 157, 162–63
slowing down, 29–30
SNS (sympathetic nervous system), 40, 41–42, 43, 67, 77–80
social anxiety, 90–91
songwriting, 209
soul strain, 53
sphere, truth as a, 139–40
spiral theory, 101–3
spiritual bypassing, 163–64
spirituality, 224–26
stacked bricks analogy, 101
"The Starless Sea" (Morgenstern), xvii

Stella Polaris (North Star), 8–9
stories. *See* narratives
sublimation, 65–67, 187
Substance Abuse and Mental Health Administration, 80–81
suffering, comparative, 141–42
suicide, mother losing son to, 198–99
summit, false, 102–3
sunny side, 2
"Supernova" (McQueen), 205
superstar caregiver persona, 46
supportive community, 243
Surface Pressure, 33
surrender, 85–87, 146
survival, 193–94
"Sweet Darkness" (Whyte), 135
sympathetic nervous system (SNS), 40, 41–42, 43, 67, 77–80
sympathy, 199
symptoms, idiopathic, 160–61

tenderness, 35

therapy: art, 5–6, 85, 206; art as, 210–11, *212,* 213, *214,* 215; sharks/bathtubs model, 176–77; as tool, 243, 247, 248, 249
thinking: binary, 35–36; logical, 147, 148; magical, 163–64; power of, 136–37; unity and connection fostered by, 147, 148
threats, 40, 77–78
three E's, in trauma definition, 81
Thurman, Howard, 231
Tibetan monks, 224–25
Tiktaalik rosae (fish species), 244–45
titration, 87–88
Tolle, Eckhart, 143–44, 175
tortured artist persona, 186–87
totems, 9–10
traffic jam story, 75–76
tragedy, dress rehearsing, 113
transition, getting stuck in, 243
trauma: ancestral, 127–31; brain and, 82–84; car accident example, 81; defined, 80–81; effects and, 81; event and, 81;

experience and, 81; self-
compassion and, 84–85;
surrender and, 85–87;
sympathetic nervous
system and, 77–80
triggers, 49, 94, 95, 97–98,
158–59
True North, finding, 8–14
True YES/True NO, 182–
85
trust, 61–62
truth, 123–24, 139–40

unconditional love, 46, 85,
191–92
unconscious mindset, 13
unity, 147, 148
Untamed (Doyle), 55, 192
Untitled (King), 211,
212, 213
Upa Guru, 239

vacations, 31, 243
values, 11–12
ventral vagal system, 40,
41, 42
vigilance, excessive, 80, 83,
163, 168–69
violence, 68

Waits, Tom, 209

WandaVision, 150
water, perspective on, 172
waves, 177–78
The Way of Integrity (Beck),
175, 179–80, 181, 189–90
Webster, Bethany, 22
weight, body, 94–95, 159
Welwood, John, 164
"We repeat what we don't
repair," 130, 131
Western culture, 19, 35, 37,
46–47, 141
"What you want wants
you," 53–54
"who you are" *vs.* "where
you're at", 89–92
Whyte, David, 135, 229
Wintering (May), 105
The Wizard of Oz, 32
working out, 66
wounds, 119, 152–53,
191–92
writing, 6, 219, 220, 243

YES, True, 182–85
"You're only as sick as your
secrets," 189
"Your Soul's Plan"
(Schwartz), 1

About Kate King

Kate King is a Licensed Professional Counselor, a Board Certified Art Therapist, and an artist and author in Denver, Colorado. As the founder and owner of *The Radiant Life Project*, Kate's mission is to create a ripple effect of well-being and empowerment to activate large-scale joy and freedom in our world. Kate is widely known for helping her clients and audience learn to cultivate radiant lives for themselves that shine so brightly they impact and improve the lives of those around them. Her work comprises an expansive array of inspiring resources, tools, and practices that provide an accessible entry point into a life of greater authenticity, fulfillment, and illumination.

Through *The Radiant Life Project*, Kate seeks to engage and empower her audience with the skill base from her more than fifteen years as a clinician and Art Therapist, as well as the wisdom she has acquired through her healing growth journey in the school of life. Kate's work incorporates the synergy of brain sciences, diverse psychotherapeutic modalities, spiritual practices, creative expression, and attuned connection. It is her utmost passion to teach others how to reclaim their truest Selves and intentionally create a meaningful life that radiates with joy, possibility, creativity, and wholeness.

Kate's first book, *The Authentic Mother*, is a creatively based companion book that offers support and healing tools for new mothers on their complex journey of early parenthood. It acknowledges and attunes to the massive stretch that happens in early motherhood, and offers an invitation toward authenticity and compassion with creative, therapeutic, and scientific resources for self-support. Kate also offers powerful offerings to help you spark next-level wellness with individual psychotherapy, group retreats, inspirational public speaking, creative consulting, and online programs.